9Q Media, LLC
10940 Wilshire Blvd
16th Floor
Los Angeles, CA 90024

Ordering Information:
Quantity sales. Special discounts are available on quantity purchases by corporations, associations, and others. For details, contact the publisher at the address above.
Orders by U.S. trade bookstores and wholesalers. Please contact Distribution Coordinator:

Tel: (800) 922-5806
Email: Distribution@9Qmedia.com or visit: www.9Qmedia.com
Printed in the United States of America
First Edition

TABLE OF CONTENTS

THE WOLF THAT STOLE
THE GOLDEN EGG

YOUR INNER FAIRY GODMOTHER

APPENDIX

In memory of my grandmother

This book is dedicated to every woman who has worked hard to support her family. Every woman who has kept going regardless of the struggles she faced, who kept saving even though at times it all seemed to go into a "black hole." I hope that within the pages of this book you will find hope, wisdom, and empowerment to plan a better retirement and be able to stand up and say to whoever or whatever it is that's trying to hold you back:

"Get your hand out of my purse, I'm not giving you my money!"

ACKNOWLEDGMENTS

As the famous saying goes, it takes a village...

This book was inspired by the stories of many women I met throughout the years. Even though, for their privacy, their names are fictitious, their stories are very real! I would like to thank all of them for their inspiring and, in some cases, heartbreaking stories and I know they will want any woman who reads this book to be aware of the "wolves" that can, in the blink of an eye, wipe away hopes and dreams.

First and most important of all, I want to thank my fiancé, who has always been there for me. He has encouraged me every step of the way. His motivation and his genuine "you can do it" attitude truly inspire me every day. Without his support, strength, and motivation this book would not have been possible. Thank you with all my heart and soul, you are a remarkable person!

I want to thank my parents for teaching me to be the strong woman who I am today. Without them, I might have never understood the importance of being independent!

I want to thank my staff who were with me every step of the way, from book design to more editing and every other small and big task that goes on behind the scenes. I offer my sincerest thanks to:

Mae Talle, who organized me above and beyond to help me achieve my deadlines for this book – her effort to make this book the best it can be was in itself enthusiastic; Silvia Park, who offered her support and many nights of long debates on subject matters; Javier Harriman, who never complained, no matter how many times I wanted the design or the colors to be changed on my cover, and Mike Ferrin, who helped with many illustrations throughout the book.

I want to give my heartfelt gratitude to my client and dear friend Alice Bryant, who helped with editing and was an incredible sounding board for many of the topics, including helping me come up with the cover idea. I appreciate how selfless her kindness was, and it has been an absolute pleasure to have someone so amazing in my group of counsel.

I also want to thank my editor, Alex Sherman, who stayed awake many late nights at the office helping me finish what seemed for a while a never-ending story. Alex, thanks for all of your hard work, dedication, and belief in our mission to empower women.

Finally, I want to thank all the women who will read this book and will choose to take control of their financial futures. Nothing makes me prouder than that, as I know that together our voices will shake down all the wolves in the financial industry, and we will be a force to be reckoned with. After all, it is you, the reader, who will help all of us pass this empowerment message and make a difference in your life or someone else's!

DISCLOSURES

Information provided herein reflects the views of the author as of the publication date of this book. Such views are subject to change at any point and neither the author or 9Q Media shall be obligated to provide notice of any change. Information contained herein is provided for informational purposes only and nothing presented herein is or is intended to constitute investment, tax or legal advice or a recommendation to buy or sell any types of securities. No investment decision should be made based on any information provided herein.

The author has not taken into account the investment objectives, financial situation, or particular needs of any individual investor and is not responsible for the consequences of any decisions or actions taken as a result of information provided in this book. There is a risk of loss from an investment in securities, including the risk of loss of principal. Different types of investments involve varying degrees of risk, and there can be no assurance that any specific investment will be profitable or suitable for a particular investor's financial situation or risk tolerance. Asset allocation and portfolio diversification cannot assure or guarantee better performance and cannot eliminate the risk of investment losses. To the extent that they are mentioned, it is important to understand that Annuities are intended for retirement or other long-term needs. They are intended for a person who has sufficient cash or other liquid assets for living expenses and other unexpected emergencies, such as medical expenses. Annuities are not FDIC Insured, and any insurance and annuity product guarantees are backed by the financial strength and claims-paying ability of the issuing company. Past performance is no guarantee of future results. Some of the information provided herein was obtained from third-party sources believed to be reliable but such information is not guaranteed to be accurate.

Any forward-looking statements or forecasts are based on assumptions only and actual results are expected to vary from any such statements or forecasts. No reliance should be placed on any such statements or forecasts when making any investment decision. Any assumptions and projections displayed are estimates, hypothetical in nature, and meant to serve solely as a guideline. Accordingly, you should not rely solely on the information contained in these materials in making any investment decision.

GET YOUR HAND OUT OF MY PURSE!
I'M NOT GIVING YOU MY MONEY!

THE ENCHANTED WALL STREET AND THE SLEEPLESS BEAUTY

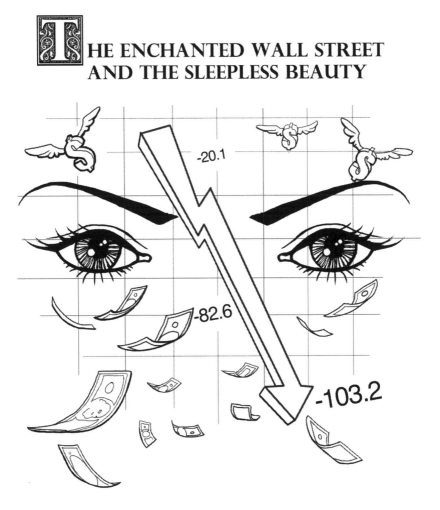

CHAPTER 1

DON'T BE SUCH A GIRL!

"With the new day comes new strength and new thoughts."
— Eleanor Roosevelt

It was a crazy-busy day in downtown Los Angeles, although a very beautiful day. The streets were very crowded, with lots of noise and cars honking as we were crossing the street, making our way to the Convention Center. I was attending an industry conference with one of my colleagues, and we couldn't wait to get inside and away from the sweltering heat! As we were walking up to the center, we suddenly heard someone yelling, and noticed that less than a few yards away, an older woman was fighting with someone. She was holding on tightly to her purse, screaming at the man next to her: "Get your hand out of my purse! I'm not giving you my money!" When we heard this, my colleague and I realized that someone was trying to rob her, but this woman was so direct and intimidating, and was making so much noise, that the man must've gotten scared, and just took off! She was one tough grandma!

We also noticed that a teenage girl was standing next to her, who we later figured out was her granddaughter. The girl was very shaken up and was just standing there, visibly upset, with tears welling up in her eyes, and a completely lost look on her face. To our surprise, as the girl was crying, the older woman turned to her and said, "Oh, stop your crying! Don't be such a girl! You've got to protect what's yours! You think I'd let some scumbag take what's mine after I worked hard for my money?" Granted, I think that in hindsight, she could have risked both their lives, so maybe her choice of action wasn't the best in that situation, but then again, they were in a crowded street and not in a dark alley somewhere.

My colleague and I walked over to them and asked if they were all right and if we should call the police, but the older lady just looked at us and said, "Hey, I did what I had to do! As you can see, there were no knights in shining armor that were coming to my rescue," hinting at the fact that on such a crowded street, not one guy tried to step in to help her. She proceeded to tell us that she didn't just resist the robbery because of her valuables, but because she didn't want her granddaughter to think it was ever okay to be a victim!

Her words really resonated with me, but it was for a different reason. It wasn't because, as someone was trying to rob this older woman, guys were just walking by, pretending not to notice so that they wouldn't have to get involved. But because this grandma had simply come to *expect* that no one would help her, and in this instance, she just took care of the situation herself – no knights in shining armor required. She didn't just roll over and give up. She didn't stand there paralyzed with fear. She just did what she had to do, and took care of herself.

This stuck with me for a very long time, and I started to wonder: how many women do we all know, no matter what age they are, who are still waiting for their knight in shining armor to come to their rescue! And I'm not talking about a situation like a robbery, where there is real, physical danger involved, but everyday situations

2

where women allow themselves to be victimized financially, because they are either too afraid to confront a bad situation, or just don't know how. I'm talking about actually managing their money and their retirement portfolios in a way that *they* want. Not just paying the bills and balancing the checkbook, but managing their wealth with the same comfort they have for making their purse choices! Doesn't the retirement portfolio do essentially the same thing as your purse – hold your valuables? We make sure that our purses have zippers so that nothing falls out and everything is protected, and we like having different compartments so that we can access our wallets or our keys when we need them! But as much attention as women give to protecting the relatively inconsequential valuables in their purses, they don't put even half as much effort into protecting their retirement money! Why? Because they keep thinking that somehow, everything will turn out all right. And they don't even realize most of the time that they're thinking this way.

I'll never forget that crazy day in Los Angeles, where one tough grandma showed me that there is still hope for women out there to stand up for themselves and to learn to think differently about themselves and their future. They just need to know that they can, and should, stand up to anyone, just like that tough grandma did. She spoke her mind, fought like hell, and didn't let anyone take advantage of her!

That day, more than ever, I set forth on a mission to find the stories of women who could have stood up for themselves but didn't, and what they lost as a result. They weren't robbed in the physical sense, and no one took their purse. Instead, they lost something much more valuable – their retirement savings, and with it, their ability to have the kind of life that they not only wanted, but had worked very hard to achieve. The enchanted Wall Street destroyed their dreams, and their knight in shining armor, also known as their financial advisor, didn't ride in on a white horse to rescue them, but in fact did the exact opposite. Why is it that these women couldn't stand up for their money like this feisty grandma did when defending her little purse on a street in Los Angeles?

CHAPTER 2

THE BEGINNING...

"... some day you will be old enough to start reading fairy tales again." — C.S. Lewis

I was about eight years old when I noticed a common thread among the women in my family. They all seemed to be very thoughtful, intelligent, and outspoken women whose voices could literally shake up a room and demand attention. Yet even though they were strong, opinionated, and always commanded respect, for some reason they all would go to their husbands to ask for money to pay the bills, go grocery shopping, or go to the salon. Sometimes, it was almost as if the man was a walking, talking ATM, and that's where the women would go to get money when they needed it. It's funny how we think when we are children, because we don't really know at that age what is right or wrong, or why things happen the way they do, and so I just assumed that if Mom does something, then because I am a girl, then maybe that's what I'm supposed to do as well.

I remember when I started receiving my allowance... I would collect it, take it to my room, count it, write down the amounts in my journal, and then... give it to my dad for "safekeeping." My dad couldn't understand at the time why I would turn around and give my allowance right back to him, within an hour. He was even more confused when I would proceed to make "withdrawals" from him (the ATM) and get just enough money for a doll or candy or whatever my heart desired. I remember him telling me several times, "You know this is your money, and you can keep it with you. That's why I gave it to you in the first place." To which I would respond, "Well, Mom doesn't keep her money with herself, so why should I?" I could not, for the life of me, see why he was telling me to keep my money in my room. Having him safeguard it for me just seemed like such a no-brainer that I was always confused by why he would make such a silly suggestion!

When I was around that same age, my grandfather passed away... At that point in my life, it was really the hardest thing I faced as a child. I loved him very much, and he was like a second father to me... I would stay with my grandparents during the summers to hang out with Grandpa, who was the best storyteller and he didn't get annoyed (or at least didn't seem to) about all the silly questions that I asked him about how cars worked and why the sky was blue, and all that other stuff that seems so strange when you're young and the world is this amazing place filled with excitement. But this is more about my grandmother... She was a doctor, a woman with a well-rounded intellect who spoke several languages and could easily out-debate almost anyone in a conversation.

On his deathbed, my grandpa asked my dad (his son-in-law) to please take care of Grandma, and make sure that she would be okay. So my grandma moved in with us, and Dad now had another member of the family to look after. He handled Grandpa's funeral arrangements, as well as the onslaught of various paperwork that comes with sorting out finances after someone's passing, so that my grandma wouldn't have to try to figure it all out while she was grieving. And now, Dad also took care of all of my grandma's bills, and as she used to do with Grandpa, she would now go to my dad to get "spending money." She was lucky because my dad took care of her very well, and did his best to make sure that she was truly comfortable. She lived a long life (she passed away at the age of 96) and her golden years were spent in a comfortable environment, with her family helping her in whatever she needed, financially and physically. I didn't realize how truly lucky she was until much later in life, when I found out that she had actually spent most of her money by the time she was about 80, and for almost two decades after that, she was taken care of financially by my dad. I am still very proud of how my father handled this situation, because he never abandoned her, didn't try to shove her off on other relatives, and wouldn't even let her go to a nursing home until she insisted on it, at the age of 96! But again, she was lucky.

As much as these events taught me about the value of family, and the importance of being there for the people you love, I can't help but feel that things could, and should have been different. There was no reason why my grandma could not have taken care of herself, or planned her retirement in advance. As I already mentioned, she was a very intelligent and confident woman, far from a shrinking violet, and at the time of my grandpa's passing, she was in her mid-70s, and was still very healthy and full of life! She could have easily managed her own money, made her own budget, and could have had complete independence from everyone! But she didn't do any of that.

The years went by and I was now a teenager who thought I knew everything. I still kept withdrawing money from my personal "ATM" (my dad), but now I was getting more and more lectures from him, especially when I was overdrawing on my "account balance" (rightfully so at many times). This is when I decided "Hey, why do I need a bank that talks back?" and I asked my dad to help me open my first real checking account. Now I was older, and the little allowance I had received before no longer worked for me, so I started getting baby-sitting and tutoring jobs to add more and more to my bank account because I had to prove to my dad that he was wrong, and that I indeed *knew* what I was doing! Hey, I was no longer his carefree little girl. So I watched my spending closely and paid my "bills" on time. I even tried to convince him that because I was so responsible and paid all my teenage bills on time, that he should buy me a pager. (Yes, you remember, we didn't always have smartphones with cool apps; we only had the coolest invention of the time – pagers!) Well, unfortunately my dad didn't think that it was a necessary purchase, and told me that when I became a doctor, then he would gladly buy me a pager! (Become a doctor…? Yuck! To me, the medical field was too bloody and gross, thank you but no thank you, I told him. If I could stand the sight of blood, then I'd rather become a vampire, not a doctor! At least I would always look young and live forever!)

So that was when making more money and saving it became very important to me. I had to show The Bank (my dad) that I no longer needed him for *any* loans... Well, he would still have to pay for the rent, the food, the cable bill, and everything else, but other than that, I could totally survive on my own. So I saved and spent wisely! Paid my own teenage bills and never asked him for any more money! Although he wasn't always happy with the stuff I bought for myself, my dad was nonetheless proud of my initiative, and I was thrilled!

On a serious note, having my parents say "no" to me whenever I wanted to buy some silly teenage thing is what actually pushed me to become more serious about my money, to budget, and to plan ahead. I didn't make all that much money with my baby-sitting gigs, and like most teenagers, I was faced with the constant dilemma of having to decide what clothing accessory or gadget I absolutely couldn't live without, so budgeting became a must. Eventually, I realized that there is no reason why a girl cannot, or should not, do this. The sun didn't stop rising in the morning just because I was handling my own money, and even though I'd make mistakes from time to time, the world did not end, and my dad never had a problem with it. So why was it that my mom still didn't know how to pay a bill, or why did she still come to Dad for money? She had a part-time job, but handed her paychecks over to her husband. I just didn't get it!

But my confusion about why women didn't put more energy into managing their own money wasn't just confined to the women in my immediate family. When I was in my early 20s, I saw my parents going through a difficult time trying to help a close family friend who became a widow at the age of 51. She was a homemaker with a 14-year-old son, and her husband suddenly passed away from colon cancer that he didn't even know he had! He just went to the emergency room one evening because he was feeling very ill, and died a few days later. No warning, no time to prepare, no time to really say good-bye. Everyone was in total shock and disbelief. He had a very small taxi business, and his wife never worked a day in her life, so she thought he had everything planned and handled for a situation like this. But as it turned out, he was a procrastinator, like most people, and obviously didn't expect to die so young, so he didn't really plan. He never bought life insurance, and because he was a business owner, he didn't have a pension plan. He barely paid into Social Security, and now his widow was left with nothing but a couple of taxicabs and a huge mortgage. Unfortunately, she didn't know how to run his business so there was no income coming in, and because there were no real savings, she lost her home and had to move into a tiny place. Because she was not very savvy, and didn't have any work experience, she had to get a minimum wage job in a retail store and she *barely* got by.

The saddest part was watching her and her son being so angry with their late husband/father, that they couldn't even grieve the right way. They went from burying the person they loved so much, and who took care of everything for them, to struggling just to stay afloat, with absolutely no time to cope with this sudden loss. The truth is, I get that, yes, maybe the late husband should have thought of all those things… But I could not understand back then, why was it just *his* responsibility to do that? Why didn't his wife at some point say, "Hey, how are we protected? How much is in our savings? What is our debt!?" Why was she not involved? Is it fair to just assume that because he was a man, he should have had it all figured out? What if he just didn't think about it? What if he, just like her, lived day to day and ignored the big picture? Again, not becoming involved was her choice too…

That is when I said to myself "NO MORE!" At least in my family, this helplessness and dependence would end right there, with me. I told myself that I would *never* be like this. I saw this dependence as a weakness – something that was not worthy of intelligent women. I saw that it was a choice; a choice that somehow throughout these women's lives, they had decided to make!

But even afterwards, when I was all grown up and living in the real world, I noticed the same thing. Except now I saw women taking the exact same approach that they took with their husbands or fathers, but they were taking this approach with their financial advisors. They didn't communicate with people who managed their money; they didn't ask questions and didn't show much interest in how their money was invested. Instead, they had complete trust that their advisor was taking care of everything for them. They used that same "He will take care of me and I have nothing to worry about" attitude!

So why is it that women continue making these choices? When I started working in finance, I began to see the common thread in all these situations. It was not just because of career choice; housewives and professional career women alike were making these same choices. Neither was it because some were more educated than others. The common thread seemed to be nothing more than habit; a habit that they learned from their mothers and grandmothers, which was amplified by the culture around them. Their upbringing taught them how to look at their money and they kept these habits, because perhaps they didn't feel confident in their abilities to take control – as if they would make a mistake and mess it all up!

I also noticed that many times these choices were made because of the relationship these women had with the people who were handling their money. It was this constant assumption that "My husband, my dad, my advisor knows what is best for me!" It was like an emotional comfort blanket that they would pull over themselves so that they wouldn't have to deal with the uncomfortable situations that made them feel lost and confused, and a "What I don't know won't hurt me" attitude that came with it. It was the pure joy of ignorance and the bliss of not worrying even though there was plenty to worry about!

The problem is that we grow up with so many unrealistic representations of the world around us, that we think everything will somehow work itself out! We see so many examples of damsels in distress who are saved by handsome princes that we think that somehow everything will always turn out for the best. But ignorance about our finances is one monster that cannot be put down once it rears its ugly head and shows its true colors. This quiet villain is hiding behind a fake sense of security and when it finally shows up, it's hard to break away from its grip, because by that time it's likely too late to do anything about it. This is one of those monsters that we have to face early, because that's the only way to be in control of it! And really, it's not a monster at all… But more like a beautiful swan that grows into an ugly, fire-breathing dragon when it's abandoned and neglected.

Think of all the stories we are told when we are kids – "Cinderella" is a great example. What do we learn? Let's just look pretty, buy a pretty dress, do our hair all nice, go to a ball and everything, including our financial well-being, will be taken care of by Prince Charming. Yay! Life's easy! Now, don't get me wrong, fairy-tale endings are great, as long as there are those around you who help shape you into a strong woman who can take care of herself. But the problem is that so many times, positive, strong influences just don't exist, and we grow up into adults who still have those same fairy-tale mentalities. We are surrounded by women who may not be the best examples of good money managers, and we naturally follow in their footsteps, subconsciously. Maybe Mom is too comfortable letting Dad take care of all the finances. Or maybe we're watching episodes of shows like *I Love Lucy*, and we learn that Lucy is bad with money, so we think that it's normal. And if you think things are completely different today, well then you haven't watched some of those ridiculous reality TV shows and all that they are teaching young girls today – to be petty, materialistic, and to completely misinterpret what it means to be independent (no, "annoying" and "independent" are *not* the same thing!)!

Our environment and upbringing have definitely contributed to the scary statistic of why so many women nowadays are having a difficult time managing their money. The sad part about this is that as women are living longer, and often alone (after a divorce or after becoming widowed), they are literally running out of savings during their retirement. So they end up spending their so-called golden years living Social Security check to Social Security check, without any freedom, and with little actual independence. But it doesn't have to be this way.

As you read the stories in this book about women who went through tough moments and made their own mistakes, one thing that I'd like you to keep in mind is the tough grandma in the previous chapter. Any time you come across a story in this book that you can relate to, think of how much better such situations will turn out for you if you just approach them from the perspective of "Get your hand out of my purse! I'm not giving you my money!" and don't allow people to take advantage of you. Standing up for yourself can be tough, but any time a solution to your problem sounds too scary or too complicated to face, I want you to think of what the tough grandma said to her granddaughter, but this time imagine her pointing at you, and saying, "Don't Be Such a Girl!" Because you can do anything you want – standing up for yourself and your retirement is, after all, just a choice!

The stories of the women in this book are real, but their names have been changed to protect their privacy. They also hope that their stories will help reshape your attitude toward your financial future, so that you can approach similar situations in a much more productive way. The thing is, many of the advisors that ultimately hurt these women's futures, and other advisors that are out there who have hurt their clients' futures in the same way, are not necessarily evil monsters. They're just humans who adopted bad habits. Some have a lazy attitude toward their jobs, which affected their clients' well-being. Some are either uneducated in the financial field or simply too inexperienced – maybe too greedy, too incompetent, or too self-centered to understand the details of what they are actually selling, and how that affects their clients. Some are just young salespeople, right out of college, working for big firms with big names and pushing whatever the analysts in their headquarters are promoting, without truly understanding the consequences of their actions. For others, this is just a side gig. They're CPAs that got financial licenses to sell financial products on the side, or even lawyers, in some cases, doing the same thing. As we all know, you cannot be a jack-of-all- trades, but unfortunately, that's the reality when anyone who can pass the test can go out there and start advising. So please keep in mind when I refer to your financial advisor or your financial professional in this book, this could refer to anyone who fits into that advising category – whether it's an actual financial advisor (regardless of experience level), a broker, or another professional who sells investments on the side.

As you read through the chapters, keep in mind that I will first share many of these women's stories and talk in detail about why we, as women, are where we are in the eyes of society and the financial industry. As you continue, you will find many chapters that will cover the solutions and offer advice on how these women could have handled some of the situations and scenarios more effectively, and you can apply these lessons to your own situation. You will learn about financial concepts, decision-making techniques and how to take control of your finances, and how to never let these not-so-happy endings happen to you.

Also, as you see references to Wall Street throughout the book, keep in mind that I am referring to the financial industry in general, not the actual "Wall Street" in New York or the stock exchange. It's a way to refer to the overall financial industry that's supposed to help you build your future, but often ends up crashing on top of you.

It is my sincere hope that by reading this book, you will become more comfortable in dealing with the monster of inaction. That you will come to better understand your strengths and weaknesses through the stories of the women who I have met throughout my career, and the lessons I learned trying to help them. I hope that you will learn from their mistakes, and that this book will help you become more involved and more aware of your relationship with your money, money management, and your advisors.

CHAPTER 3

A RUDE AWAKENING

"Fairy tales since the beginning of recorded time, and perhaps earlier, have been 'a means to conquer the terrors of mankind through metaphor.'" — Jack Zipes

Since we all love fairy tales so much, let me tell you a quick story about a fair maiden who I once knew. I won't share her real name, but her name isn't as important as her story.

Once upon a time, in a faraway land, there lived a fair maiden who dreamt of an early retirement so that she could live her life to the fullest. She didn't come from a wealthy family, but was an extremely hard worker and diligently contributed money into her retirement account, or a "401(k)" as it was called in this fairy-tale kingdom. The fair maiden had great dreams for her golden years: traveling, taking up new hobbies, relaxing in the hot sun with cold piña coladas (yum!), and living life to her heart's content. In fact, she didn't just *hope* for financial independence, but was *sure* that she would reach her goals – after all, she regularly set aside money into her retirement account and had a financial advisor who she thought was as concerned about her retirement as she was.

From time to time, the fair maiden would check in on her nest egg to marvel at the amount of money that she had accumulated, and every time it seemed as though she was getting closer and closer to her dream of real financial independence. In fact, she had grown so accustomed to seeing increases in the value of her account, that her dreams seemed almost within reach. The magical stock market was ever increasing, and her account followed suit. When her net worth had surpassed the $1-million mark (after all, she had been diligently contributing to her 401(k) for over 20 years), she could hardly believe her eyes. "Looks like all of my hard work is finally paying off," she would think to herself while imagining what the hot sand would feel like beneath her feet at the beach on the tropical island where she was going to take her first overdue vacation.

Unfortunately, as in most fairy tales, evil was lurking in this fairy-tale land – an evil that showed itself in the form of account fees, stock market volatility, and an ugly toad pretending to be a diligent financial advisor...

When you think about it, for a girl, childhood is really quite a sham; almost like a Ponzi scheme. Growing up, we're told a whole bunch of things and get all these promises about the world that we later find out aren't really true, and we're surrounded by magical stories about heroes and villains, and all the warm and fuzzy fluffiness that comes with them. But the thing that really stands out about these magical worlds is that they are very clear-cut. There are good people, and there are bad people; people who only want to help us and those who only want to take advantage of us, and it's always easy to distinguish between the two: the good characters in these stories are almost always handsome and flawless, while the bad ones are usually fat, ugly, and have crooked teeth. On top of that, these fairy-tale stories incorrectly teach us that life is inherently fair. That at the end of the day, good will triumph over evil and that everything will turn out just fine; that the handsome prince will come riding in on a beautiful white horse and we'll live happily ever after. Just imagine, for a second, that if instead of ending like a perfect love story, the Prince decided to tell Cinderella that he didn't really like her, and gave her some lame excuse – how differently that would have shaped your outlook on life at an early age? Now, I'm not saying that the best solution is to destroy fairy tales for kids – that would be a downright evil thing to do. But what I *am* saying is: just think about the difference in perspective!

UMM... SORRY, CINDERELLA, I MEAN I REALLY LIKE YOU AS A PERSON AND EVERYTHING, BUT I'M JUST NOT READY TO SETTLE DOWN YET. YOU KNOW... IT'S NOT YOU, IT'S ME... BY THE WAY, HERE'S YOUR GLASS SLIPPER.

It's no wonder that many of us go through a somewhat angry and rebellious phase when we become teenagers! Sure, some of it is because of the changing hormones in our bodies, but a huge part of it is also that we start seeing the world for the complicated and disappointing place that it can be sometimes, and now the real world actually begins to clash with how the world was originally presented to us when we were young girls. We begin to realize that people can be very mean and selfish, and our relationships with others aren't always clear-cut. In real life it's often truly difficult to tell who has your best interests in mind, or if someone really doesn't care about you at all. After all, in real life, selfish people don't always look ugly, and don't always have crooked teeth.

Unfortunately, as much as we hate to admit it, even as we mature into intelligent and independent women, these childhood stories continue to affect our way of thinking and continue to shape our judgment for the rest of our lives. Let's be honest, ladies, no matter what your age is and no matter how silly it may seem at times, we still like to believe that our life will turn out just like a magical fairy tale. There's a reason why movies like *Kate and Leopold, Ever After,* and *Enchanted* are so successful! We *want* to believe that good will triumph over evil, and that the world *is* inherently fair and full of wonder. And maybe you're not exactly thinking of a knight in shining armor, or maybe the knight in your life turned out to be a bit of an ugly toad (who no matter how much you kiss him never seems to turn into a handsome prince), but we all like to stop and pretend from time to time about how wonderful it would be for our dreams to somehow come true.

Now, there's nothing wrong with stopping to dream once in a while, because that's what makes life magical – even if it's just for a moment. But unfortunately, this same way of thinking can sometimes cloud our judgment, by allowing us to lull ourselves into a false sense of security; and into believing that at the end of the day everything will turn out all right – even when we should know better. It's this same way of thinking that helps us turn a blind eye to things that would otherwise eat away at our sense of logic. This isn't a big deal when your husband or boyfriend decides that giving you a toaster on your birthday is a great idea, but can turn into a huge problem when we begin to apply this "it's not that big of a deal" mentality to serious topics that will have a truly profound effect on how our lives turn out, like our decisions about planning our income in retirement, or not taking the time to understand how the mere fact of being a woman basically *guarantees* that you will miss out on hundreds of thousands of dollars' worth of earnings, pension, and Social Security benefits.[1]

I am not here just to tell you to "shape up" and start penny pinching so that you can save more money. Nor am I going to only tell you to start using coupons, to cut back on your morning lattes, or to find some other feel-good ways of saving more of your hard-earned dollars. Instead, I'd like to show you how to take control of your future in a much more meaningful and productive way by helping you understand the dynamics of your retirement planning not just from a financial perspective, but from the perspective of choices. The choices that you make every day regarding your relationship with the financial professionals in your life and your inner relationship with money. Choices that can either help you grow your wealth, or constantly leave you lagging behind. Even more importantly, choices that will determine how you feel about yourself and your future.

So here is how the fairy-tale story at the beginning of this chapter ends: the deterioration of financial markets in 2008 destroyed nearly two-thirds of this fair maiden's portfolio. By the time she realized what was happening, instead of having over a million dollars for retirement, her portfolio had shrunk by over 60%, and she now had less money in her account than she actually contributed over the years. Her early retirement plans were forever ruined. She wouldn't be able to take all those vacations that she wanted, her piña coladas would have to be just regular pineapple juice, and the worst part – she would *have* to continue working way past her expected retirement age. The real human tragedy of her situation was that her dreams weren't destroyed because she was careless with her spending or didn't earn enough at her job, but because she made the mistake of blindly trusting someone with her money without realizing that no one else really cared about her dreams and what she wanted. She didn't review her portfolio allocations, didn't understand the risks of the investments she was placed into, and hadn't the slightest idea of what fees she was being charged, because she thought that someone else was taking care of it for her. Her kind nature and a desire to avoid asking tough questions for fear of confrontation, or for fear of seeming dumb, caused her to place one of the most important aspects of her life – her retirement plan – into someone else's hands, without understanding the sad reality that no one cared about her nest egg as much as she did. And because no one cared, no one took the steps to protect her retirement portfolio from significant downside investment risk exposure.

The sad truth behind this story is that it happens every day. It is a story that I have seen all too often over the years as a financial advisor. Hard-working, intelligent, independent women who made all the right career choices, but had their retirement plans completely ruined because they trusted someone with their entire nest egg and either were afraid to ask questions because they didn't want to look silly, or simply trusted that the person with the title of "Financial Advisor," or "Pension Specialist," or "401(k) Manager" actually cared about their future as much as they did themselves...

CHAPTER 4

CAN YOU HEAR ME? CAN YOU HEAR ME NOW?

"Whatever words we utter should be chosen with care for people will hear them and be influenced by them for good or ill."
— Buddha

When Sleeping Beauty fell asleep, a sleep that only came because her trusty fairy godmother had the power to battle back against a fatal curse, she left behind a family, a social life, a set of expectations about the world, and the role she played within that world. Hidden away until she reached young adulthood, just about to burst into the world as an individual rather than a part of her father's household, Sleeping Beauty stayed in her perfect youthful state, suspended for a hundred years, until the dashing Prince Charming came to her rescue. Honestly, I'm already thinking that these hundred years of restful sleep sound fantastic, but add in the never aging part, and I'm looking for the sign-up sheet!

Crashing through overgrown weeds and entering a castle that had been snoozing for a century, Prince Charming rescued Sleeping Beauty from her hundred-year slumber with a true love's kiss. But when she finally awoke, she found a world that was hard to understand. Outside of her castle walls, the world had moved on without her, but inside, her life had stayed entirely the same. Frozen in time, Sleeping Beauty's castle and its inhabitants had not progressed one day...

Although we may not seriously compare ourselves to legendary fairy-tale princesses (well, maybe just once in a while), as women, we do often occupy two opposing worlds – one that has progressed forward and allows us so many opportunities, and another that is still frozen in time and sees us as passive observers to our own destinies.

As I mentioned before, I grew up around women who were opinionated and outspoken. Women who were educated, and a few who were very successful professionals. Today, success for women is more attainable than ever before. Women are better educated, have better jobs, and honestly, well... are even more outspoken. So why is it that in the financial industry, we are still not really being heard?

One Hundred Years Ago... and Now

Let's take a detour, hop in a time machine, and go through a quick historical timeline! Take your seat, strap on your seat belt and let's take a quick ride... Well, actually, better yet, put on your *Titanic*-inspired dress, and let's stroll down memory lane! You won't have Leonardo DiCaprio coming to rescue you from the freezing-cold reality and offer you a floating board. You will just have to face the cold hard truth on your own... good or bad.

The last one hundred years have made an enormous difference in the daily lives of women, ranging from winning the right to vote to having legal control over their finances. Though many women had started working outside of the home by the 20th century, until the 1960s, women had no real protection in their workplaces. Laws were eventually passed to "protect" women, but they often did so by keeping women away from supervisory positions. In the last hundred years, lawmakers have increasingly worked to protect women's rights in the workplace in a more real and productive way. I'm guessing that's a result of the most important change of the last one hundred years – a woman's right to vote! Of course, with more women voters came more attention to issues unique to them and their financial lives. In the early 1960s, for example, the Equal Pay Act and Civil Rights Act promised women equal access to jobs and, when they got those jobs, equal pay for the same work as a man (a promise that's only been about 80% achieved).[2] And more recently, the Lilly Ledbetter Act of 2009 further strengthened the ability of women to seek better protections when it comes to gender pay inequality.[3]

When you really think about it, it's because of women like Lilly who had to fight so hard, and in so many cases unfortunately weren't able to correct their own situation, but raised a loud enough voice to give others a better opportunity in the future. What women like Lilly were basically telling the world was "Get your hand out of my purse! I'm not giving you my money! I'm not going to work hard for less, just because I'm a woman, and you can't steal from me just because you think that it's okay!" And this was still recent – just a few years ago! But many things have changed for women when it comes to money, especially if we go even further back. For one thing, the way a woman deals with her money has become very different in the last century. When you get a paycheck, you probably don't even think about the fact that you have complete control over what happens to the money you have earned. You might direct deposit it, divert some to a savings account, decide to buy an astonishing amount of delicious-smelling bath beads at your local Sephora (hey, you *earned* it!), or lump it all into a wad of cash and stick it under your mattress. The point is that today, whatever you choose to do with your money is *your* choice. That's because the law is on your side – today. But a hundred years ago, that wasn't the case. Forget about being able to spend your money how you'd like; before the 20th century, married women weren't even considered as individuals! The way it used to work, when a woman got married, she fell under the coverture laws, which essentially created a family unit where the woman had absolutely no legal voice![4] In the eyes of the law, she was considered her husband's dependent and was treated like one.

If you think that was a *long* time ago, think again; in Texas, until the late 1960s, the laws were written in such a way that gave a husband sole control over any money earned by his wife![5] While single women may have been a bit better off, married women have been consistently, even in the late 20th century, considered totally incapable of managing their own financial destiny. That destiny was placed squarely in the hands of their husbands, to the extent that if a wife was going to be hired, an employer technically had the legal obligation to ask the husband's permission!

You might be thinking at this point, "Ugh! A history lesson!? Jeez! What's next? Are we going to review geometry as well? Why is Crystal talking about all this stuff anyway? It was all a long time ago… definitely before Facebook. Of course the attitudes were old-fashioned and sexist!" Well, the reason why it's important is because we have to understand how history shaped attitudes toward women, but even more importantly, to understand how history shaped women's attitudes toward themselves. Although it's sometimes almost unbelievable how far we've come in such a short time, in many ways, things have stayed very much the same.

As far as industry and law go, we are definitely worlds ahead of where we used to be. Women can own property. We can take out loans and establish credit in our own names, married or single, without answering to anyone. We have the legal right to start a business, and many of us do. In fact, women own about 29% of all businesses in the U.S., a proportion that has seen a huge increase over the last two decades![6] And now, in 2013, the head of the Small Business Administration is, you guessed it, a woman. Women have definitely come a long way from the days of coverture laws.

But the problem that remains comes from the fact that laws are much easier to change than attitudes, and some attitudes are still frozen in time, like Sleeping Beauty's castle and its inhabitants…

Still Frozen in Time

The road to equality and a real change in attitudes has been difficult to pave, and would still be just a small trail if it wasn't for the likes of Marie Curie, who won the Nobel Prize in 1911 for her work with radiation; Amelia Earhart, who flew across the Atlantic; Frances Perkins, who served as FDR's Secretary of Labor, the first female Cabinet member; Valentina Tereshkova, a Russian civilian cosmonaut, who became the first woman to orbit the Earth; Sandra Day O'Connor, the first woman to sit on America's highest court, and many other trailblazers who helped break old stereotypes about what a woman could do. Throughout history, there are literally "binders full of women," who bravely challenged expectations, traditions and critics – and they did these things at a time when it wasn't acceptable for a woman to stray too far from the kitchen. Their sacrifices and toughness are what got us to this point in time, when more and more women are becoming doctors, lawyers, teachers, soldiers, scientists, and continue to push the boundaries of what is considered acceptable for a woman to do with her life.

Now, a new generation of women moves even further ahead.

Think about this: in 2010, nearly half of all law students were women[7] and 34% of practicing physicians were female.[8] Three women now sit on the United States Supreme Court, three women have served as the Secretary of State, female CEOs head up Fortune 500 companies, and women can be found in every profession from the ranks of the military to the halls of government. It's almost mind-boggling how many changes took place in such a relatively short period of time, and the next several decades will probably be an even more amazing ride, as women continue changing traditions and building a completely different world for the next generation.

But attitudes take a long time to change, because we learn so many of our values when we're very young, and these worldviews, even if misguided, shape our perceptions of what we can and cannot do. I remember when I was a kid and playing make-believe with all my cousins who by the way are almost all boys (I have over 20 cousins and only four are girls!). We would sit around and play one of those silly games where we would guess what we would become when we grew up, and I would always yell out, "Financial advisor!" Okay, just kidding... I didn't really say that. I actually would always say that I wanted to be an astronaut. Something about space just always fascinated me so much – I've watched *all* the *Star Trek* episodes! But in any case, whenever I would say it, my cousins would burst out laughing, saying that girls can't be astronauts. Of course, we were just kids at the time, and it was just a silly game. But it's amazing how day by day, the things that all of us as children would hear at school and on TV actually shaped our attitudes, and we weren't even out of elementary school yet! Even in my early 20s, when I was certain that I would work in the financial field, some of my family members were trying to discourage me, because they just didn't think it was a woman's job, and they didn't think anyone would take me seriously. This wasn't like a hundred years ago, by the way!

These same attitudes continue to affect us on a daily basis, even when we're all grown up. Let's be truly honest for a moment; even if you have a great job where you're happy, and even though no one can tell you what to do with your life, you probably have the same attitude toward your finances as your grandmother had... I mean, sure, you've probably got a 401(k), you've got your bank account, and your credit cards, and when you go to the mall, no one tells you whether you're allowed to buy something. But for most women, that's pretty much where their financial empowerment stops. Just like my grandma, and my mother's friend who lost her husband early, women still don't really get involved in the big picture when it comes to their wealth. I see this problem on a daily basis, and it's true for women of all walks of life.

Choosing to Be the Scullery Maid

We all know the Cinderella story. It's become a part of our cultural consciousness. Cinderella loved her father, and her father saw the greatness in his daughter. Determined to give her everything he could, he decided that what she really needed was a mother – someone to help her grow up into a strong woman. He married a woman who had two daughters of her own, but rather than creating a happy, blended family, à la the Bradys, this fairy-tale marriage instead created a literal family feud (talk about a reality show!). The death of Cinderella's father made everything even worse, as she was permanently divided from the inheritance that was rightfully hers and was forced to work as a scullery maid. Cinderella only escaped this horrible situation through a glass slipper and a prince with a lot of determination and time on his hands.

Imagine, instead, a world where Cinderella had legal access to her inheritance and the gumption to go after it. Instead of sleeping in the attic and cleaning toilets, Cinderella might be drawing up an eviction notice for her stepmonster and taking back her room from her stepsisters. She would be managing her father's estate, hiring staff and supervising them, and interacting with that determined prince as a landowner rather than a desperate and penniless maid. But that's about as far from our comfort zone as we can get. Updated versions of this fairy tale, even the ones that embrace a strong Cinderella, only let her near her money when some twist of fate convinces her that she deserves it.

Cinderella's sad tale of financial desperation isn't that far-fetched. Historically, women were at the mercy of the men in their lives, which led to real situations of poverty and hopelessness. So it makes sense that a woman's fear of being victimized by someone who has access to her money would become a kind of cultural Big Bad Wolf. Mixed fairy-tale metaphor aside, the fear at the heart of all of these bedtime stories has ironically become a self-fulfilling prophecy. The truth is that we really could be the evicting, land-owning, smart-aleck Cinderellas, because the law is now on our side. Yet we keep choosing to remain scullery maids, leaving our glass slippers in the closet, apparently waiting for a later, better occasion to put them on. Since we all know there's no time like the present to wear a fabulous pair of shoes, this failure to act must be rooted in something much deeper. Either because we still don't believe ourselves capable, or because we don't see how separated from our financial lives we truly are; women simply do not take control of their money the way they can and *should*.

If you doubt this, I challenge you to ask a few girlfriends, neighbors, or co-workers, and see who handles their investments. I bet you anything, you will hear mostly these three things: "Oh, my husband does it. I don't worry about that," or, "Oh, I have my accountant for that," or, "Oh, I have an advisor that handles my investments!" Very rarely will you hear, "I am in charge of my entire financial picture: I have an accountant who *helps* me with my taxes, and I have hired a financial advisor to *help* me grow my portfolio according to *my* goals! And I ask my husband for his opinion from time to time, but I'm the one who makes the decisions about all my investments." That would be a rare answer you most likely will not get! Finding women who are *that* attuned to their finances is almost like looking for a unicorn… Even if you *think* they exist, somewhere, you can't really be sure because you've never really seen one… Trust me, test it out, and make a list!

Scenes From Our Childhoods

A big part of this financial hesitation comes from growing up surrounded by cultural messages and family traditions that taught us how to deal with our money. Fairy tales and folk tales used stories about wolves, giants, and ogres as a way of subconsciously dealing with fears and worries, but in the process, these stories tried to teach women how to look, act, and behave. Nowadays, instead of just fairy tales, we also have television, which tries to tell us, over and over, and in varied ways, how we should behave as women in society.

What do we see all the time? Well, the typical portrayal of a woman and her money managing abilities is basically Lucy Ricardo, who stays home (even before having children) and seems totally incapable of managing the small household budget that Ricky gives her. She's constantly overdrawing their account, spending frivolously, and receiving lectures from her husband about the need to be financially responsible (poor guy, he suffered so much!). And when she really screwed up, Ricky didn't hesitate to give her a well-deserved spanking. Because that's how a grown woman should be treated by

31

her much more intelligent husband; just like a child, because how else will she learn, right!?

Portrayals of female business owners, like Harriet Oleson on the incredibly popular show *Little House on the Prairie*, often saw women constantly supervised, and reined in, by a long-suffering husband who was clearly more of the "adult," and had the cooler head for business. Nowadays, when we see women on TV solely responsible for their family's financial success, it's accompanied by a lot of hand-wringing and anxiety about how much they earn and how they can make ends meet. But rarely are we presented with an example of a woman who seems to have financial savvy, or the know-how, to find the resources she needs to get her financial act together.

In the same way, our childhood experiences taught us how women should interact with money. Maybe Dad went to work while Mom stayed at home, and because he earned the money, he made the financial decisions. It may have even seemed to us like Mom just didn't care, so the lesson we learned was that we didn't need to be involved either. You likely didn't have in-depth financial talks at home, and your sole interaction with money as an impressionable child was probably a weekly allowance that was spent as quickly as possible on something completely frivolous. We may look back at those financial decisions with a mixture of envy and amusement – how excited we were to buy a tube of lipstick or a new magazine! How nice it would be to have "mad money" to spend on things we can't justify anymore! Our lifelong attitude toward money began early, and those lessons continue to influence our behavior to this day.

Recognizing Our Self-Fulfilling Prophecy

The same thing may be happening now – you're looking around

at a world full of smart, savvy investors who are making the most of their money and wondering why that's not you. Trust me, *many* women share your feeling of financial disconnection, as if their financial future is at the mercy of the crazy stock market, a sluggish economy, or an inaccessible advisor. (And they say women have mood swings! Someone seriously needs to talk to Wall Street!)

If in the last hundred years women have come a long way, one thing that still hasn't changed is a woman's lack of confidence about her own financial savvy. Just like Sleeping Beauty's castle, in this area we've been unfortunately pretty much standing still. Like a girl who knows in her heart that she can ride the bicycle all on her own, but is still afraid to take the training wheels off. As a result, the financial industry has just not made that much effort to include us, or ask us to be more involved. And why would they? After all, the financial industry is made up of people – people who grew up with the same male/female stereotypes as you did...

And when you *do* feel motivated to act in your financial life, ask yourself what reception you receive. Think for a minute about the last few major financial decisions you've made. Maybe you bought something big – like a car, a boat, or a house. People often joke about taking a man along for the ride when going to purchase a car, just so that they'll get a better deal. "They'll see you coming from a mile away," someone snickers. I don't think a guy would need to take a woman along in order to be taken seriously. These kinds of attitudes drive me absolutely crazy, precisely because of how common they are, and the fact that they are still perfectly acceptable, and are most of the time brushed off as some comical fact of life!

Trying to Take Control – and Failing

When women do talk to financial advisors, having decided to finally get some answers to their questions and tackle the uncertainty surrounding their financial situation, the reception they get is often very different than the attention and respect given to their male counterparts. Imagine, for a minute, that you visit your advisor's office tomorrow with specific questions about the performance of your investments, maybe concerned that you are not getting a large enough return, or to be sure that you and your husband can retire early enough to enjoy some years together and pursue your dreams. Instead of showing you concrete numbers about your investments and their rates of return, to either encourage you to stick with them or to encourage you to adopt a different strategy, you'll probably get a very broad explanation of what's going on with your portfolio, and hear that you shouldn't worry so much because you have left your money in capable hands. Coffee and condescension, all in one short visit... until you're back for a free refill of both, the next time around.

Now that's efficiency for you!

Here are some re-enactments of a few conversations that I've heard women recount over the years about what happened to them during their visits to their financial advisors. I want you to imagine the following scenarios, play them in your head, and ask yourself whether the reception you would get is all that different from these…

<u>Mary's Story</u>:

This is a story of a woman named Mary, who described typical interactions that took place when she and her husband would visit their advisor.

ADVISOR: *Good to see you, Mr. Thomas! Did you see the stock market numbers today? Wow! What a day we had!*

MR. THOMAS: *Hi, Bob* (ADVISOR). *Oh yeah… my goodness, Apple is just rocking.*
(BY THE WAY, BOTH SIDES ARE USING TYPICAL MEANINGLESS JARGON.)

ADVISOR: *So good to see you, Mrs. Thomas! Nice that you wanted to be a part of this.*
(REALLY…? "PART OF THIS?" UMM… EARTH TO BOB, IT'S MRS. THOMAS'S MONEY TOO, AND HER LIFE, AND HER RETIREMENT… HECK YEAH SHE WANTS TO BE A "PART OF THIS!")

MRS. THOMAS: *Hi, Bob, so how is our portfolio doing?*

ADVISOR: *Oh great, really great, so Mr. Thomas, do you want to buy some more Apple shares?*

35

MR. THOMAS: *Well you know, Bob, I am not sure, maybe I should just stick to what we have.*

ADVISOR: *True, but let's think about this; Apple is always good and I feel it going even higher… They're number one in the industry!*

MRS. THOMAS: *Umm, Bob, so what do you mean we are doing great? Are we on track with retirement? What's the plan?*

ADVISOR: *Oh, don't worry Mrs. Thomas… We've got it all handled… (smile)… So, Mr. Thomas, back to Apple...*

This may sound comical and you may be laughing, either a cynical laugh because you know exactly the feeling of what Mary went through, or maybe a "No way!" laugh, because you're thinking that in this day and age such situations just can't be real! "Crystal must be joking. This never happens anymore, not now!" Well, unfortunately I've heard many versions of this situation over and over again, and they *are* happening regularly, to women of all backgrounds, regardless of their education level or how far they've gotten in their careers. Their only common thread is that they're women – women who kept trying to take more control of their finances, but whose efforts were being disregarded as those of some pesky Lucy Ricardo!

Let's look at another typical scenario:

Sandy's Story:

ADVISOR: *Hi, Sandy. How are you? So I heard you wanted to see me?*

SANDY: *Hi, Bob, I wanted to see you today because I wanted to reevaluate my portfolio. I'm concerned if it may be too risky because of all the recent news, and at this point I need to see if I am on track.*

ADVISOR: *Oh, don't worry about what they say on the news, that's not relevant to you, and you know we are on the track.*

SANDY: *Actually, Bob, I am really not sure what my portfolio consists of at this point.*

ADVISOR: *Ha! Sandy, you know… mutual funds… and bond funds and some REITs, typical, run-of-the-mill stuff we talked about before.*

SANDY: *Well… I know that, but I am not sure how risky they are… and…* (FEELING AT THIS POINT UNCOMFORTABLE THAT HE IS LAUGHING AND WONDERING "SHOULD I ALREADY KNOW ALL THIS?" "IS THIS MY FAULT?")

ADVISOR: *Well, they were based on that questionnaire that we did at the beginning, don't you remember, Sandy? Ha! I know it's been a while but we did them…*

SANDY: *I know, Bob, but I am not sure what I answered and I can't really read my statements correctly as far as the fees and so forth…* (FEELING AWKWARD AT THIS POINT)

ADVISOR: *Sandy, you know the fees. They have not changed since you started and we manage your account diligently and everybody's portfolio goes up and down. You have to be able to have a tough stomach or you won't have any earnings… This is normal… Don't worry, just let me handle it. We know what we are doing... don't you trust me anymore? We've known each other for years now, come on, Sandy...* (TYPICAL BEHAVIOR, I MAY ADD)

SANDY: *Umm... Of course I trust you, Bob* (NOT REALLY...) *But I was just wondering, I just want to make sure I can retire according to my goals and needs...* (FEELING COMPLETELY THROWN OFF AND GUILTY AT THIS POINT)

ADVISOR: *Don't you worry, we have it covered, you will have an amazing retirement!*

If this hasn't happened to you, consider yourself lucky. And I really mean that. But I challenge you to ask your friends, your family, or your colleagues about their recent experiences. I bet you'll find that about one out of every three women has experienced these feelings of dismissal, and that one of those women will be in your immediate circle.[9]

By the way, if you ever want to test out how seriously your advisor is taking your ideas, research an investment product that you think is a good fit for you, and then ask your advisor about it. If they give you alternative solutions, ask them why the solution they are suggesting is better than the one you came up with. If they don't give reasons *why* your idea is worse, but just go into extolling the virtues of whatever they suggested, you will quickly know that they immediately brushed off your suggestion without really taking the time to understand what you wanted.

Mirror, Mirror on the Wall, Who is Responsible for It All?

The most famous mirror in fairy-tale history, of course, is the one owned by the Evil Queen in "Snow White." Enchanted, the mirror had to repeatedly answer the Queen's now-famous question: "Mirror, mirror, on the wall, who's the fairest of them all?" Stroking her ego, and not wanting to get shattered with a brick, the mirror told the Evil Queen that, of course, she was the fairest. Who wouldn't love a mirror like that? A constant self-esteem boost and fashion advisor in one – I'll sign up now! But the Evil Queen only wanted to hear that pre-programmed response, and when she didn't hear it, she was unwilling to accept the reality of her situation.

In contrast, in the story of "Beauty and the Beast," when the Beast gave Belle an enchanted mirror so that she could see her home once more, Belle saw the hard, uncomfortable truth. Far from the happy, thriving home she remembered and desperately wanted to see once again, the home she saw in that enchanted hand mirror was rundown and her once cheerful father was sick and lost without her. The magic that she found was the ability to see the truth – and then to do something about it. Yes, the truth was difficult, and yes, taking action wasn't easy. But without being honest with yourself, can you be truly happy?

Let's not be like the Evil Queen. Our mirror is not telling us that we're the most beautiful or fashionable; our mirror is telling us that the relationship we have with our finances, detached and disconnected, is someone else's responsibility. And even worse, it's telling us that this is okay!

When it comes to the financial industry, many advisors aren't purposely evading questions or keeping their clients in the dark (some bad seeds may be, but most of them are normal people). They, like you, have simply been immersed in the quicksand of the status quo, but that doesn't change the negative consequences of such attitudes.

They have not seen any reason to change because most women have not demanded to be heard, and they've grown up in the same culture of "Dad takes care of the finances." So there's nothing really pushing them to change their attitudes, because despite all of our progress, and the fact that we make up about half of the workforce,[10] women still often feel incapable of investing or managing their own money so they have no option but to hand this responsibility over and feel like they have to accept the direction that someone else feels is best for them.

So what do we do now? Well, I would start with my favorite saying, which is, as you know by now: "Don't Be Such a Girl!" Now, let's get to a real solution! It's time for us (you, me, all women) to claim our financial responsibility and change society's perception of women when it comes to our investment needs and the relationships we want with financial professionals. From refusing to laugh at stupid "Oh, you should take your husband with you, or you'll get ripped off" jokes, to simply investing more energy into taking care of our finances. These changes of attitude can't just be legislated into our daily lives, but have to start with taking deliberate steps to gain confidence and reshape these attitudes – and the first place to do that is within ourselves.

I still hear my mom laughing and saying, "Why do I need to do all this? That is what I have your dad for." Nope, not funny, Mom. Just imagine if my 12-year-old nephew was hearing this? I wonder what he would think of his future wife if she decided to be in charge of her finances. How would he raise his daughter if he had one? This attitude is what needs to change. We all have people in our own circle like this. I know you may say, "But this is what they grew up with," and you're completely right! That *is* what they grew up with, just like the rest of us, and now it's time to update those views.

The Happily Ever After Starts With You

The bottom line is that if your financial advisor doesn't know your priorities (either because you feel uncomfortable sharing them or because he or she is not listening), then you are very likely to end up with a result that you don't want. As women's wealth and spending power increase, and life expectancies continue to rise, so will the need for solid financial plans. It's unavoidable. And no matter how much you trust your instincts, no matter how on the ball you are in other areas of your life, you need to *know* that your financial plan will get you where you want to be in your retirement.

It's time to abandon the worry that you'll offend an advisor by questioning their suggestions and to abandon the idea that you don't have the right to clear, timely information when you ask for it. Somehow, we've grown up with this idea that when women want something done, they have to negotiate or charm their way into success. "You'll catch more flies with honey than with vinegar," they tell us. If you're an exterminator, maybe this advice is worthwhile. But who else is interested in catching flies? I don't know about you, but I want to get rid of those disgusting insects! So if you're a woman looking to steer her own financial course, abandon the baking ingredients and make sure that your financial professional is actually listening to what you have to say. It's your money, not a recipe for a scone. And if a more aggressive attitude is what it takes to get the results you need and to create the relationship you want with your advisor, then forget about being Miss Goody Two-Shoes! "Don't Be Such a Girl"; put on your stilettos, and kick the metaphorical door down.

This, by the way, goes for all the other aspects of your life where money is involved. Whether it's buying a car or a house, applying for a loan, or negotiating your salary,[11] demanding respect can go a long way. Unfortunately, whenever a woman does demand respect, her tenacity is usually attributed to her being a bitch. A guy can be rude and say whatever he wants, and that's called being a "tough negotiator," while a woman doing the same thing is just a bitch. So, then, if I remember high school algebra correctly, I can set this equation up as follows: If women are equal to men (Women = Men), and in the same situation Man = Tough Negotiator while Woman = Bitch, then Bitch = Tough Negotiator. And by that formula, the logical conclusion is that if you want to be an even *tougher* negotiator, then you just have to be an even bigger bitch. Math *is* fun!

And you know what? Honestly, it's a word that guys use whenever they don't have a real point to argue, but don't want to admit the woman is right. So they either blurt it out or think it, while rolling their eyes, as a way to make *themselves* feel better when they can't come up with a valid rebuttal. So if you happen to be in a situation where someone either dares call you that, or is obviously thinking it, then that's your validation that what you're saying is 100% correct, because they obviously can't come up with a valid reason to prove you wrong.

Things to Keep in Mind

It is time for us to be heard by ourselves first, and then have society listen by demanding it through our new, changed attitudes!

In the last hundred years, women have gained legal rights and social acceptance, and now can seize complete control of their financial destinies. These are rights that were nothing more than a fantasy for hundreds of millions of women, for thousands of years. Yet, our complicated history of forced alienation from our finances, along with a cultural message that women are incapable of successful money management, has left women detached from their financial lives. This detachment has created a similar inaction in financial professionals, who often see their female clients as a bunch of Lucy Ricardos, incapable of making intelligent decisions, and definitely not to be taken seriously. It's a perplexing, frustrating cycle – and one that only we can change through regular action and involvement in our finances.

The reality is that even though we now have extensive legal rights, women have remained complacent about their own money. In almost every other area of women's lives, they have demanded attention and forced change – in law, in politics, in healthcare – but in this key area, they are mostly mute. If women are going to take control of their own financial futures, if we are going to teach the next generation of girls that managing their money is indeed *their* responsibility, then we must step up and require the attention and respect of the financial professionals in our lives; whether it's your financial advisor, the manager at your local bank, or your CPA.

It's time to be the gutsy Aurora, a Sleeping Beauty who prefers the modern world to her ancient kingdom; or the Rapunzel[12] who comes up with a battle plan, cuts off her hair, and makes a rope out of it to escape her tower. Stepping up and taking control of your own finances is not only possible, it's necessary. You can make your own fairy-tale ending, but you have to believe in yourself enough to try.

CHAPTER 5

WALL STREET VILLAINS

"If the lessons of history teach us anything it is that nobody learns the lessons that history teaches us." — André Gide

I remember when I first set foot on Wall Street, in New York. I was 12 years old, and I remember how excited my dad was when he was telling me about it! "Oh honey, this is where all the action happens," he told me. He could not wait to show me the trading floor of the exchange. We went on a tour, and of course, it was a really interesting experience – for my dad. Me, I was just confused about all the commotion, the excitement, and the yelling and screaming of the traders! As a kid, of course, I didn't fully understand what was going on. I just thought it was one big playground where adults could scream and yell at each other, and throw papers on the floor because they were excited about something! "Tag! You're it! You own this stock now! Ha-ha! Now, try to tag me back and see if I'll buy those shares again at the same price!" It's ironic how innocent and fun it all looks from the outside, but in reality it can devastate lives with just a push of a button or a crumpled piece of paper that is tossed away.

The glamorous kingdom of Wall Street – full of villains, ogres and dragons, all cleverly disguised as handsome princes and brave heroes. With all the hype, glamour, and crafty deceit it is so easy to be lulled into a false sense of security in the middle of such a financial Wonderland. You never know when your precious nest egg is going to be cracked open, cooked, and eaten by an ugly ogre. Oh, but if only there was a warning label big enough to actually see: "Swim at your own risk, no nest egg lifeguard on duty!"

In this dazzling world of Wall Street, if we believe the movie by the same name – the box office blockbuster starring Michael Douglas[13] – we seem to have an almost unhealthy fascination with what we see as sexy. "Sexy" in a sense of the huge gains that are dangled like carrots in front of us; "sexy" as in wanting to be a part of that alluring and often impenetrable world where the big dogs play, and "sexy" as in the feeling of power and importance that comes from being part-owner of a national or even multi-national business.

Most of us are too busy being captivated by the glory to notice the ugly monsters that are hiding behind the scenes. And over the years there have been plenty of these scoundrels lurking in the shadows. Let's revisit some of the once-upon-a-time ugliest characters of Wall Street – those villains disguised as heroes.

We'll start by traveling back in time only a few years, to consider a story that many of you will be familiar with – the story of Bernie Madoff, or as I like to refer to him, "The Prince of *Mad*ness":

> In March of 2009, Bernard Madoff admitted to having defrauded thousands of investors of billions of dollars in a ridiculously massive Ponzi scheme. Now although most of us are probably familiar with this story, it's important to understand exactly what a Ponzi scheme is. Let me try to explain it simply… and it really is quite simple. The Ponzi master, who outwardly appears to

be a highly intelligent and enigmatic prince, convinces his subjects to jump on board the latest and greatest investment opportunity. And although these people are not really his subjects, as no one forces them to invest, they become beholden to the prince because he makes it appear as if he has figured out a way to consistently make money without too much risk (and of course the prince never shares the details of his strategy, which makes him even more enigmatic). By promising either excessively high returns with little risk, or remarkably stable returns, he lures his faithful subjects into his evil scheme. After the first subjects invest, the prince fakes account statements showing sizeable returns on investment, and even gives cash payouts to these investors to make the scheme look more real. But of course, the payments aren't made from any actual investment growth, but from the investors' own money that they gave the prince originally. Investors see their account balances increasing, and nice payouts, and they think to themselves "Wow, this prince must be using a magic spell! I still have my original principal in my account *and* the prince gave me a nice chunk of money because he was able to earn a great return on my original investment." What the subjects *don't* realize, is that although the cash they received is real, the account balances shown on their paper statements are completely fake, because that money doesn't exist. They just got some of their own money back, and nothing else!

Of course, no one was screaming "Get your hand out of my purse! I'm not giving you my money!" but instead, the loyal subjects tell their friends and family about the wonderful investment they have found with the unbelievable returns, and they encourage them to become investors too. What really drives this are two things: 1) the original investor wants to do something nice for his or her family and friends, and 2) the original investor wants to have some of the prince's enigmatic appeal rub off on him or her as well. The original investor wants to be regarded as being "in the know," just like the prince was originally regarded. Now, this really works to the evil prince's advantage. Instead of having to continue working hard on his image, his loyal first-investor subjects will do the work for him. They will sing his praise to anyone who will listen, free of charge!

The scheme continues, with the new investors' contributions being used to make dividend payments to the previous investors, and so on, and so on. Inevitably the scheme master uses some of the money to make himself look more impressive and believable – bigger castles (his offices), more servants (his assistants), and the finest clothes other people's money can buy. For this pseudo-prince, the beauty of a scheme like this is that his subjects' human nature plays right into his hands, and the human desire to be perceived as intelligent and special will sustain his ruse for a very long time. When his investors (who might as well now be his disciples) tell their friends about the amazing opportunity, and their friends begin to express doubt, the subjects will vehemently defend the prince, even if the deceit is pretty obvious. Why? Because we all want to be in the know, and most humans crave that positive attention that comes from appearing somehow special. And most of all, we *hate* admitting our mistakes. That's just human nature; we want to make believe that we have something amazing at our fingertips, and even when the ugly truth is right there in plain view, we will sadly deny it just so that we can hang on to that amazing feeling a little longer (this is called cognitive dissonance). Without this human quirk, massive Ponzi schemes would be simply impossible.

Eventually, because all honeymoons end sooner or later, some people do become suspicious and begin to withdraw their account balances. Because the fake prince has to keep up appearances, he will pay their fake balances in full, but with other people's money! At some point, it becomes impossible to pay everyone because there simply isn't enough money available to pay the dividends, pay out account balances, and keep up the prince's lavish lifestyle, and the scheme crumbles in a roaring thud. Some people might get a portion of their money back, but it becomes such a tangled web that people who have invested a large chunk of their wealth are basically financially ruined.

In some cases, the scheme may collapse earlier if any of the subjects begin to get suspicious or if changes in the economic situation cause the subjects to want a return of their capital sooner. But in most cases, the schemes go unnoticed for too long and the losses are simply unrecoverable because the money has either been spent or hidden from everyone under several layers of untraceable offshore accounts and shell companies.

Now let's get back to the fairy-tale nightmare of Madoff; he admitted to having started his massive scheme in the early '90s and pled guilty to 11 federal felonies. It was determined that there were an estimated $18 billion in losses to investors and it was believed that in reality his scheme may have actually begun as early as the 1970s.[14] On June 29, 2009, Bernard Madoff was sentenced to 150 years in prison. His legacy is one of ruined financial futures, ruined lives, and very likely ruined marriages that could not handle the stress of this financial disaster.

So think about this… It is very easy for anyone who was not involved in that mess to look back and say, "I would have totally spotted him a million miles away," but as we know with the benefit of hindsight, most investors didn't do this. Why do you think that was? Well, think about it. Madoff presented himself exactly as we would expect for a Wall Street guru; he was perceived to be "sexy," and he offered an undeniably attractive get-rich-quick, no-questions-asked adventure. Everyone was so blown away by the promises of stable, double-digit growth that they did not care to stop and question the methods of this "Prince Charming" and ask exactly how he was making these incredible profits. Furthermore, his aloof attitude of "I don't need your money" only added to the allure.

"O, what a tangled web we weave, When first we practice to deceive!"[15] Except in this tangled web, Madoff's deceit won him even more followers. Followers in the form of high net-worth investors with many insecurities of their own, lusting after a sense of belonging and a VIP status. Followers who with Madoff's intriguing attitude of "don't ask" were drawn further and further into wanting to be a part of that insider club, not caring that the Big Bad Wolf was lurking within, just waiting to get them when they least expected it.

So who is to blame? Madoff? Definitely! The misled investors? To a degree, because many of them likely did have an inkling that something was off, but chose to turn a blind eye to their instincts anyway. What about the banks and the major players involved – those who suspected that he was a crook and yet did nothing to stop him? Why? Maybe because it was easier to do nothing and profit from the money he was depositing with them than to take action and be a hero. Or maybe even they, themselves, began to doubt their own suspicions, and didn't want to challenge Madoff on the off-chance that somehow their suspicions were incorrect, and that this guy really did come up with some amazing system to make money. So at the end, it is no surprise that once this house of straw had been huffed and puffed at, and all blown away, there wasn't going to be anyone left who was completely blameless.

Now you may think that Madoff was new or rare, but that is certainly not the case. There are many villains that have existed, hidden away in the dark shadows of the Wall Street towers. Let's go back a little further, shall we…

A long, long time ago in a land far away where swing-like music was heard in every lounge and smoking cigarettes made a statement… that's right, I'm talking about the Jazz Age… the Roaring '20s, the era of change, where women first abandoned the restrictions of fashion and embraced the comfort of trousers or shorts for the very first time… Yet the times were not as innocent as they seemed… This was the era of the fraud that gave rise to the term "Ponzi scheme."

Although there were a few similar schemes in the past, the first recognized Ponzi scheme involved Charles Ponzi, the infamous swindler after whom the term "Ponzi scheme" was coined. He promised his investors phenomenal returns: 50% return in 45 days. He explained that his method involved buying International Reply Coupons ("IRCs") from overseas countries at a cheaper price and selling them in the U.S. He recruited investors and sales agents who brought in significant amounts of cash ($250,000 per day at one point!), and built an image of a confident and savvy businessman. He then used new investors' money to repay earlier investors, and to fund an extravagant lifestyle. His scheme lasted less than a year because people quickly began to suspect that something just wasn't right, and Ponzi was arrested in August of 1920, owing an estimated $7 million. He pled guilty to mail fraud, and spent 14 years in prison. In today's terms $7 million may not seem like a really significant amount, but it's equivalent to about $82 million in today's dollars, when adjusted for inflation.

What is so interesting about Charles Ponzi was that he came to this country with a dream. He said, "I landed in this country with $2.50 in cash and $1 million in hopes, and those hopes never left me." They obviously did not, except that instead of working tirelessly for his good fortune, this young immigrant's confidence and charisma ended up helping him pull off one of the greatest financial swindles at the time.

And somehow he got away with it too for a while, but at least not as long as some of the ugly villains that wreaked havoc after his time, including Madoff.

By the way, these are by no means the only two villains out there; the list goes on and on:

Many, many people have been defrauded over the last century, in countless Ponzi schemes of various sizes. For example, David Dominelli defrauded investors out of $80 million in the 1980s, and served about a decade in prison. Reed Slatkin, co-founder of EarthLink, cheated the rich and famous out of almost $600 million by creating fake statements and referencing fake brokerage firms. He was caught in 2000. Michael E. Kelly defrauded thousands of people, many of them seniors, out of about half a billion dollars, while using their money to buy properties for himself.

One thing all these swindlers had in common was a charming and confident personality, which played a big part in the success of their Ponzi schemes. In the world of investments there are many villains and they come in many shapes and sizes, and somehow they always seem to find some poor suckers who are ready to jump in with both feet. These villains are basically magicians who create an illusion, and many smart people just choose to believe. Maybe because it has a certain sense of magic; a sense that the opportunity to reach their dreams is finally here, and that they have to take the chance no matter what the warning signs are (some people really misinterpret the saying "fortune favors the bold"). Or maybe the people who fall for this are so insecure that being part of some magical illusion gives them a sense of worth and a sense of belonging, which makes these schemes all the more tragic. Just like in fairy tales, they go ahead in blissful ignorance, or worse yet, just lie to themselves when the evidence is so obvious, and only stop to question things when something looks so odd that it's no longer possible to make-believe, at which point it's probably just too late to save their money.

The funny thing is that some fairy tales already have prepared us for dealing with situations like this. Consider the older version of the infamous Little Red Riding Hood story, where she is in fact eaten by the wolf at the end of the story, and the dialogue in the cabin goes like this:

Little Red says to the wolf disguised as her grandmother: "What a deep voice you have."

The wolf says: "The better to greet you with."

Little Red then says: "Goodness, what big eyes you have."

The wolf says: "The better to see you with."

Little Red then says: "And what big hands you have!"

The wolf says: "The better to hug you with."

And lastly, Little Red then says: "What a big mouth you have."

The wolf says: "The better to eat you with!"

At which point the wolf jumps out of bed, and swallows her up too. Then he falls fast asleep.

There are some obvious comparisons between the scene in Red Riding Hood's grandmother's house and the scene that has been repeated so many times throughout history between the Ponzi villain and the unfortunate potential investor:

The unfortunate potential investor says: "What a convoluted investment method you have."

The Ponzi villain says: "The better return you shall have."

The unfortunate potential investor says: "Goodness, what big and ever increasing gains you pledge me."

The Ponzi villain says: "The happier you will be with me."

The unfortunate potential investor says: "And what big promises you make!"

The Ponzi villain says: "The better off you will be."

This is the point in the story where you need to stop and listen to the alarm bells going off in your head, your built-in early warning system. Remember, when something sounds too good to be true, you need to *stop* and *think*. If you have any doubts just kick the "investment opportunity" to the curb before your life goals are eaten alive like poor Little Red Riding Hood was, before the original ending of the story was changed to make us happier. Now, in a fairy tale we may have the luxury of being able to change the ending, but in cases like Madoff and Ponzi et al., we most certainly do not!

That's why it's important to never just assume that bad things can't, or won't, happen to you. And I don't mean just Ponzi schemes. I'm also referring to very risky investments where the potential gains are heavily promoted, while the possibility of losses is glossed over as almost non-existent, with a wink and a nod, as if to suggest that it's a "sure thing" but that the risks are being disclosed just because of regulations, but aren't really that serious. Remember, if it looks too good to be true, it probably is. We all know that in order for us to have a fairy-tale ending we need to save money, accumulate our wealth, and protect our portfolios from huge losses. But we also need to remember that unlike in fairy tales, there is no Prince Charming riding on a white horse coming to our rescue. Trust me, most investors who lose money due to bad or risky investments do not have the Securities and Exchange Commission (SEC) knocking on their door to help. There is no one holding a bouquet of roses waiting to give them a big rescue kiss and return their life savings in the form of a check. Most of the time the SEC doesn't even answer all the complaints they get; not because they don't care, but because with their limited resources they can only really focus on the truly big cases, like Madoff. So it's really up to you, the investor, to protect yourself. Especially since as a woman you have even more hurdles to watch out for.

In the glamorous world of Wall Street, you have to remember that what may normally be considered hot and sexy is not necessarily a good fit for you. Unlike a new pair of the season's trendiest and hottest heels – that pair of Louboutins that look hot and sexy and the only price you pay for them is at the end of the night when you have to soak your feet in hot water to recover, or possibly rethink your showy investment – with your portfolio you can't just

56

toss the wrong investments away and easily purchase some new ones. Sometimes it's just too late.

So making sure that you are always educated and understand the risks associated with growth, and ensuring your eyes are wide open when it comes to the secrets that Wall Street holds, will keep you safe from the witches' spells and the villains and the storms associated with collapse.

Talking about collapse, let's not forget the mortgage meltdown that occurred in the not-too-distant past. Think about it carefully... when do you really think the Wall Street insiders knew that there was a really serious housing bubble happening, and that they could potentially benefit from it (by betting *against* the market)? Some figured out that a bubble was growing by 2004.[16] But remember that you can only make money betting against a bubble as it unravels and as far as Wall Street was concerned, if there was room for the bubble to grow, their overwhelming intention was to keep it going. And of course, that is when the nightmare began... When they saw that the bubble was about to pop, their intentions and methods changed. By 2006 many on Wall Street started massively betting on its collapse.[17]

As all this was going on, what do you think was happening, or starting to happen, to the new homeowners and all the little people that were not insiders? They were all starting to drown financially because they too got caught up in the real estate frenzy, and bought homes at prices they couldn't afford. And the smaller investors that were trying to take advantage of the mortgage industry paid the price for trying to swim with the big fish.

It is truly sad how many investors were so drastically affected by the credit crunch that grew out of the real estate bubble, and it is even worse when you realize that without a doubt, Wall Street saw it and felt it coming. So the best lesson to learn from this is to forget about the big players, and instead think of *you*, <u>the most important investor</u>. In everything that you do, you need to know that you are the only one who can keep your money safe and sound. Listen to your instincts and trust your gut feeling.

And by the way, if you happen to be like some of the investors I talk to, who compare themselves to Warren Buffett and say, "Well, I listen to Buffett and he says this and that... he does this when the market is down... and he does that when the market is up...," well, guess what? When you have the big bucks that can get you seats on the boards of directors of the companies you invest in, then, and only then, you can invest the Buffett way. For now, be honest with yourself, realize that you're not a big fish, and please start investing appropriately for the size of fish that you are. Because folks who aren't honest with themselves are taking a real chance of being served up on a plate to the sharks of Wall Street. There's no shame in admitting to yourself that you're a smaller size of fish. In fact, that will separate you from the average investor, and will make you an astute decision-maker.

<u>Things to Keep in Mind</u>

- Ask questions, lots of them, and do not let any know-it-all "experts" peer pressure you.

- Watch out for the typical sex appeal of Wall Street – there's nothing sexy about being broke.

- If you decide to swim with the big fish, be aware that you can end up as dinner.

- Never stop taking notice of your gut feeling – in most cases all of the victim investors had a bad feeling about the bad investment but decided to ignore their instincts.

- Unlike some government agencies, please try to learn from history's mistakes.

- As I like to say, when you dress your size and invest your size… that is when you will look your best!

Most importantly, remember, in the real kingdom of Wall Street, there are a lot more Gordon Gekkos and a lot less Bud Foxes[18], if in fact there are even any, who are willing to stand up and say "no more," speak up, and come clean!

You may ask, "Why?"

And the answer is relatively simple… because money will *always* win on Wall Street, because unfortunately some of the players just don't care who they have to use or abuse to get what they want!

And in this kingdom of not-so-righteousness it's every player for himself and herself. There are no loyalties and there are no guarantees, there are no princes and most definitely there are no heroes. There are only investors… <u>ONLY</u> investors, with no one to save them but themselves… So be wise about where you invest your money and be mindful about who you trust.

Be smart and be savvy! And more importantly, "Don't Be Such a Girl!" especially when it comes to Wall Street!

DOES THE GLASS SLIPPER FIT?

CHAPTER 6

THE TALE OF TIMID-ELLA

"Beware of false knowledge; it is more dangerous than ignorance." — George Bernard Shaw

In a faraway land, many years ago, there lived a fair maiden by the name of... let's call this woman "Timid-ella." Through a friend, she was introduced to a financial advisor who she thought was a real Prince Charming, but little did she know that this "prince" was nothing but an ugly toad, only pretending to be a financial professional.

Now, Timid-ella was an intelligent woman, who had built a successful career, and was an otherwise confident, well-rounded person, but who became very, shall we say, timid, when it came to insisting on real answers from her financial advisor prince. And how could she not feel a little bit intimidated? After all, he had everything you could imagine! He had a fantastic castle (his office), had great servants (his assistants), and he talked the talk, walked the walk, and constantly showed off all the big portfolios he was handling! "Oh, yes, Timid-ella, I'm handling the Duke's portfolio, and I gave the Earl a great stock tip, and I even attended a conference where the keynote speaker was the Oracle of the magical lands of Omaha, by the name of Warren Buffett! I am definitely quite important! Now let's take a quick look at your portfolio..."

Many times this pseudo-prince even told Timid-ella that her account was way too small, and that she was not the caliber of the people that he usually did business with, but that he did business with her anyway because she was his friend... Poor Timid-ella felt pretty sad that her account wasn't large enough; but she always felt gratitude to the prince because he was taking care of her accounts even though he was of royalty and she was obviously just a tiny fish in a very big pond. "What a nice fellow that prince is," Timid-ella would think to herself. "There he is, such an educated, confident man, who knows all about the markets... He doesn't even need my tiny account, yet he's taking the time out of his busy day to help me out."

So, understandably, many times Timid-ella felt awkward pressing for answers about her investments, because the prince would purposely use unnecessarily sophisticated lingo when explaining them, and she would still be confused afterwards. This made her uncomfortable and she either felt too embarrassed or too frustrated to ask for more clarification. But it wasn't all her fault. The problem was that when she did ask the prince questions regarding various account fees, or about how risky her investments might be, and tried to talk about her actual financial goals to see if her portfolio was on track for *her* future, the prince always did pretty much the same thing... He would look at her with the same comically dismissive smile, the kind usually reserved for silly questions from little children, and would proceed to briefly explain things in general terms. The moment that Timid-ella began to appear even slightly confused, he would stop his explanations and say that it was his job to manage her money anyway, for Timid-ella not to worry, and for her to stick to what she was good at. He would then proceed by telling her that he had everything under control and would suggest that it was silly for her to ask any more questions about these things, as it would just confuse her more, because she wasn't a professional. This would make Timid-ella feel silly, almost as if she was interfering with a doctor during surgery, so she would just tell herself that there probably wasn't anything to worry about anyway, because the prince was a professional and that she shouldn't meddle so much. Even worse, sometimes she would feel guilty (yes, *guilty!*) and humbled, thinking that because the prince was kind enough to take care of her small nest egg, she really should not be questioning him or his methods because he had to have been an expert, at least based on how confident he was.

After some time, Timid-ella just stopped questioning things altogether and would just walk out of the prince's castle not understanding exactly what it was that she was planning for her future. Even though that little voice inside her head, which is called *a woman's intuition*, told her that something just didn't feel right, she stayed with the prince for many years, hoping that things would somehow work themselves out.

Sadly, many, many, *many* years later, after contributing more and more money into her retirement account, Timid-ella made a startling discovery. After the markets became highly volatile, after yet another investment bubble, her portfolio experienced a significant decline in value. "How could this have happened!?" she exclaimed to herself. "Wasn't the prince looking after my interests?" With huge losses so close to retirement, Timid-ella grew furious. Finally, after many previously missed opportunities to set things right, she became angry enough with the prince to confront him and obtain real answers – because walking away and just hoping for the best was simply no longer an option. After learning all the details, she realized that all this time she had been invested in a way that she never intended to be. The investments in her portfolio were too risky for her age, and were significantly beyond her comfort level. Finally, she realized that the prince was never really a prince at all.

He wasn't even a court jester – just an ugly toad who got along in life through mere confidence, but very little actual concern about what his clients wanted.

As she kicked herself for being so complacent about these issues before, she also realized that now it was unfortunately too late to fix anything. She was simply too close to retirement, and there was not enough time to wait for a market recovery. Too late even for her fairy godmother to save her. Her portfolio had turned into a pumpkin, and there was nothing she could do about it.

Sadly, this fairy tale is based on a true story of a woman I had met at one of my seminars. I won't reveal her name, but the moral of this sad tale is: when it comes to your financial security, you simply can't afford to act like a TIMID-ELLA!

Unfortunately, her situation is a very common one, and many women get sucked into a bad relationship with their financial advisors because they don't feel like they can speak up. Either they don't feel confident enough to demand answers, or they slowly get bullied into feeling insecure about their decision-making abilities, and the results to their portfolios can be devastating because their financial plan doesn't match what they want.

The only way to avoid a disaster is to ask questions, lots of questions, when you see your financial advisor. You are smart enough to understand what you are invested in; it takes a little effort, but it's definitely a lot easier than brain surgery – and you won't faint from the sight of blood (unless your portfolio is bleeding losses from an overly risky allocation). Even more importantly when working with a financial advisor, don't just blindly invest in things that you don't understand. Always ask questions until you are clear about *all* the investment features. It is essential for you to form a productive relationship with your advisor, so that you can use their experience to brainstorm ideas for your financial future and take the right steps to get you to your goals.

CHAPTER 7

WAKE UP, SLEEPING BEAUTY!

"He that is good for making excuses is seldom good for anything else." — Benjamin Franklin

Have you ever fallen asleep, and dreamt that you were being chased, or in some other scary situation where you're trying to run away or hide, and in the dream you're trying to say something, to scream out for help, but you just can't speak? You're trying so hard to say something, but all that comes out is either complete silence, or a barely audible whisper? And then you wake up in a cold sweat, trying to make sure that it was all just a dream, and saying "Thank goodness" that it wasn't real...

It's Time to Wake Up!

These dreams are like situations where someone is in a bad relationship with an advisor, but feels powerless to do something about it. They feel like they can't speak up and can't run fast enough to get away from that nightmare. But in this case the bad dream isn't a dream at all – it's reality, with genuine feelings of fear and helplessness. Fear that comes from having no certainty about the future, and helplessness that comes from feelings of having no control over the situation. Unfortunately, when people in these situations do wake up, the harsh reality does set in, but by then it's just a little too late because they have lost their financial security. You see, losing your financial security is not like losing a wallet. A wallet gets lost all at once, in a moment of carelessness. But losing financial security is something that happens over time. A person gets chance after chance after chance to fix the situation and speak up, but for whatever reason they can't bring themselves to take action – their voice is just a faint whisper. Eventually, they cross a point in their life when taking action may help somewhat, but if the damage has been done, there will simply be no time to rebuild their finances and recover from mistakes.

Over the years, I've had the opportunity to meet with many women who came from various walks of life and have achieved various degrees of professional and financial success. Some of them were entrepreneurs, some were teachers, nurses, doctors, homemakers, lawyers... you name it (although I've never met a woman astronaut – but there's still time!). And the one thing I've noticed over and over again is that no matter how successful a woman may be, most of the time it is very difficult for her to stay in control of her professional relationships that involve her finances. It's quite fascinating, and this trend has baffled me for many years. I could not, for the life of me, wrap my head around how is it that well-rounded and intelligent women, who in some cases have built even better careers than their male partners, can have such a difficult time getting what they want from the people they hire?

Of course, the obvious answer that comes to mind is a person's upbringing, the way that our society portrays traditional female roles, and the social cues that women get all the time as to what is acceptable or unacceptable for a woman to do. As I've already talked about in Chapter 4, all of these things have made an impact on how women see themselves, and affected how they interact with people handling their money. But as I kept meeting more and more women who wanted better control over their finances, I began to realize that the problem was really twofold. Yes, a big part of it is simple lack of self-confidence when it comes to investments because of the traditional male/female roles that have been ingrained in our minds from the time we were young girls (Dad handles the money and the big decisions, while Mom does "woman's work"), but a big part of it is also because our thought process, and the way that we approach relationships, is fundamentally different from how men approach the same situations.

As human beings, we are very social, and our lives are basically built on interaction with others. We have friendships, romantic part-ners, our family, our professional relationships, and we spend a large chunk of our day interacting with others in one way or another. And because we're dealing with different types of relationships all the time, it's sometimes easy to blur the line as to how these relation-ships *should* work.

Let's look at it this way, there are three very basic types of re-lationships: personal, romantic, and professional. Each one of these types works differently and has its own set of rules. For example, your relationships with your friends are different than the one you have with your husband or boyfriend. Your relationship with your family is different than the one you have with your doctor. But all relationships are founded on the same idea that people end up ben-efiting more if they are together than if they are on their own. Really think about that for a second... <u>The whole point of any relationship is that two people will decide to interact together because they *both* benefit at the end</u>. This can be as simple as enjoying an engaging

71

conversation with a friend (just try having a fun conversation with yourself...) or something as complicated as love, where both people experience that nuanced elation that comes from finding their soul mate.

The reason why all relationships work this way is because they are founded on a subtle *give and take* system among all the people involved. You fulfill your friends' emotional needs by being there for them, and they fulfill yours by being there for you. You provide a shoulder to cry on when things are bad for them, and they should do the same for you. The same thing happens in a romantic relationship; you fulfill your partner's needs for stability, family, and the warmth of love, and your partner should (ideally) fulfill your needs in the same way. So the first thing you've got to realize is that relationships are like a very delicate barter system, and for a barter system to work, everyone has to play fair. Simply put, the idea is that when everyone *does* play fair, the whole (the relationship itself) becomes much greater than the sum of its parts (the people in it) because what we're essentially saying is: "I'll be there for you when you need me if you'll do the same for me, and we'll both be happier by being in each other's lives than we would be on our own."

But here's the thing... if in a romantic relationship or a friendship this exchange of benefits can be very subtle, and is based largely on emotions and trust, the barter exchange in a *professional* relationship is very different, because it's much more straightforward: the professional provides you with a service in return for a fee, allowing you the use of their expertise to make your life better. No feelings and no emotions should be involved. Pretty straightforward, right? Well, from what I've routinely observed over the years, the answer to that question depends on whether you are a man or a woman.

72

For men, this exchange is pretty simple; they are able to compartmentalize their feelings into separate little boxes inside their brains, and if a professional doesn't deliver on their promises, a guy will easily call them on it because the situation is unfair. Men tend not to allow feelings to get in the way of their judgment just because they like the person they are working with, and they will usually have no problem telling their professional if they are unhappy about something. But for women, professional relationships can sometimes become affected by emotions, feelings of insecurity, and awkward loyalty. Perhaps it's because we are hardwired by nature to be mothers, to be caretakers to our children, and to bring stability to our families. So this desire to avoid commotion for the sake of stability can sometimes make its way into other aspects of our lives where being non-confrontational and forgiving is absolutely the worst strategy. To avoid this, it's important to learn how to better control your professional relationships so that your financial future can stay on course, without being sidetracked by misunderstandings, or pure laziness on the part of your financial advisor.

Your Relationship With Your Advisor Should NOT Work Like a Relationship With Your Family

Because professional relationships are a straightforward exchange system, make sure to ask yourself from time to time if you might be cutting your professional too much slack by treating them just like you would a family member who's doing you a favor. A great way to do this is to ask yourself the following questions:

- **Am I Forgetting to Step Outside the Situation?**

Being able to step aside and observe what's really going on in your relationships can do wonders for your decision-making, because it will help you notice things that you hadn't before, when emotions kept tugging at your heartstrings and clouded your judgment. If you think back, to your younger and much more naive days, you'll probably remember one of those seriously messed up relationships where one person was clearly taking advantage of the other, but the relationship just wouldn't end! If it wasn't you specifically, you probably know at *least* one person who was in such a situation. If you think back to a relationship like that, the most interesting thing is that the person who is being taken advantage of is the only one who doesn't realize what is going on and keeps playing make-believe, pretending that the bad parts of the relationship just don't exist, and will not listen to anyone!

I remember my best friend was going out with this jerk (I'd rather use a different word, but I will keep it clean), and it was so obvious to all of us that this guy was trouble and up to no good. Too many disappearing acts, not showing enough interest in her... and also wearing many feminine-inspired clothing items: rhinestone belts, very low-cut V-neck shirts, and very well-groomed nails... Come on! He was from Italy, and obviously desperately seeking a quick and convenient marriage to stay in the States! We all saw this! All of us, well, except my friend, she was the only one who didn't! She was a well-educated, intelligent woman who worked as a CFO at a major corporation, and made over $300k a year. But even with all those achievements, she still felt insecure in some ways, and this guy would play games with her that kept her constantly confused about the nature of their relationship, and because she was so emotionally involved, she couldn't step outside the situation, and was oblivious to all the red flags!

Now, she had some really good friends who tried to help her, yours truly is one of them, and we actually did an intervention to get her to see what was going on. Thankfully, she eventually realized the problem! The funny thing is that later she was like, "What was wrong with me? How did I not see all those things before!?"

Just like in a bad romantic relationship, feelings of insecurity and self-doubt can make you blind to the fact that you're in a bad professional relationship. So from time to time, especially if you already feel anxiety about your finances, take a moment to step outside the situation and look at it objectively. A good way to do this is to make a list of all the specific things that bother you and then set up a call or a meeting with your advisor to address those specific items. After the call, or the meeting, ask yourself if the advisor genuinely addressed your concerns, or if you just got the runaround with no real answers.

- ## Am I Feeling Guilty for No Reason?

Remember the classic fairy tale "Beauty and the Beast?" Beauty was always the most generous of her family, waking up at the crack of dawn to take care of her country home and asking very little from her poor father, even when her sisters kept asking for a new wardrobe and accessories. And the poor thing didn't even have a skinny, "double caf" latte with extra foam to help her start the day! When one day, her father returned, having made a deal with the Beast that one of his daughters would return in his place so that he could save his own life, Beauty volunteered – and refused to show any sadness because she didn't want to make her father feel worse (by the way, this is how the original story went, not the Disney version). Okay, I seriously admire Beauty's dedication to her family, and of course things definitely worked out to her benefit in the end. But, seriously, she thought she was heading off to her doom, and to make her dad feel better, she didn't express any of her own feelings. "Umm... Yeah, I'm going to die a horrible death, Dad. But, you know... don't feel bad about it, or anything." She felt *guilty* for being sad. What kind of life lesson is that? If you're shaking your head at this, as I do, think about all of the times you've done the same thing! We've all felt guilty about stuff that wasn't our fault, and instead of getting pissed off at the situation or the person responsible, we'd substitute guilt for anger!

If at any point in time you do find yourself feeling guilty about "bothering" your advisor with phone calls, or repeated requests for explanations, then that should be a clear sign that you are treating them the same way you would treat a friend. Whether your advisor made you feel this way, or these feelings are driven by a sense of insecurity about your finances, doesn't really matter, because the end result of this will be the same: your financial future *will* suffer. Feelings of guilt will prevent you from asking all the questions you'd like to, and that means you won't have all the information that you need to make smart decisions for yourself. In a professional relationship, there is absolutely no place for feelings of guilt. So when it comes to your money and asking questions about it, all I have to say is: "Don't Be Such a Girl!" Especially a girl with guilt; because then you'll be found guilty, and sentenced to a substandard retirement, when your retirement portfolio dies and you are accused of its murder!

• Am I Just Making Excuses for the Other Person?

Now, the situation that just drives me up the wall is when it's completely clear to a woman that her advisor is obviously ignoring her, but instead of becoming upset, she will begin coming up with excuses for their actions. The advisor was too busy to return her phone calls, or maybe the advisor had already explained the investments to her and now she feels dumb for not understanding. Regardless of how complicated something related to your portfolio is, you have every right to ask as many questions as you need until you do understand what is going on. No need to make up excuses for why what you asked for wasn't done.

I remember one of the first times when I really started paying close attention to how I approached situations, and accidentally realized that I was making excuses for someone else, for no reason at all. I was working very long hours, and started getting bad back pains from sitting in a chair all day long. So when one of my co-workers suggested I go to her massage therapist to help loosen up all those stale back muscles, I was more than happy to do it. She told me that her massage therapist was just great, and that all her clients loved her! Well, great! Relaxation? Tension relief? You don't have to tell *me* twice! So I made an appointment and couldn't have been happier – until I actually got the massage.

It's kind of hard to describe what that first massage session was like. Let's see, imagine that you went into a massage place, fully expecting a gentle touch to slowly ease all the tension, and then a rhino ran in, tossed you all over the table, and then stomped on your back. Yes... I think that's a pretty accurate description. I didn't feel relaxed at all! But yet I still paid the lady, and told myself that maybe I didn't complain loudly enough when she was digging in too hard into my fragile muscles, or that her fingers felt like daggers in my back. Or maybe I was the one who didn't understand how a real massage should feel, and that maybe it takes a day to really feel the difference. Making up all these excuses definitely made me feel better. Now, instead of feeling like a pretzel that's been untwisted and then twisted again, I could calmly tell myself that "No, the massage was completely worth it, I didn't just pay someone to torture me, and it was totally worth the money." This way, I didn't have to feel so bad about it anymore.

Well, unfortunately, I did such a great job making up excuses that I went to this masseuse two more times. And every time, I felt the same way. As if the Spanish Inquisition had set up a massage parlor, and I was just going there to suffer. No matter what I said to her, no matter how I tried to explain what I liked or didn't like, no matter what cues I was giving her with the pained grunts I'd make, she just wouldn't listen! But, me, I did the same exact silly thing when I'd get home. I would just think to myself that maybe she didn't hear me well. Maybe because English was her second language, she didn't fully understand what I was trying to say. Maybe it's all in my head!?

Finally, I realized that I was just making excuses and the fourth time I went in, before the session started, I just told her that I had now asked her several times to do the massage the way I like it and she had ignored me, and I flat-out asked her if there was miscommunication or an issue!

To my surprise, she apologized and said that she *did* hear me all those times, but that she knows how to do a massage the right way because she's a professional and so she knows better. She told me that she's been doing this for many years, and that's why she was ignoring my requests, because all of her clients like her techniques. I promptly thanked her, said, "Thanks, but no thanks," and left.

But all painful and annoying experiences have a silver lining, because every bad experience is an opportunity to learn, and I was so upset with having spent several hundred dollars on her barbaric services that I could not stop dwelling on it. That's when I realized that, yes, the massage therapist was a fool for treating her clients that way, but that I was an even bigger fool because I am the one who wasted my own money by making up excuses for her. Had I just stopped making excuses and confronted her right away, then I wouldn't have wasted all that money!

The moral of the story: if you want to be in control of your future, then you've got to train your mind to catch yourself when you start making excuses for others, *especially* your financial advisor, because your money is on the line. A great trick to doing this is to pay attention to how you think throughout the day. The next time you find yourself trying to rationalize your advisor's actions (or anyone else's, for that matter) because they did something that makes you uncomfortable, ask yourself if you might just be making excuses for the other person

This is What Happens When You Make Up Excuses For Your Professional

because you're feeling a little helpless about the situation and the only way to stifle your anger and discomfort is to rationalize the other person's actions. At first, it may take you a little while to get the hang of it, but if you're genuinely honest with yourself, you will find this trick very useful in all aspects of your life.

Things to Keep in Mind

- Your relationship with your advisor is a professional one, so treat it as such.

- Your advisor's job is to take care of your financial needs – NOT to just be friendly and chitchat, while giving you no answers. Bedside manners are always good, but only when done in conjunction with good practices, not in place of them.

- Never feel guilty about asking your professional for help, or about asking questions, even if you didn't understand the answer the first time.

- Learning to catch yourself when you make excuses for others will help you make better decisions. This skill is absolutely invaluable.

- Don't forget to step outside the situation from time to time and look at your professional relationships objectively.

CHAPTER 8

WHO IS WORKING FOR WHO?

"This above all; to thine own self be true."
— William Shakespeare

In the previous chapter, I talked about common mistakes that women make when working with their financial advisors, and gave tips for being honest with yourself about the level of service you are getting. In this chapter, I will focus on proactive steps that you can take to improve your interaction with your advisor so that you can build a long-term professional relationship that truly benefits you.

As I already mentioned, the whole point of hiring a professional is to gain the benefit of their education, their training, and their experience over the years – to make your life better. It's that simple! You use their experience so that you don't have to learn everything yourself, right? You *could* go to medical school and complete residency requirements so that you can be your own doctor, but it's easier to just hire someone who's already done it: your physician. You *could* take classes on auto repair, and learn to fix your car, but it's easier to just take it to the mechanic. So when you hire a professional, you're paying them because you, yourself, don't want to invest all the time and energy to become an expert in all these fields. You pony up some money, and they pony up their expertise, and you're both better off!

If you have a financial advisor, the purpose of working with them is, first and foremost, to use their knowledge and their experience to build a better future for yourself. To use all the experience they've accumulated from seeing thousands of different client situations over the years, to help you avoid rookie mistakes and make your life better. The purpose of hiring them is definitely *not* to spend your meetings having personal, feel-good conversations, or to just chitchat about the stock market without addressing your specific situation. So even if they happen to be your friend, or if you develop a friendship with your advisor later in life, it's important not to blur the line between both of those relationships, so that your finances and your retirement plans don't suffer because of misplaced trust.

Ensuring Your Relationship With Your Advisor Is a Productive One

A big part of your financial success is building a good relationship with your financial advisor. A relationship based on respect, and true concern about your financial future. Here are some hands-on tips about working with your advisor and structuring your relationship with them in a way that will help you get the most out of their expertise, without feeling pressured or overwhelmed.

Whenever you feel concerned that an advisor may not be addressing your needs, or is not being responsive, try some of the following techniques:

- MAKE IT CLEAR THAT YOU EXPECT TO WORK AS A TEAM.

    Working with a financial advisor is a lot like working with an interior designer. They should give you current trends, and their opinion, and then you can brainstorm the best design ideas, together. For example, imagine your interior designer said something like, "Umm... Darla, I have some new drapes here for you... Don't worry about what color they are or what the fabric is, I'm the professional, I know what I'm doing, so why don't you just let me handle it from here." Would you just let them do as they please? No chance, right!? So in the same way, if your advisor brings an investment proposal to you, keep in mind that you don't have to blindly agree to it or make any decisions right away, especially if you don't fully understand an investment. Don't be shy about asking questions, even if you think a question is silly.

Whether you are starting out with a new advisor, or would like to improve your interaction with your current one, feel free to openly tell them that you expect to work as a team. Let them know that detailed explanations are important to you and that you expect your comments or concerns to be addressed fully. Being direct about this doesn't mean that you're being rude, it just means that you're openly sharing something that is a big concern for you. And actually, the way that they react to you bringing this up should tell you a lot about how they will react to your concerns in the future.

• *EMAIL IMPORTANT TOPICS AHEAD OF MEETINGS OR CALLS.*

If you'd like to get the most out of your meetings or calls with an advisor, send them an email ahead of time to let them know specifically what you would like to talk about. This is such an easy and simple practice, but I'm amazed at how many people don't take the time to do it! Sending an email ahead of time helps you in two specific ways: 1) it helps you organize your thoughts, and remember detailed questions that you might have forgotten otherwise, and 2) it helps you make sure that you actually get answers to those questions, and that your meeting doesn't go off topic!

- *TREAT YOUR ADVISOR THE WAY YOU WOULD YOUR HAIRSTYLIST – SPEAK UP!*

The most important thing to remember is that if you feel something is wrong, you should always feel comfortable speaking up and resolving any concerns. You already do this in your everyday life, and telling your advisor about your concerns isn't all that different from dealing with your hairdresser.

For example, when you go to a hairstylist, you have a certain image in your mind of what you'd like your hair to look like, right? So when you go in for your haircut, and as your hairdresser is working, you notice that she's doing something you don't like, your first thought will not be "Well, she's so busy and fit me into her busy schedule, so I'll just stay quiet and let her do things her way." Heck no! Every woman I know, and every woman that I've ever seen at a hair salon, will *continuously* give feedback about how she wants her hair done, exactly how she wants the highlights, and the haircut, even down to the style of the blow-dry! *That* is how engaged and verbal we are as women: "No, not too short. No, not that dark. No, not that style." So just apply that same approach to your money and be that verbal when it comes to your portfolio! "No, not that risky. No, I don't like those fees. Why is this investment better? Is there another similar investment but with less fees or less risk? How does this investment match my retirement goals?" You didn't find that great, sassy hair style by being silent, right? And you can't build a great portfolio without being assertive and clear about what you want. Both should reflect you, your personality, and your goals!

What If You ARE Friends With Your Advisor?

If you're friends with your advisor, sometimes it may feel a bit awkward to act very professionally, because you might feel like that may affect your friendship. But most of the time, that fear is misplaced, and you really have nothing to worry about. Doing so is totally fine and helps make sure that your advisor is doing their job, that they don't become lazy when it comes to your needs *because* you are friends, and that they're taking care of your financial needs in a real and meaningful way. A businesslike attitude won't just help your professional relationship become stronger, but will help keep your friendship intact as well! If your financial advisor is also your friend, but is not fulfilling your retirement planning needs, or is not addressing your concerns, then your financial future is being jeopardized, which will have very real consequences for how you live your life in retirement. And what do you think will happen to your friendship then?

Here's a good example for how to structure your relationship with your advisor if you already are friends, or may become friends in the future. One of my closest friends, Bobbie, is also my client. We have a great friendship on a personal level as well as a great professional relationship, and we're able to have both of these seemingly opposite relationships without any awkwardness at all. Here are some ground rules that we use to help make sure that there aren't any misunderstandings:

- *SET THE AGENDA IN ADVANCE*

    Whenever she comes to visit me at the office, we always label it ahead of time as either a personal, "meet you for lunch" visit, or a professional, "I need to look at my finances" visit. This helps both of us get in the right mindset in advance, and prevents any miscommunication. And if it's a professional meeting, it also helps us figure out in advance how much time we'll need to set aside to cover all the important stuff.

- *DURING BUSINESS MEETINGS, KEEP PERSONAL CONVERSATIONS TO A MINIMUM*

    Sometimes, even when we determine in advance that we are having a professional meeting, there is obviously a desire to chitchat and catch up, because yes, we are friends and it's hard to just meet and get right to business. But it doesn't have to be awkward. We'll talk a little bit about personal news, but very quickly we will, no matter what, turn the personal chatter off, and delay it until after the professional meeting. This helps us ensure that we have enough time to cover all of her financial business first. And then afterwards, when we've covered all the important stuff that pertains to her finances, we can relax and chat about life, the weather, the family, shopping tips, and all the really fun stuff.

- We Have a Zero-Tolerance Policy for Sugarcoating

The great thing about Bobbie is that she is a strong woman and she would never hesitate to make sure she gets the answers that she needs! But nonetheless, when we started working together, we both openly agreed that if something was bothering either of us on a professional level, that we would speak directly, and would not try to communicate by using hints or assumptions. So if either of us has a professional concern, we just say exactly what's on our mind, without trying to soften the message. Bobbie would have no problem calling me out on something, if she felt that I wasn't addressing her concerns, and she would say it directly. And if *I* felt that she was slacking on some part of her financial plan, I'd have no problem frankly telling her that she needs to shape up. Neither of us gets offended, because it's *her* future, and *her* retirement, and the point of our professional relationship is to get her to her goals – the chitchat is reserved for the friendship. This openness and directness helps keep peace and harmony for everyone.

When in Doubt, Imagine Your Portfolio is an Ailing Puppy

When in doubt as to how you should act, imagine that your nest egg is a cute little puppy by the name of "Retirement Portfolio." And imagine that you took your sweet "Retirement Portfolio" to a veterinarian because she was sick. Well, if the vet didn't feel like helping her and told you "Oh, you shouldn't worry about it, I'm sure she'll be okay" as your poor, sweet, little puppy was howling in pain on the floor, well you'd have no problem calling the vet's B.S. (that doesn't stand for Bachelor's of Science), and would immediately confront them about it, right? You would demand immediate attention to your poor, little puppy – no question about it! So, if you're not getting the level of service that you need to keep your actual Retirement Portfolio safe, then just imagine it as a cute, fluffy puppy, and you'll have no problem demanding answers from your advisor.

Things to Keep in Mind

1) Remember that you are paying for your advisor's services, either through fees or commission. So even if you don't pay them out of pocket, it doesn't mean they're just doing you

a favor – it's their job to make sure that all your questions and concerns have been addressed. In one of the upcoming chapters I will outline things to look for when working with an advisor.

2) Organize your meetings with your advisor beforehand, so that you stay on track and get the maximum benefit from your conversations.

3) Treat your advisor like your hairdresser – speak up any time you don't like something, or simply want to double-check an answer.

4) If your advisor is also your friend, there are easy ways to keep your personal and professional relationships separate, without any awkwardness.

CHAPTER 9

MONA AND THE ENCHANTED SPELL

"Follow your honest convictions and be strong."
— William Makepeace Thackeray

I'd like to share with you a true story about how, sometimes, things can get really out of control. This doesn't happen often, but once in a while, you or one of your friends might encounter a professional who will blatantly try to take advantage of you. Again, this doesn't happen to everyone but it happens often enough, and this is a cautionary tale of a real nightmare experienced by one of my prospective clients.

I met Mona when I was doing a presentation at an event in Los Angeles, and even though I didn't catch on to the situation right away, Mona was in the kind of relationship with a financial professional that was blatantly detrimental to her finances, and frankly, to her emotional health. When we first met at the event, we did the typical small talk, exchanged contact information, and went about our day. Well, to my surprise, I got an email from Mona the very next day, where she not only said the usual "Nice to meet you," but also asked if we could set up a time to go over her portfolio. About a week later, we met at my office, and that's when I started to notice that something was very odd about her situation.

What I found out was that she had already seen at least two other financial advisors who had made great proposals that would reallocate her investments to be more in line with her comfort level. So, by the time I met with her, she had already considered changing her investments on more than one occasion and seemed ready to move forward. But for reasons I did not understand at that time, Mona could not take action. So we came up with a plan and decided that we would make changes step by step, so that it wouldn't be a drastic change for her all at once.

Now, adjusting Mona into investments to better fit her age and risk tolerance made perfect sense, and she agreed that she was not comfortable with where she was invested at the time, but as we started making changes to her portfolio based on the plan, she would get cold feet and would call me saying that she wasn't sure what she should do. This seemed very strange to me, because Mona wasn't asking any additional questions or telling me what bothered her; she was just in limbo and couldn't make up her mind. This alarmed me, because when it comes to financial planning, if clients are hesitant to proceed with something, it's usually because they have valid questions that need to be addressed. They want to understand something better to make sure they are taking the steps that are right for them. But in this case, Mona just seemed stuck for no apparent reason at all – or so I thought at the time.

You may have already seen this coming, but it turned out that Mona's previous financial advisor was pulling her puppet strings. Poor Mona had herself a seriously manipulative financial Geppetto, who was telling her that she was making a huge mistake by leaving, that he had always watched out for her best interests, and that she was now going to lose everything by making this decision. He wasn't actually telling her logical reasons for why her decision was supposedly incorrect, but was simply building up fear inside this poor woman who already had a hard time dealing with the transition.

Does this story remind you of anything? If this was a romantic relationship that one of your friends was in, you would probably get furious, because you would see how blatantly obvious the emotional abuse and manipulation were. What makes situations like this difficult is that there is a real gap in knowledge and experience between the client and the financial advisor. In a romantic relationship at least both people are on somewhat equal footing, so if things get really bad, you eventually realize that the constant put-downs and manipulation have no truth behind them. But, because Mona thought her previous advisor was very smart, and doubted her own know-how, she became overcome with fear of losing her entire nest egg (a fear that her advisor had instilled in her). She basically became paralyzed, like a deer in the headlights. She was so scared of making the wrong choice that she simply couldn't make a choice at all.

But she didn't get into this situation overnight. She had been with this advisor for about six years, and had allowed herself to become bullied into decisions with which she wasn't comfortable. Remember when I mentioned that you should set the rules about how to work with your advisor? Unfortunately, Mona was a "Timid-ella" and had allowed the professional relationship to get seriously out of control. But she wasn't entirely to blame. She had grown up being constantly reminded that it wasn't a woman's place to make major decisions, so she didn't really learn how to stand up for herself when she felt that something was wrong. Mona never really learned that she was fully entitled to ask questions and make her own decisions.

Every time she agreed to make an investment that she didn't understand, it became easier and easier for her advisor to pull another string, and get her to make more decisions about confusing investments. He became more and more her puppeteer, and she became less and less independent.

Mona's situation had become so obviously unhealthy for her, that it was really no different from a relationship with a manipulative boyfriend; she became so confused and insecure about her ability to make the right choices that she became stuck and didn't know what to believe. She didn't have a group of friends, though, who were looking out for her and telling her to drop the jerk, because we normally don't talk to our friends about our feelings when it comes to professional relationships. So she stayed in this relationship for almost six years without ever really feeling secure or happy. Eventually, thinking about her finances became uncomfortable and stressful, so she just turned a blind eye to her concerns because they became too frustrating to deal with! At some point, the stress of Mona's situation became so bad that she started having mini breakdowns, because she was feeling completely lost and didn't know who to trust or what to do.

My advice to her at the time was that she needed to go and discover what was going on with her; to really take a step back and think about her experiences clearly. She had to cut unhealthy ties and feel comfortable and confident in her ability to make decisions that were right for *her*. She needed to feel empowered enough to be able to start thinking clearly about her money, without being bullied, and that meant getting out of the professional relationship that she was in. Because she was in an erratic state of mind, and felt completely unable to take any steps, I told her to just take some time off, stop thinking about the situation, and clear her head. Believe me, I really wanted to tell her exactly what I thought of her advisor and what she needed to do. But I couldn't force her to do what I knew was right, because after all, it was *her* decision to make. If I forced her to make up her mind, then I would really be no different from the bully who was her advisor at the time. Trust me, I would love to have screamed at the top of my lungs, "Don't Be Such a Girl, Mona!" but that would not have done anything in this case, because at this point, she had become a little girl who was pulling the blanket over her eyes to escape the monsters in her closet. She was no longer a grown woman who could open up the closet door, face the monsters in the closet, and say "No more!" And if you really want to empower someone, you have to give them space to learn how to think for themselves.

Mona listened to me, but honestly, she was so manipulated, confused, and helpless that I wasn't sure if she would follow through with my advice. It was very sad to see an otherwise strong woman like her being derailed by this situation, financially and more importantly, emotionally. I believe, unfortunately, in her case what will eventually have to happen before she can stand up for herself and make a decision, is for something drastic to occur to shake her up! Something drastic in this case sadly will be a huge loss, and maybe then she will have enough courage to make decisions that are right for her. I doubt that she will recover from a huge loss, and she will have to readjust her lifestyle to account for it. But sometimes in abusive relationships no one can help the victim until they decide to help themselves!

CHAPTER 10

WHEN THE PRINCE TURNS OUT TO BE A FROG

"Actually, it's not me, it's really you." — Anonymous

As young children, we've all had those moments when we were super afraid of something silly. Maybe you were afraid of the dark, and every time you heard a creak or some other noise, your ears would perk up and you'd lie perfectly still in your bed, thinking that a ghost was walking around. Or maybe you were afraid when your mom or dad would leave the house, because you were very attached to them, and felt very anxious when they were away. Or perhaps whenever there was a thunderstorm, you felt so scared that you'd run looking for your parents, because you just didn't want to be alone. Whatever the case was, you probably had one fear or another, and like all fears, it was based on feeling weak and vulnerable, as if you weren't in control and couldn't protect yourself.

My biggest fear wasn't of the dark or some monsters or ghosts – that stuff never bothered me. But one thing that absolutely terrified me growing up was public speaking. Until I was about 12 or 13 years old, I absolutely hated going up in front of the class to answer questions or to do presentations. I don't know why people say that you get butterflies in your stomach when you're nervous. I definitely felt something, but it sure as heck wasn't butterflies. This feeling was more like my stomach was twisting and turning in every which direction as if it was trying to jump out of my body, so that it wouldn't have to witness my public speaking skills. Every time I had to speak in front of the class I could feel my face getting red and my temperature rising. And the redder my face would get, the more I felt everyone focusing their attention right on me, to the point that I thought I'd throw up right then and there. It was like this terrible cycle that fed on itself and grew bigger, and bigger and bigger!

Well, I hated that feeling so much, and I became so frustrated, that one day I realized that I just had to do something about it. The only way to fix the problem was to become in control of the situation instead of letting the situation control me. To do this, I decided to face the very thing that scared me so much; so I joined a drama class and volunteered to help with announcements during assemblies. I figured that if I could learn to be comfortable speaking on stage at the auditorium, in front of all those people, then doing an assignment presentation in front of my classmates would be a piece of cake! And you know what, after I did a couple of auditorium announcements, I realized that it wasn't really that scary to speak in front of others. After a few more times, it became quite enjoyable, because now I was in control of the situation, and even though I'd still get nervous, the fear just didn't bother me that much anymore.

You probably had your own fears about one thing or another as you were growing up, and you eventually got over those fears by either realizing that they were silly things to be afraid of, or better yet, by confronting them head-on and realizing that you weren't weak, but actually stronger than the things that scared you. But growing up and letting go of your childhood fears is only half the battle, because even though you're not a little girl anymore, you still have to face fears on a regular basis – except they're a little different now. As an adult, your fears become more complex, and instead of monsters you become afraid of certain situations, or confrontations. The funny thing is that these fears are based on the same feelings of weakness and vulnerability you had as child, except that as an adult, you call them insecurities. So as that monster in your closet goes away, insecurities about your physical appearance might take its place. Or that fear of the dark might be replaced by feelings of not being smart enough, or not being strong enough to deal with a bad situation. And just like you'd sometimes feel stuck as a kid when you were afraid, you now become stuck in your mind when faced with an uncomfortable situation.

When it comes to your money and your ability to build a good future for yourself, having your insecurities prevent you from making the right decisions can turn into a real-life nightmare. Remember the story of Mona, from the previous chapter, who was being manipulated by her advisor? Well, her advisor quickly latched on to her insecurities and manipulated her to the point that she didn't know how to make the right choices for herself anymore. In the same way, you may find yourself in a bad professional relationship with a financial advisor who is manipulating you, or maybe invested your money without your permission and then told you it was a misunderstanding. You can tell that you're in a bad situation, but your fear of confrontation and your fear of losing your money, or insecurity about your ability to make the right choices, can paralyze you. These worries begin to eat away at you, and build themselves up to the point that you want to make a change, but you just don't know how.

If you're stuck in a bad situation, and you realize that your financial advisor is hurting your financial future, then it's important that you confront the problem head-on, and either change it or get out of that professional relationship. As uncomfortable as the confrontation may feel, and as worried as you might be that you won't be able to assert yourself to make a clean break, you have to realize that your financial future is at stake. The longer you stay with an advisor who is detrimental to your financial future, the more chances you are taking with your money.

But there's no reason to dread this type of confrontation to do something good for yourself. Confrontations are not a bad thing. Instead, they give you the opportunity to correct a situation that otherwise eats away at your sense of well-being, and a way for you to assert yourself and regain the sense of confidence that feelings of doubt and insecurity can sometime shut off. It's the same exact thing as opening up your closet door and confronting a big scary monster; you realize that you are much stronger than you give yourself credit for, and that your fears sometimes have absolutely no basis in reality. So when, and if, you do conclude that your current financial professional isn't the right person for you, and you decide to break things off, here are a couple of points that can make the process a lot easier on you.

This is what I call using the 3-Step, "Don't Be Such a Girl!" technique, which can help you walk away with your head held high and feeling completely in control, confident, and empowered!

Step #1 – You Don't Need to Say "I'm Sorry"

When I was about 18, working as a teller at a major bank, I had a real issue with my then-manager! I felt like she pushed me around a lot and gave me few shift hours because I was younger than everyone else. This was very frustrating for me because I had consistently good performance. Even though I did a great job at opening new accounts, and was one of the top-performing tellers in the branch, she just wouldn't acknowledge it. Then I discovered I was not the only one who felt frustrated. There were several other tellers who had the same issues with her management style. So when an opportunity with a nearby branch opened, the three of us applied for transfer!

But, it wasn't as easy as we thought it would be. Sure enough, we were confronted by our manager, and when that happened, the other two who had applied for the transfer told her that they were really sorry, that they loved working with her, and that they only did it because the other branch was closer to their homes (without realizing, by the way, that she had their addresses in the employee files, and this lie could be easily revealed...)! Obviously the two tellers were young ladies themselves, and they were scared, didn't want to upset their manager for fear of retaliation, and didn't know how to have a professional confrontation. Neither did I, but when my turn came, and my manager asked "Let me guess, you want to go too, because it is more convenient distance-wise for you?" I replied, "Actually, no, not really. I am asking for this transfer because I know that I do a great job, and I believe that I deserve more hours, and quite frankly, a promotion. But for whatever reason, you're not noticing my effort, or how hard I am trying, and I want to go somewhere that may give me a better opportunity." I didn't say "sorry," and I didn't try to soften the situation. I stood up for myself, remained professional and respectful, but in a sense, almost demanded that transfer. Well, guess what happened? At the end of the day, I was the only one that was chosen for the transfer! (And I was promoted within a month at the new branch!)

That was truly a great learning experience for me, and it taught me that I should never compliment someone or say nice things if I don't actually mean it. It also taught me that even in uncomfortable situations, where your instinct may be to try to soften things, sometimes it's better to avoid the sugarcoating for the sake of your own sanity. But most women don't feel comfortable being blunt when dealing with professional relationships, especially when trying to end them. They start to feel guilty, or awkward, so they start apologizing. They try to make the other person feel better, and let them know how great they are, and that they like them as a friend but as a professional, they just "want to see other professionals." See, it's just like a real breakup! And just like in a real breakup, saying "I'm sorry, you're such a great person" just confuses things.

Forcing yourself to be nice when you don't actually feel that way makes you feel kind of stupid afterwards. Have you ever ended a romantic relationship with someone, a person who you didn't like, but went on and on about what a great person they are? How did you feel afterwards? I bet it didn't feel all that great, because you just told someone who wasn't right for you what a wonderful person they are, and suggested that you're sorry for letting them down. But that's not the case in a bad professional relationship, because when you get to a point where you feel the need to leave your advisor, it's pretty clear that they let you down, and it's not your job to apologize for someone else's mistakes. You're not a little girl who didn't let her friend play with her dolls; you don't have to say "I'm sorry." That's absolutely the worst thing you can do in a situation like this, because if you are unhappy, and if your financial advisor has been ignoring your needs, then what the heck are you sorry about! They should be sorry because they were too foolish, or too selfish, to care about what you needed as a client and didn't take your needs seriously. So no, you're not sorry; you're just doing what's right for you, and your financial future.

Step #2 – You Don't Owe Anyone an Explanation

Remember the fairy tale of Rapunzel? The girl with super-long hair who just sat in her tower until a prince showed up? Well, just imagine if Rapunzel had to stop and explain to the evil witch why she needed to escape and leave the tower; she would have never gotten out and she would have been stuck there forever!

So I'd like you to take this point very seriously: once you've made up your mind to do something that you feel is right for you, you don't owe anybody an explanation. So as you initiate a breakup with a professional who doesn't seem to have your best interests in mind, you don't really need to go into too much detail as to why you are leaving them. Remember, this is not a romantic relationship, so you don't need to make anyone feel better. This is not the same thing as when you are breaking up with a boyfriend or going through a divorce. In a romantic breakup, when done properly, the talking is important because it gives both people closure, which is essential when genuine feelings and emotions are involved. But in breaking a professional relationship, your professional is not really emotionally vested, so there is no need to talk things out. That's why going into detail is absolutely unnecessary – it just makes the process more difficult on you for no reason at all.

Here's why this is important: if you do go into too much detail, then they will try to talk you out of your decision, and this will make you feel insecure and will make you doubt yourself. When you make decisions on a whim, a little self-doubt is a healthy thing, because it helps you avoid mistakes. But in a situation where you've already thought carefully about your decision, unsuccessfully tried to fix the problems, and now decided to make the break, then at that point you know that it's the right step for you. And if someone makes you second-guess your decision after you've already clearly made up your mind, it will make you feel beyond lost, to the point where you won't know what to do at all. That was exactly Mona's problem; she second-guessed herself into decision paralysis!

I have seen many situations like this where, instead of staying firm, women would fall into this trap of "talking things out" and answering their advisor's questions when they would try to leave. So these poor women would pour their hearts out about what bothered them, only to then be ridiculed about their reasoning for moving on: "Oh, you should have told me sooner, I had no idea you felt that way about such and such investment. And I never received those voicemails, so that's why I didn't return your calls." The stupidest part about all this is that the ridiculing happens not because these women's real reasoning is incorrect (their current advisor being inconsiderate and not focused on the client's needs), but because in their attempt to sound nice and make the professional feel better, they come up with alternate reasons that sound softer. Because these reasons don't truly come from the heart, they are harder to back up by facts.

If you're trying to leave a bad professional relationship where you have been constantly ignored, and you just want to end it, here's how the situation can go very wrong for you and leave you feeling weak and insecure:

YOU (trying to be nice): *"Well, you know, I just don't think these investments are the kind that I want, and there are other things I'd like to try, because it wasn't what I really wanted."*

FINANCIAL PROFESSIONAL: *"Oh, not a problem, I didn't realize that you felt that way, you should have told me earlier. I can definitely fix it for you."* (Only taking the concerns seriously now because you are leaving.)

You: *"Well, I did mention during our meeting that I wasn't really comfortable with it, but maybe I just didn't explain myself correctly. In any case, I just want to move along in the new direction I found."* (Still trying to sound nice, and blaming yourself so as not to be confrontational.)

FINANCIAL PROFESSIONAL: *"Hmm, well you did sign the paperwork saying that you understand what the investment is about, and all the risks. I guess I just don't understand why the change of heart, and why you're leaving altogether instead of just asking me to change your allocation."* (Now making you second-guess yourself as to whether they were unresponsive when you voiced your concerns, even though you've already tried explaining what bothered you, and making you feel like the miscommunication was on *your* end.)

You (now flustered and uncomfortable): *"Yes, but I would just like to continue with moving the accounts anyway, because it's just not for me."*

FINANCIAL PROFESSIONAL (with a confused and indignant tone in their voice): *"I don't understand what you mean by that, but sure… I guess… I mean it's your money, you can do what you want."*

Do you see the potential of what will happen in that conversation!? If you try to be nice during a professional breakup by trying to explain things, and offer explanations that aren't what you're really feeling, then the professional that you are leaving will offer solutions on how to fix the situation and start pointing out why you are incor-

Which one would you rather be?

rect. Because you are trying to be nice and are not explaining the real reason (you want to leave), then there is absolutely no way that they can offer a solution that will make you feel better. So in their mind they will feel like you're being unreasonable, and will make you feel as if you're being a jerk because they're offering up solutions and you're just rejecting them.

The bottom line is that you should only bring up concerns when you still think there is a chance that there may have been some genuine miscommunication, or some legitimate misunderstanding, and you still believe that once they understand your concerns, the professional will attempt to rectify the issue. But once you've made up your mind, there is no point in going into detail, because you should no longer care what the other person does with that information. You have already found a solution that is best for you – leaving.

Even if that advisor is also your friend, they should be able to understand the difference between your professional and your personal connection. They should be able to see that on a professional level, they are simply not satisfying your needs, should be humble enough to accept your decision, and understand that a split on a professional level doesn't mean that your friendship has to end. If they can't see that, and don't want to maintain the friendship after the professional relationship has ended, then they were probably never a real friend to begin with. Seriously, would you want to be friends with someone who has a requirement that you do business with them to remain friends? Of course not! It means that the friendship isn't real!

When in doubt, remember: you don't owe anyone an explanation, except your "future self" – the person who will have to live with the decisions that you make today and deal with any issues that might come up because there isn't enough money during retirement. And the only thing that separates you from your future self is time. You will have to meet your future self one day, and it's up to you whether that meeting will be a happy one or one filled with regret and self-kicking.

Step #3 – It's Not Your Job to Teach Them

If you're breaking up with a financial advisor, one thing they may ask is what they did wrong. They won't make it sound like they want to talk things out, but as if they just want some friendly tips on how they can improve themselves. Just like you don't owe anyone an explanation, you also don't owe them free training about how to treat their clients. You want your advisor, just like your doctor or lawyer, to be proactive about helping you, rather than being reactive after they know you are leaving. Think about it this way, if someone in your life does something that's detrimental to you, like talking about you behind your back, is it better if they feel guilty and come to you to tell you the truth and apologize, or if they apologize after you confront them? In both cases the person might genuinely feel sorry for their actions, but in the first case, where they came to you to apologize first, it's their own conscience that makes them uncomfortable enough until they need to come to you to fix things, because they truly are thinking about you. They, themselves, feel uncomfortable to the point where they need to be proactive and set things right. And that's what you want from your financial advisor, and any other professional you hire; you want people whose character drives them to take care of you proactively and to make sure that all your needs are met rather than waiting for a threat of losing you as a client to start caring about your needs.

That's why I always say that when you are breaking a bad professional relationship, it is absolutely not your job to teach somebody how to provide better service. They should know how to do their job and if they have not been able to learn by listening to the questions that you have been asking prior to this "breakup," and they've been ignoring you, then it's not your responsibility to sit down and explain what they can do better. It's not your duty to improve their business or to help them grow, because a person who really does want to learn and grow will do so themselves, without losing clients.

Let me give you an example about a problem I once had with my previous dentist. I had been going to her for several years, but felt that she didn't really listen to me. I kept complaining about ongoing pain in my teeth and she would always just say, "Oh, you're probably grinding them at night," but would never really recommend any solutions. One time, when I visited her office after years of feeling like I had been ignored, I again complained about sensitivity in my teeth because it had become a real problem. Again, she barely examined them, and had her assistant take some x-rays. Then, she came back and said, "Oh, it's your fillings… They need to be replaced." I asked her, "Are you sure?" She said, "Definitely," and went on to tell me how fillings eventually become loose, and cavities continue to form. I then asked her, "Are you 100% sure those are my x-rays, I just want to make sure before we do any work." She looked at me with a quizzical expression on her face, and said, "Of course, we just took them!" This is when I realized this situation was out of control, because as my dentist, she should have known that I never had any fillings, ever! So why would they need to be replaced!? Well, that's when I knew that it was time to "break up" and get a new dentist before my teeth would suffer any drastic consequences.

At that point, I decided that no explanation was needed as to whether she had the wrong x-rays, because she was about to perform unnecessary work on my teeth. It didn't matter what the situation was – honest mistake, incompetence, or laziness. So I said, "Thank you, but I will not be doing that work today, and I will not be coming back, so you can close my patient file." I then paid my co-pay, and left. There was no point in explaining to her what the reason was, as it wouldn't have done anything good for me, and wouldn't have solved my problem. Because after all, it was about my well-being – not her feelings.

Things to Keep in Mind

At the end of the day, ending professional relationships that are bad for you and having to confront someone because they're not meeting your needs is never a pleasant experience. There's no way around it. But you know what… neither is taking your car in for service. Neither is it a pleasant experience to sit down with your checkbook to pay your bills, or to do laundry, or to go to the dentist to get a root canal. So if you're stuck in a bad professional relationship with your financial advisor, and you just can't seem to get the attention or the answers you need, then at some point you have to make the decision of what's more important to you: avoiding an uncomfortable situation, or protecting your financial future, and ultimately your retirement.

If you do end up in a situation where you have to make the break, just keep the following points in mind to make it as simple as possible:

- You don't have to apologize. Saying "I'm sorry" won't make you, or them, feel any better, and may make things worse.

- You don't owe anyone an explanation once you've decided to take action that you know is right for you. Talking things out only makes sense if you still want to fix a broken professional relationship.

- It's not your job to teach your advisor how to be a better professional.

- Confrontations, whether it's with your advisor or some other professional in your life, will never be as scary or uncomfortable as you think. And the relief you feel after confronting a problem will make it worthwhile.

THE WOLF THAT STOLE THE GOLDEN EGG

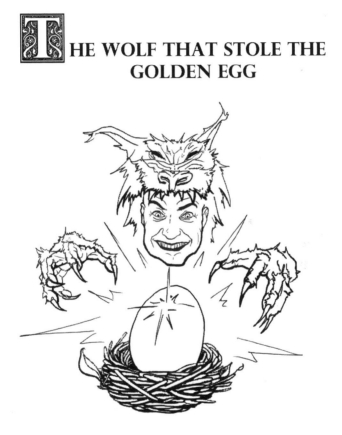

CHAPTER 11

THE YELLOW BRICK ROAD TO INNER PEACE

"Everyone who wills can hear the inner voice. It is within everyone."— Gandhi

Whether you just got out of a bad relationship with an advisor who wasn't paying attention to your needs, or maybe you haven't had an advisor for a while, the best thing you can do for yourself is to take a little time and figure out what you want out of life before you form another professional relationship. In your romantic life, one of the best ways to avoid bad relationships is to become comfortable in your own skin. To love yourself, to respect yourself, and to feel confident to a point where you don't *need* someone in your life just to feel complete, but *want* someone in your life because they genuinely make you feel better. Being in a relationship just because you feel lost when you are on your own is when you're likely to let things go more often, and are less likely to command respect from your partner because you are afraid that if you assert yourself, they will leave you and you will once again feel alone and drowning.

When it comes to your finances, it's very much the same thing. If you don't feel confident about your understanding of basic financial concepts, and more importantly, if you don't feel in control of your financial situation, then you're likely to end up in another bad professional relationship. Instead of feeling empowered and in control, you will look for a savior; someone who will solve your problems *for* you, rather than *with* you. The danger of this is that you'll end up in a hopelessly frustrating situation, where you will feel weak and lost, and that is something that you can't afford to do, emotionally or financially. The only way to avoid this situation is to take steps that will make you feel strong and empowered. Steps that will help you feel in control of your future, and ultimately, in control of your destiny. When you feel confident and strong, you will choose relationships that are right for *you*. That is why it's so important to have at least a basic understanding of financial concepts.

Do keep one thing in mind... Before you decide to drop everything and get a PhD in finance, remember *why* you decided to take action. Remember why you decided to do more about your finances than just the status quo. And even more importantly, remember that you did not set out to learn all there is to know about the world of investing in a couple of weeks and try to figure everything out on your own. It is very important that you keep this in mind, because nothing ruins a good nest egg like a newbie investor who is overconfident and knows just enough to do some damage. This is something I've seen happen before, and it's not pretty. It's kind of like using the internet to self-diagnose your health problems, and then not actually going to the doctor. Yeah, you'll get *some* useful information, but you won't necessarily have the experience to carefully analyze that information from all angles to come up with a prudent action plan.

You should first take some time to familiarize yourself with basic financial concepts; and even more importantly, before rushing into a professional relationship, you'll definitely want to spend some time interviewing and getting to know other financial advisors so that

you can find one who really understands your needs and life goals. Remember, the whole point of having a good financial advisor who is right for *you* is that you want to have a professional on your side who is genuinely interested in helping you achieve your goals and dreams, and who listens to your concerns. This is someone who acts like a trainer at the gym and uses their experience to help you fine-tune your workout routine to get the most out of it. But just because you have a personal trainer, that doesn't mean that you shouldn't know why it is that you are doing the exercises and whether the exercises are helping you toward your personal goals. We all need professionals in our life to help us plan various important factors. Eating healthy and taking vitamins can help prolong your life, but this does not mean that you don't need a doctor. Brushing your teeth and flossing regularly will give you healthier teeth, but this doesn't mean that you do not need a dentist. And it's the same thing with your money; you should be the one working diligently to improve your finances, but having an experienced financial professional watching out for you, and helping you avoid pitfalls, is priceless – it just has to be a person who is right for you.

During the next few chapters you will be provided with a basic overview of some of the more common financial concepts with the idea that this will give you a better understanding of investments and budgeting, and will help you to have a more productive conversation with your advisor when you finally find your financial soul mate. Remember, you might not know everything about navigating financial waters, but having a compass and a map is way better than just sitting in the boat with a blindfold on. (I have included additional information and definitions in the Appendix section of this book if you would like a more in-depth understanding of certain financial topics.)

Now, there are two big reasons why you should understand at least the basic financial concepts: 1) it will help you be more confident when it comes to discussing your retirement, your investments, and your portfolio allocations, which will help prevent rash decisions or decisions based on feelings of insecurity, and 2) it will enable you to better interview and select a financial advisor who meets your needs, because you will be able to ask them more meaningful questions during the interview process. It's important that you keep in mind that you should devote some time to hiring the right person to help you take care of your finances and not just try to figure everything out on your own. I have seen many people throughout the years who have become their own financial advisor, and the problem that I see over and over in these situations is that a person will get lucky because the market just happens to be doing well at that time. Instead of realizing that the stars just happened to be aligned in their favor, these folks will start to think that they've got the entire stock market figured out. However, most people can't consistently beat the performance of the market, and a novice who gets lucky a couple of times is making a huge mistake when they start thinking that everyone else who is actively investing (at least tens of millions of people over the last few generations) is just too foolish to get the magic formula right, but that *they* somehow figured it out based on intuition and by reading obscure online blogs. Even Jack, from the fairy tale of "Jack and the Beanstalk," probably thought that he was savvy for getting those magic beans that grew into a giant beanstalk, but he obviously just got very lucky.[19]

I want you to take this very seriously, ladies; if you start managing your own money and see some early success, please don't let it go to your head. Many people make this error of mistaking luck for actual ability to beat the markets. There are tons of professional money managers out there who have delivered amazing short-term results, but who can't do so regularly, because a lot of short-term investment success is based on timing and luck.[20] Even experts who study and follow the stock market and the economy all day long still can't accurately predict what will happen next. They are definitely not dummies, but rather people with PhD's who devote their lives to studying the markets, statistics, and all that other fun stuff that makes for great party small talk. I once heard a great joke that went something like this: "An economist is someone who can explain to you on Wednesday, why the prediction they made on Monday, didn't happen on Tuesday." So if they have a hard time beating the markets, what makes you think that you can do better? There have been very, very few investors throughout history who were able to consistently beat the markets, and who nonetheless also have at times incurred disastrous losses. If it were truly easy, we all would be rich, right? Better yet, anyone who could figure out the perfect formula for making money would probably keep it a secret and be the richest, most powerful person in the world! So let's take our naive hats off – consistently predicting the market is an illusion, no matter how luxurious and couture it may feel. Such a notion is simply fake, just like most of the Louis Vuitton bags you see teenagers carrying in downtown Los Angeles. So as you begin to learn various financial ideas and concepts, just keep reminding yourself *why* you're doing it: to be better equipped to protect your nest egg and keep it on the right path – not to become the next Warren Buffett.

Remember when I said earlier that it's all about the choices we make? There are many intelligent women who are making the wrong choices because of their lack, and fear, of understanding the financial implications of retirement and financial planning. But it doesn't have to be that way. A little bit of effort and a desire to be in control can get you a long way into having a better grasp of your financial life. With that in mind, put your learning hat on, sharpen that pencil and get your lunchbox ready, because you're about to learn some really fun stuff! Actually, forget the learning hat and the lunchbox; just pour yourself a glass of wine, cozy up under a warm blanket and get ready to learn about your finances! And if you're already thinking "Ugh, finances are boring, why do I have to read about this stuff?" then really, "Don't Be Such a Girl!" I promise it will be fun! There is nothing more fun than being on the right track and in control of your money, and you can only do that with good old-fashioned solid planning. The only way to begin to plan better is to gain more knowledge and a better understanding of the financial world around you, which will help you make better and wiser choices!

CHAPTER 12

401(K) – YOUR NOT-SO-MAGIC-BEAN

"Even if you're on the right track, you'll get run over if
you just sit there."— Will Rogers

We have all heard of the fairy tale of "Jack and the Beanstalk" – how Jack's wondrous magic beans grew into a giant beanstalk that gave him access to an enchanted world where he found treasure. Despite knowing that fairy tales are fiction with no basis in reality, there are still many of us who mistakenly believe that our 401(k) is our very own magic bean. And so, we live our lives with the idea that if we just plant this magic bean, it will grow all by itself, and will eventually become a pile of treasure that will provide for a very comfortable retirement. We think that if we work hard and regularly contribute our hard-earned money into our 401(k) accounts, that everything will work itself out and a lifetime of income will magically appear for us! But remember, ladies, life is not a fairy tale, you're not Jack (or Jacqueline) and your 401(k) is not a magic bean; a happy outcome is not guaranteed. Just because you're contributing money to your retirement account on a regular basis does not mean that you will accumulate wealth.

Let me give you one of the more glaring examples of this lack of attention toward a 401(k) that I encountered in my career... I once had a client, Irene, who genuinely believed that because she was contributing money into her 401(k), that it somehow meant she would automatically get exactly the amount of income she desired when she retired. She believed that, even though her contributions were less than 10% of her salary and her company only matched 5% of that amount, that her 401(k) would grow large enough to the point where it would generate sufficient income during retirement to cover her rent and all her other expenses. Apparently, she had heard somewhere, probably from someone who was as confused as she, that if she just saved with a 401(k), the magic bean, that it would automatically give her the money that she would need in the future. She did not understand that it wasn't just about contributions, but about how much she contributed, where she allocated her portfolio, and for how long she saved! In her head, just the mere fact that she had a 401(k) meant that she would be okay. Now, it may be really tempting to laugh at her, until you realize that her outlook could have had very tragic results, and especially when you realize how many women also have this same outlook! Fortunately for Irene, she still had about nine years until her retirement, and after I explained to her why her assumptions were incorrect, we were able to figure out a plan of action to get her retirement on track. She increased her contributions, cut back on unnecessary spending, and started saving more in her regular savings account. Doing this wasn't super easy, but it helped her avoid the disaster of running out of money during retirement.

But, unfortunately, this story is very representative of how most people think about their 401(k) accounts, which is especially dangerous since, for most people, their 401(k) is one of the biggest retirement assets that they will have when they get to their golden years. Whether you retire with one huge 401(k) account after working at a company for decades, or have lots of small Rollover IRA's where accounts from your previous jobs accumulated, you will likely have saved up a large chunk of your retirement nest egg through the 401(k) program during your working years. Because of this, it is very important to take good care of your 401(k) in a way that will actually get you to your retirement goals. Growing your retirement plan contributions into a mini-fortune that can sustain you throughout your retirement requires more than just stuffing contributions into your account. It requires your time and attention, just like a real beanstalk, or any other plant, would. You have to water it regularly, make sure there is enough sunlight, and check the leaves regularly to make sure that your plant is healthy and that there aren't any bug problems. You should tend to your 401(k) account on a regular basis and constantly check to make sure that there aren't any small issues that can eventually become big problems and prevent you from enjoying your retirement.

Mistake #1 – Thinking That Someone Else Cares About Your 401(k)

Let's break it down, shall we? First and foremost, it is essential for you to realize that your 401(k) is not a magical solution whose sole purpose is to look after you in your retirement. It is not! Your next wake-up call is to grasp that your 401(k) is not being managed specifically for you. The company you work for is not watching your portfolio's investments carefully to ensure that you avoid any risky situations should the stock market collapse. Trust me, Joe Schmo from Human Resources is not sitting there watching *your* account and thinking about *your* retirement and lifestyle goals.

When I talk to most people about their 401(k) accounts, I just love it when they say, "Oh, my job has people for that. I don't need to worry about it – it's all taken care of." Umm… NEWSFLASH: it is not! No one at your job has "people" looking over your account, and *nothing* is being taken care of the way you think it is! What your company has are several general staff members who handle general account tasks (you know… the really important things, like printing statements and sending you reports), and that is all! All accounts are treated the same regardless of your personal circumstances. Whether you're 20 or 50, single or married, have children or not – nobody gives a hoot. They have zero idea about what your retirement goals are, what kind of lifestyle you would like, or when to warn you that your allocations are too risky for your age. Your 401(k) account is just one of many, and as such, it is treated with the same lack of interest as everyone else's. So if you want your 401(k) to really work for you, you've got to accept the fact that making sure that your 401(k) is on track is all up to YOU! *You* need to watch your magic bean, nurture it, and protect it from the ogre; you need to watch it like a hawk (a ninja hawk, who's been trained in martial arts!) and question its allocation and growth; you need to find out whether you are contributing the right amount and whether that amount is being invested appropriately for your circumstances. Only your actions can make a difference, and the sooner you start taking steps to keep your financial future on track, the sooner you will begin to be in control of your retirement.

I remember when I had just met Irene, one of the first things she told me was that there was no reason to review her 401(k) because the "people" at her work were taking care of it. I had, of course, heard these kinds of comments before, so I was not surprised that Irene thought that someone was watching her account. I explained to her that there was actually no one at her job who was specifically dedicated to monitoring how her 401(k) was doing, and I helped her figure out how to read her statements. When we sat down to go over her paperwork, what we realized was that she was only contributing 7% of her salary, and she was shocked! Yes, shocked! Until that day, she was always under the impression that as she was getting closer to retirement, which was now only about seven years away, that the "401(k) watcher" was automatically increasing her contributions every year! That someone was sitting in the back office at corporate, and saying "Hmm… looks like Irene's account isn't high enough, and she's getting close to retirement, we've got to increase her contributions! Stat!" What was even worse was that because her contributions were invested in a mutual fund that had the word "growth" in its name, she thought everything was fine. In reality, she was still invested in the original, aggressive, mostly small-cap stock fund that she selected when she set up her 401(k) in her late thirties! Yes, she was less than a decade from retirement, taking the same risks with her money as if she was in her late thirties! This was a huge wakeup call, or what I refer to as a Rude Awakening. Irene made this mistake and will have to work an extra four and a half years to make her nest egg large enough to retire comfortably! And when you think about it, just a couple of hours a month spent on reviewing her 401(k) would have saved her four and a half years of work! Don't let this to happen to you.

Mistake #2 – Confusing Accumulation With Growth

It is imperative that you learn how to read your 401(k) statements. I am not just talking about gazing nonchalantly at the numbers and thinking, "Wow! They look good – I'm sure they've increased since the last statement…" But I'm talking about reading and understanding the *Growth* (the return on your investments), and being able to differentiate it from a simple increase in your account balance.

Think about it this way; your 401(k) can grow only in two ways: 1) from your contributions (and your employer's matching, if you're lucky!), and 2) from the growth in the value of the investments in your portfolio over time. There really isn't any magic to it at all. Now, out of these two things that affect your accumulation of wealth, you can only directly control the first one – the amount of your contributions. The second force, growth, is only partially controlled by you, and like a moody boyfriend, it can be very unpredictable at times. So when you're looking over your 401(k) statement, and you see that your account balance has increased from the last time you checked, it's incredibly important to understand how much of that increase came from your contributions, and how much of that increase came from your investments growing in value. If you don't take the time to review your statement carefully, you might not even realize that your 401(k) has become a giant black hole that sucks in your hard-earned dollars, never to be seen again!

When you look at your 401(k) statement, you should expect the account balance to be higher than the previous statement because you've been contributing money into your 401(k) on a regular basis. But what you need to understand and focus on is the actual capital growth on your hard-earned principal investment (i.e., how much your investments have increased in value). You need to look at the growth on the contributions, and don't forget to subtract any fees that you may be paying. Sometimes it is not obvious that you're losing money, because the contributions made by you and your employer are masking a drop in value of your investments – the account balance will increase even though there is zero or even negative capital growth. This means you don't necessarily notice the big drops in value as much as you should, because at first glance, your account balance is up.

This is why watching your 401(k), your magic retirement bean, and understanding your 401(k) statement is really important. Remember, no one else is watching it like you may think they are! And even more importantly, no one cares about it as much as you. By reading your statements correctly you will be able to find out what you are truly earning on your investments and where you are heading when it comes to your retirement target.

126

Mistake #3 – Not Taking the Time to Understand the Risks in Your 401(k)

Let's go back to the beginning. Once upon a time you started a great new job somewhere; you were excited, filled out the new-hire paperwork, and by the time you got to the benefits applications, the process probably went something like this:

Human Resources representative:

> *"So, welcome aboard. Just a few more forms to fill out. Here is your 401(k) paperwork, the company matches up to 3% of your contributions, if you'd like to take advantage of that... You just need to put down how much you'd like to contribute from each paycheck and select your investment allocations."*

The new hire then looks over the paperwork and thinks about how much money she can "afford" to set aside; and I use quotations because I just want to tear my hair out when people say "I can't <u>afford</u> to set that much money aside." Then, after devoting about three minutes to reviewing her options, which is probably less time than you spend on choosing what to order at a restaurant, she selects a few mutual funds from the incredibly limited number of investment options offered by the company. The thought process is pretty much something like this (and you *know* it's true):

> *"Hmm... This fund has 'growth' in its name, and I do want my portfolio to grow, so let me put some money here. Oh, and this one says 'value'... I definitely want value because value is better than no value, so let me put a few percent here. Hmm... who could help me*

with this… maybe I should call my friend, she has a son who is majoring in business so he must know about this stuff… Yeah, that should get me to a good retirement…"

Okay, maybe the example above is a little bit exaggerated, but you get the point. Most women make their 401(k) retirement portfolio selection without taking the time to understand what it is they are investing their money in (and most men do the same thing for that matter, even though they won't admit it – because they're great at faking confidence. You know… when you hear something like "Don't worry honey, I can totally fix the roof myself without falling off and breaking my legs in the process. Trust me, I know what I'm doing"). A few of us will actually try to read the investment prospectuses, the long-winded documents full of legal language describing these funds, which are also a great cure for insomnia… a cup of hot cocoa, a mutual fund prospectus, and you'll pass out in no time! Even fewer will actually understand what these funds invest in, or the risks that are involved. Just think about the implications; the funds you choose will directly impact two things about your portfolio: growth, or how quickly your investments could appreciate, and risk, or the possibility that your investments will lose money at some point, which could be a lot, as we've seen with the meltdown of 2008. And because most women don't really know much about the funds where they are putting their hard-earned contributions, and the risks associated with those investment funds' strategies, they are basically throwing a Hail Mary and praying for the best.

Remember, a little while ago, when I mentioned that you can only increase your 401(k) through: 1) your contributions, and 2) growth of your investments…? Well, most people leave the growth portion of their wealth-building strategy completely to chance! If you went on a cross-country road trip from Los Angeles to New York without a map or a GPS, and just decided to drive down any random road, do you think that might be a risky thing to do? "Ooh, 'Mulholland Drive' – that sounds like a good street name! I think I'll take that one! Why? I don't know! But it sounds nice! I'm sure it will take me where I need to go!" Well, when you're selecting random funds for your 401(k) without really understanding where those funds invest, that's exactly what you are doing: driving down a random road that will get you *somewhere*, but likely not where you want to go!

And just to be clear; this is your *retirement portfolio* we are talking about! This is not a lottery that you hope to win, or a game of bingo, but money that you will need during your retirement. These are your hopes and dreams, and the way that you allocate your mon-

YOUR 401(k) WON'T JUST GROW ON ITS OWN. IT HAS TO BE NURTURED.

ey will directly affect how those retirement hopes and dreams turn out. This is your future! Remember, life isn't like a fairy tale, and taking the time to understand your portfolio may be annoying, and sometimes downright frustrating, but if you approach your retirement planning with an "I'm sure it will all work out" attitude, then you're leaving your future completely to chance.

Mistake #4 – Setting Your 401(k) on Autopilot

Now this part is what really gets me; after setting up their 401(k) account, some women will just set it on autopilot, and won't bother to adjust their contributions or investments as time passes by. Think about how silly that is. As you move along in your career, you probably received a promotion or a raise, or moved to a better-paying job, and of course you increased your 401(k) contributions in line with your increase in pay, didn't you? Well, if you're smart, you will always deposit the maximum amount possible; but if you have more of a "set and forget" mentality, then your contributions to your 401(k) account are probably not the highest priority in your life. And what happens to things that aren't a priority? Well, the same thing that happens to your plants when they're not a priority and you forget to water them. Irene learned that lesson the hard way, and it cost her dearly, but she was still one of the lucky ones, because she had at least some time to fix her situation. Had she found out about her problems on the day of her retirement party, well, then her story would have had a much sadder ending.

If you haven't looked over your 401(k) recently, or haven't increased your contributions in years, ask yourself "Why not?" Perhaps you forgot to increase your contributions or maybe you decided to buy a brand-new car, upgrade your kitchen, or take an exotic vacation instead. For most people, their contributions usually remain the same as they were when they first started working. Since no one ever comes along to take your hand and let you know that you should be investing more money and into different allocations, you remain blissfully unaware that you may be aimlessly adding your contributions to a black hole.

Whatever your point of view when you started cultivating this 401(k) bean, you were certainly younger and less concerned about funding your retirement. As you get older, it's important to make sure that you're making the necessary changes to avoid major mistakes. Think about it; you wouldn't wear a short miniskirt in your mid-60s, would you? Of course not! As the years have gone by, you have updated your fashion, you have changed your style, your hair color, maybe even your taste in music to match your sophisticated age. So why are your 401(k) contributions and investment allocations stuck in the late 1980s, wearing power shoulder pads and huge, poufy hair!?

There really isn't any magic to selecting a proper 401(k) strategy; the simple truth is that the long-term growth of your account and the risks associated with your investments are very much intertwined. Just like Jekyll and Hyde, they are the flip sides of the same coin. One has the potential to bring you positive returns in the form of growth, while the other has the potential of causing your 401(k) value to drop. These two will always go hand in hand: the bigger the possibility for growth, the more risk you are likely taking. At the same time, the less risk you would like to take, the less growth you are likely to see (you will read about risk in more detail in Chapter 16). It's kind of like watching movie stars on the red carpet; the more attention they want to get, the more ridiculous their outfits will be. But when they do decide to wear something that stands out too much, they're also taking a risk that the attention they get will not be the attention they want. So when you are accumulating your wealth, you have to watch your magic bean like a hawk and make sure that the amount of risk that you are taking is appropriate for your age: the further away you are from retirement, the more risk you can take. As you get older (in age only, not at heart, because we're all 18 forever and ever), it is important to start reducing the amount of risk you are taking because you have less working years left, and less time for your portfolio to recover from potential losses.

When it comes to allocations, generally speaking, when you are between the ages of 30 and 50 your focus should be on accumulation, which is more of an aggressive growth allocation that accepts more risk for a higher potential return. You can afford to be more aggressive when you are younger, because you have the luxury of time on your side, to be able to deal with any potential hiccups along the way. Then, between the ages of 50 and 65 your focus should be on preservation, which is a conservative growth allocation that reduces the overall risk, as well as potential returns. It is important to exercise more caution as you get older and make sure you don't lose any of your principal, because as you get older you don't have the time available to grow your 401(k) bean if the market collapses again. I can't stress this enough; making sure that your portfolio is properly allocated to match your age is one of the most useful things you can do for yourself. Finally, after age 65, your focus should be on distribution, since by this age you are retired and most likely will have to use your retirement accounts as supplemental income.

Now, let's consider what would happen if you left your allocations the same as they were when you were in your 30s and 40s and never made any changes as you got older. If the market crashed, you would stand to lose way more than you could afford to without having the time available to recoup your losses. How fun do you think your retirement would be then?

Mistake #5 – Not Contributing the Maximum Amount

When it comes to investing for retirement, time is your biggest ally. The more time you have until retirement, the less work you have to do, and the less risk you need to take to reach your goals. Remember when I said there is no magic to growing your 401(k) portfolio? Well, there *is* just a little bit of magic, or something very close to it, and it's called *compounding*. It is a magical little tool that requires you to do very little, but works very hard on your behalf and goes a long way to help you achieve your goals. It's almost like the ultimate magic bean; it helps your money grow faster and bigger, like a magic growth potion.

Now, this is *very* important: compounding is the concept of earning returns on top of returns. In the simplest of terms, I can explain compounding this way: a dollar contributed to your 401(k) account 20 years before retirement is worth much more than a dollar contributed five years before retirement, and this is all because of compounding. For example, if you invested $10,000 into your 401(k) in Year 1, and earned a 5% annual return, you would have $10,500 by the end of the year, or a net gain of $500 ($10,000 x 5% = $500).

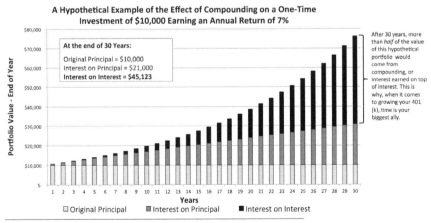

A Hypothetical Example of the Effect of Compounding on a One-Time Investment of $10,000 Earning an Annual Return of 7%

At the end of 30 Years:
Original Principal = $10,000
Interest on Principal = $21,000
Interest on Interest = $45,123

After 30 years, more than *half* of the value of this hypothetical portfolio would come from compounding, or interest earned on top of interest. This is why, when it comes to growing your 401 (k), time is your biggest ally.

Note: This is a hypothetical example, and is not intended to reflect the actual perfomance of any specific investment.

133

If in Year 2 your investments earned another 5%, you would have $11,025 at the end of the year, or a net gain of $525 ($10,500 x 5% = $525). Notice that in Year 2 you've earned $25 more than in Year 1, because you had an extra $500 (your growth from Year 1) sitting in the account at the beginning of Year 2. And here's the awesome part: you didn't have to do anything extra for your portfolio to earn this extra $25. What you are doing is putting time on your side, and letting the investments in your portfolio work for you over a longer period of time, which lets you earn more growth on top of the returns that your portfolio generates.

Now of course, the example in the previous paragraph doesn't do much justice for the true benefits of compounding. After all, what can you buy with $25? Two movie tickets maybe, not even enough to add on the popcorn. But over long periods of time, and with regular contributions, compounding can help generate stunningly better returns on your investment, because again, you're making time work for your benefit.

Take a look at the example in Chart 1. If we took a hypothetical investment of $10,000 that pays 7% on an annual basis, then after 30 years it would have grown to over $70,000. But the important thing here is to pay attention to how much of that return came from compounded interest, which is interest earned on top of interest. In this scenario, over half of the total return comes from compounding! When it comes to making your 401(k) work for you, time is one of your biggest allies. That's why contributing as much as possible, as early as possible can really go a long way toward building your retirement nest egg.

Mistake #6 – Leaving Your 401(k) Behind

Now that we have covered 401(k) contributions, allocations,

and not confusing account increases with growth, let's talk about what you should do with any previous 401(k) accounts.

For those of you who may not have rolled over your previous 401(k) account, from a previous employer, into an Individual Retirement Account (IRA), find a mirror, and shake a finger at yourself in an admonishing way! Look at it like this: when you change jobs, you wouldn't leave your personal belongings like the pictures on your desk behind, would you? So why would you *ever* think of leaving your most precious belonging behind – your nest egg for retirement? I mean, it is a no-brainer, right? Wrong! You'd be surprised how many people do this regularly and just leave their 401(k) accounts behind after changing jobs!

So what should you do with a previous 401(k) account? Some people choose to roll it over into their current 401(k) account at their new job. You can do that, but in my opinion it makes more sense to roll it over into an IRA outside of the confines of an employer. Why? Because by doing so you will have more investment options to choose from than what most 401(k) plans offer. By moving your funds into an IRA in a brokerage firm outside of your work, you can have your choice of different stocks, mutual funds, ETFs, etc. – you are not restricted to the limited options of an employer-provided 401(k).

But whatever you do, don't simply cash out your 401(k) unless you have no other options and unless you've spoken to your tax preparer or a CPA ahead of time. Cashing out your 401(k) early can result in higher taxes as well as penalties. So the vast majority of the time it's better to just roll it over into an IRA and allow your nest egg to continue growing.

Let me tell you about a client of mine, Anna. I met her about five years ago, around the time when she had just retired. She was so happy to finally be done with work, and that she could now spend time on herself and her family. We reallocated her IRA into several funds that made more sense for her age and the stage of her life. As part of the process, she had also asked me to help her locate an old 401(k) from one of her previous jobs, so that she could roll it over, since she wasn't working there anymore. Well, as it turned out, she had left that account with her previous company… when she left 13 years ago! I was shocked! I couldn't understand how she was so comfortable with that fact, and I was even more concerned when she couldn't show me a recent statement for that account. I remember specifically the conversation I had with her, because of what she said to me. It was right around the Thanksgiving holidays, and I remember asking her if she could give me copies of her statements, and she replied with something like "Hmm, I can't do it until after the long weekend." And then she jokingly followed it up with a phrase that would make her cringe just a few weeks later. She said, "Eh, the money's been there forever, I'm sure it can wait another week or two." After the holidays, I met with Anna, and she showed me her documents, but all she had was an old 401(k) statement that was dated from about eight years prior, which showed that just under 85% of the portfolio was invested in company stock and as of the date of that statement, it was worth about half a million dollars!

Well, without naming the major hotel where she had previously worked, and where she left that 401(k), when we tried to find out why she was not receiving her statements, and where the account was being held, we learned that the hotel chain had filed for bankruptcy years ago! That hotel was then bought out by another major hospitality brand, and all of that company's stock, where most of her portfolio was allocated, was now valued at less than $20k, because it basically became valued at pennies on the dollar, after all the bankruptcy proceedings were finished. So instead of having a value of about half a million dollars, her portfolio was now a pittance in comparison. Anna was devastated and shocked. And by the way, so was I. Witnessing someone think that they have hundreds of thousands of dollars in an account, and helping them track down the information only to find out that it had pretty much become worthless, was a very emotionally wrecking experience, because there was nothing I could do to help her recover any of that money. It was gone! Anna couldn't believe this actually happened. It never occurred to her that something like this *could* happen! She didn't break down, or cry, she just had this lost look of disbelief about her when we found out.

Her unfortunate mistakes were: 1) leaving her account at her last job, and 2) just setting her account on autopilot and completely forgetting to check in on it from time to time. The other problem is that she was a product of her environment, and like so many other people I've met over the years, she simply believed that *someone* was watching over her money, and would alert her if there was a problem. But no one was watching, and no alert ever came. So I hope you learn from Anna's tragic story, and if you even *think* of leaving your 401(k) behind, understand that you can lose all of it.

The problem with leaving your account at an old job is that you simply don't know what's going on with your previous company. At least the present employees will know something is up and can get out of the company stock when they feel trouble brewing. But how could Anna have done that when she was no longer working there, and had no contact with previous co-workers? She had a false sense of security, and it unfortunately cost her close to half a million dollars. If Anna would have had the attitude of that tough old lady at the beginning of the book, protecting her precious purse and yelling out loudly, "Get your hand out of my purse! I'm not giving you my money!" then Anna would have had her retirement intact! By leaving her money behind, she subconsciously told the universe, "I don't really care what happens to my money. Go ahead, take it away from me. See if I care." Of course, she didn't actually say that, but that's certainly the attitude that she projected out into the world.

If you don't believe in the power of intention and the messages you put out by your actions, then I suggest reading books about many success stories that started out simply just by setting forth the right mindset and intention. Keep reading and you will get to a great success story in Chapter 18 about my client's experience that at first glance would appear as a hopeless cause, but you will learn how she changed the course of her life significantly by using the right thought process of intention, followed by meaningful actions.

Mistake #7 – Treating Your 401(k) As Your Emergency Fund

It is important for you to understand that your 401(k) is your *retirement savings*, not your emergency savings! I know this may sound elementary, but to many people, these two concepts pretty much mean one and the same thing. Over the years I have met many clients whose thinking I've had to shift to ensure that they really understood the concept that their 401(k) is their funding for retirement, not a contingency fund for emergencies. I completely understand that sometimes dipping into your 401(k) may be the only choice open to you, but if you plan ahead and build up an emergency fund in a savings account, then you may be able to avoid this issue. Your 401(k) is meant to supplement your income during retirement, because, trust me, Social Security alone won't be enough, unless you love an all ramen noodle diet – yum! But it's definitely *not* there to help you deal with the challenges you may encounter along the way.

So touching your retirement money should be reserved only for true emergencies, where you simply have no other options. Because every time you dip into your 401(k) before retirement, you are putting yourself a step behind.

Now let's assume that there is an absolute emergency and you have to decide whether it is better to borrow from your account or to take a distribution. Notwithstanding special circumstances, if you're under age 59½ and you take a distribution from your 401(k) then you will be penalized by the IRS, and there may also be other tax consequences. So in this case, borrowing would likely make more sense. Most 401(k) plans have an easy way to pay yourself back and you're not really paying interest because you borrowed from yourself. Borrowing is sometimes better even in cases when you are aged over 59½, as long as you are still working. Again, the first preference would be that you do not dip in your 401(k) at all, and that you treat it the same way you would treat a soufflé while it is baking in the oven, and not open the oven door until it's fully baked, or it will collapse! But if you absolutely had to, then you need to ensure that you discuss the situation with your tax preparer before you do anything, and seriously consider any tax consequences and any penalties that may be involved.

Things to Keep in Mind

I hope this has helped to shed some light on how to treat your 401(k). Remember, if you love your 401(k) and treat it well, it will love you right back, and will be there for you during retirement. The bottom line is that understanding how your 401(k) works and how the choices you make *now* will affect your lifestyle *later* doesn't require a very high IQ or some secret, magical knowledge; just a little bit of common sense, and a desire to be in control of your own future. In fact, the concept is very much similar to learning how to read a map before going on a road trip; you can make all the right and left turns that you want, but if you don't know how to read the map, or at least buy a GPS, you'll never get to your destination, and you might just drive off a cliff! And no, it won't be in the cool *Thelma and Louise* style.

The effects of risk, growth, and contributions can mean the difference between a good retirement, and one where you have to make heart-wrenching decisions about whether to pay the electric bill or to purchase medication. It can mean the difference between staying independent and making your own decisions for many more decades, or becoming dependent on your children and having to go ask for help all the time. Sure, you raised your kids, and they definitely owe you for all your hard work and patience, but if you think that after a while, asking them for help won't become humiliating, then you're in for a very rude awakening.

Remember, your 401(k) is not like a magic bean, it won't grow exponentially by itself; it is more like an ordinary bean, requiring a certain level of care and attention, as well as some understanding of proper cultivation techniques, to ensure that it grows into the tall, healthy beanstalk that you need it to be.

CHAPTER 13

THE "B WORD"

"I hear and I forget. I see and I remember. I do and I understand."— Confucius

Budget, I know that most people don't like to talk about the "B word." But if you're looking to be successful in your financial planning and to move forward to a happy and healthy financial life, there's no better sidekick than your trusty budget.

Knowing how much money you spend, and what you spend it on, is one of the most critical pieces of information you can have. Being "in the know" about your spending habits and understanding how your money flows through your hands is what lets you have a clear picture of your financial situation. Even more importantly, understanding your cash flow is the very first step to understanding how much money you will need during retirement. And if you know how much money you'll need, then you'll be able to prepare for your golden years, or what I refer to as your Life Vacation, in a much more meaningful way.

In the tale of Rumpelstiltskin, a greedy king believes that a young woman can spin straw into gold, because her father told him she could, in a mind-boggling attempt to impress the king. Most dads brag about a daughter's grades or fabulous soccer-playing skills, so in the story of Rumpelstiltskin, I've always been a bit confused about the miller's choice to tell the king that his daughter had supernatural powers of alchemy. I mean… what did he think was going to happen? That the king would just take him at his word? Well, the king was a greedy guy, so he decided to swallow his morals and kidnap this beautiful girl so that she could fill his treasury with lots of glittering gold. Threatened with all manner of danger and destruction if she didn't come through for him, the young girl is locked in a dungeon and is desperate. Of course, she jumps at the chance to take the help of a slightly maniacal elf-like creature, Rumpelstiltskin, who agrees to do this impossible task in return for payment in things precious to the young woman – a necklace, a ring, and, finally, her firstborn child. Wow, Rumpelstiltskin was really quite the negotiator!

But however reprehensible he may have been, Rumpelstiltskin did have an amazing skill; he could make money out of basically nothing! Sometimes, I think we all wish we had a magical imp in the basement who could take our yard clippings and turn them into gold. And sometimes, many of us for some reason act like we actually do! We'll spend our money on completely frivolous stuff, or we won't plan ahead, as if somehow, magically, there will always be enough money in our checking accounts to cover it all. We'll log on and check our balance on the bank website, and eyeball it to see if we can reasonably assume that we can afford some purchase, but this process is rarely methodical for most women.

In many ways, we tend to think about the way our money works as this magical straw-into-gold formula. While we may understand some fundamental basics about what's going on with our money, a lot of the time we act almost as if there's some unknown magic that is the reason why our account balance either grows or it doesn't. And at the end of the month, or sometimes in the middle, we are often totally confused about why we have the amount that we do in our bank account. Instead of trying to understand it better, we seek out our own Rumpelstiltskin – we try to make money out of nothing by purchasing lottery tickets, going to Vegas to play roulette, searching the couch cushions for money, or looking around our homes and attics for some long-forgotten antique worth thousands! I don't know about you, but I've never seen anyone have much luck in these attempts to turn nothing much into something substantial. Usually, they are just out more time, effort, and money. I've never been into gambling or buying lottery tickets, because although it may be fun, I could never see how counting on pure luck makes any sense. I'd rather make my own luck by effort, and effort requires knowledge, and most of all, persistence!

One of the most important things you can do when it comes to your personal wealth is to understand your expenses, because your expenses are the key to accurately understanding your income needs, now and in the future. So if you want a genuinely solid foundation for your financial plan, you absolutely have to start with understanding how, where, and on what you spend your money. By doing that, you will begin to see how much money you will need in retirement to maintain the kind of lifestyle you want. No one wants to get to retirement and be unhappily surprised, so this element of your financial planning could not be more important. Being able to effectively plan a budget and work that plan is crucial to your financial happiness, so it's absolutely vital to take this step seriously.

I've always been bothered by the fact that the financial industry still fails to recognize that their clients' spending habits and lifestyle are a major part of their retirement. It's not just about investing money somewhere and hoping that it will grow over time. Why are you buying an investment in the first place? Just so that it grows and you have more money? By that rationale, you should also go to the gym and just aimlessly do exercises without any plan at all. Do some squats here, and some yoga there, and maybe it will eventually address the reason why you went to the gym in the first place (oh, and don't forget to grunt loudly during your workout so that the entire gym knows you're exercising, at least that seems to be the latest trend...). But if you go to your workout with a plan to improve your health in a specific way, like get some cardio, or build up strength, or maybe make those love handles less handle-ey (yes, I just made up that word), well then you'll do exercises that are meant to address those specific goals. When planning for your retirement income needs, it's very much the same thing. You need to look at your future work pension, if you've got one; estimate Social Security benefits, and then compare your total estimated income in retirement to how much money you will need to cover your living expenses. And only after that will you actually be able to make a genuinely smart decision about how to invest your nest egg.

With that same idea, you can't really plan what investments are most suited for you if you don't know exactly what your future expenses will be and how much income you will need during retirement. We are living longer and healthier lives and planning for lifetime income is essential for everyone. And the most important step to a good plan is understanding your expenses now, and in the future. So this is one area where you really have to hop in the driver's seat and figure out what your future income needs will be for the kind of lifestyle that you'd like.

Budgeting – The Poor, Ugly Duckling

In a lot of ways, budgeting is like the little ugly duckling – seriously misunderstood and neglected. If you are like most people, you probably look at budget planning like you looked at eating your Brussels sprouts when you were eight; yes, you know you have to, but it's no fun at all! However, budgets unfairly get a really bad reputation because most people incorrectly believe that budgets are a source of deprivation rather than a source of wealth. A budget has somehow become synonymous with the idea that you absolutely cannot have anything you want, when in reality the opposite is true! It's a way to have more of what you really *do* want by eliminating the spending on things that don't mean much to you, and which you only buy impulsively. Strategic budget planning is the key to success for companies and individuals who understand how to grow their money.

Take, for example, Google. By anyone's definition, Google is a hugely successful company (just "Google" it), which recently overtook Microsoft in market value; a huge feat since Microsoft had a 20-year head start.[21] In order to become one of the industry leaders, Google has certainly had to strategically plan their expenditures. But imagine, for a moment, that they didn't. For the next three, or six, or even 12 months, Google just did whatever Google executives wanted to do, in the moment. They tossed the plan out of the high-rise window, so to speak, and just operated the business based on whim and guesswork. Revenue projections are suddenly a thing of the past. Checks are written whenever someone requests one, perhaps all at one time, regardless of when the revenue has been received. If this strategically brilliant technology giant operated like this, do you think the company would be able to keep its doors open? Do you think that Google would be as successful as it is today? Of course not! It would be shuttered before we knew it, having wasted away its opportunities because it failed to plan a budget. Well, you're a successful person, an individual Google so to speak, so why should your financial activities be any different? Unless you have an elf spinning straw into an everlasting slush fund of gold in your basement, you should be mindfully planning your budget the same way.

Much as you may wish it to be true, your financial life is not a fairy tale. The only one with the capacity to increase your wealth is you, and you are entirely capable of doing it. You do have some tools at your disposal that will help you increase your net worth with a little bit of effort. Even Rumpelstiltskin had to put his shoulder to the wheel all night long – and it's important that you too put in the effort to make your money work for you. Understanding your finances in detail will help you do just that; taking a step toward a more lucrative outcome for your financial future.

Money Comes In, Money Goes Out

The first and most important part of budget planning is to understand what money is coming in, what money is going out, and what that money is earmarked for. First, let's talk a little bit about the types of expenses you encounter each month. Fixed expenses are just what they sound like – bills you are responsible for, which for the most part are a fixed amount each month. These expenses might include things like your mortgage or rent, your car payment, your phone bill, or your utility bills. Again, I'm not talking about credit card bills, that may radically change from month to month, but the things that change very little from one month to the next. Of course, inflation rate changes may cause some of these charges to fluctuate over time, but for the most part, you can count on fixed expenses to be about the same, most of the time. Most people tend to have a good grasp on these bills, because these are usually the *Needs*, the things that you know you always have to plan for and pay. Because they are fixed expenses, these might also be the bills that you have automatically debited from your account, simply because they are so regular that you can anticipate them with confidence.

Now, flexible expenses are an area where most people tend to go a bit off the budgetary rails. That's totally normal, because these are the hard-to-pin-down expenses like entertainment, eating out, and shopping. If you're like most people, you don't sit down on the first day of the month and say, "This month, I am going to purchase three pencil skirts and a fabulous bag, for a total of $300." Of course not! You saw that beautiful purse in the store window or you signed up for that new set of dance classes, all on a whim! Sometimes we get a bit carried away with our flexible spending habits, much like that storybook emperor who wanted some new clothes, but ended up strolling around naked.[22] We hear some buzz about a new play, or a designer with amazing handbags, and decide that we just *have* to have it. We want it. We deserve it. So, darn it, we're getting it! Because flexible expenses are the *Wants*, and aren't planned, we tend to behave like the emperor with no clothes did – we pretend that everything is okay, even if we are suspicious that maybe that purchase wasn't the smartest financial decision we've ever made.

Where Did It All Go?

The only way to really understand the state of your finances is to start tracking your expenses as you pay for things – there's just no way around it. If you're already a list-maker, and many of us are, this won't be too much of a challenge for you. If you aren't, this process may feel a bit uncomfortable at first, but definitely not brain surgery. Nevertheless, it's important for you to make a list of your fixed expenses and track your flexible expenses in order to get an accurate picture of your financial life. Once you do, you will have a much better understanding of how your money is currently working, and even more importantly, where you could cut impulsive spending on things that you don't really care for, so that you have more money for the things that you do want.

Keeping track of your finances is as eye-opening as tracking your calorie intake. A few years ago, I gained 20 pounds, like overnight. Ha! Well, that's how it felt, anyway – like it happened within a day! When I had a hard time figuring out why this was happening, my trainer gave me a food diary and committed me to writing down everything that I was eating. All of a sudden, my morning latte was not just a daily dose of caffeine – it was 480 calories! Going directly to my thighs! I suddenly realized that even a simple cup of delicious coffee in the morning could have a substantial impact on my goals – it was almost a third of the daily calories that I was allowed under my workout plan. It was no wonder that I was gaining weight… I was going merrily through my day, not realizing the large amount of calories I was consuming, thinking everything was just fine. Only when I started writing things down, did I realize my mistakes. Just imagine, a latte here and there, then a protein bar (or a chocolate, depending on my mood for the day), then dinner, maybe a glass of wine… maybe two… and now, my "nothing" calories were really like 2,000, or even more many other days! Well, no wonder I was gaining!

Your spending habits are the same thing! When you take the time to write down what you are spending your hard-earned money on each month, you will begin to see your finances in a completely new light. Physically keeping track of your expenses each day, writing them down in one place, is really eye-opening. Some people prefer to use an app on a smartphone or an Excel spreadsheet; whatever you want to use, the most important thing is to be consistent. However, I strongly suggest to my clients that, in the beginning, they write it down on paper. Remember your time in school – if you needed to remember something, you took notes. You highlighted the textbook and wrote in the margins. You probably do the same thing now when you are sitting in a meeting or a seminar – it's just human nature, because when you write, you learn. Our brain registers the information differently than if we type it or swipe it into an app or program.

Since this is definitely a learning process, and I wanted my clients to learn in the most effective way possible, I actually created a tool that I call Your Personal Money Diary because so many of my clients needed a tool where they could organize their spending notes. You'll catch your mistakes faster and nothing is preventing you from translating those handwritten notes into software or an Excel spreadsheet later on! But whatever system or software you decide to use, really make it work for you. I guarantee you will love the result even more than the Tory Burch wallet you just bought, because now you can get the matching purse since you have more cash flow, since you are spending more wisely!

At the end of each day, take a few minutes to write down what you've spent, keeping track of the expenses as either fixed or flexible. If you wrote a check to pay the mortgage, that goes in fixed expenses. If you went to Starbucks and bought a scone, or found a pair of shoes you loved at the mall, those purchases should go under flexible expenses. It doesn't matter what you've spent or how you spent it – just record it. No judgment, just accountability, to no one other than yourself. I promise, no one will steal your notes and expose them to the world.

Seeing your strengths and weaknesses in black and white each day, as you record your spending, may really jar you in the same way that my epiphany about the latte did for me. Suddenly, your successes – and the failures that you have been blind to until that very moment – are staring at you in all their glaring truth. It's not always an easy thing to come to terms with your spending habits, and to realize that you've been throwing your money away on things that you don't really need. You may even feel a bit like the emperor with no clothes after the little boy in the crowd told the truth that no one else had the courage to say – feeling naked, silly, and a bit foolish for not

149

seeing it all along. Well... don't! Instead, be grateful that you had the courage to start the process, and face any previous mistakes. Those failures will soon turn into opportunities for wealth building and budgetary success in no time. The first step is to start, so that you can make smarter, better decisions with more information.

Planning a budget, even if it's not 100% complete, will help you see and make better spending choices in the future! If you need help, you can take this new information to a financial advisor to fine tune your budget planning. But I can tell you this, though: most of my clients who commit to recording their expenses in this way end up making all of the changes that I would have advised them to make, on their own – they learned what they needed to learn through the process. You will too!

I'm including a few sample worksheets from the Money Diary at the end of this chapter to help you get started. Grab a pencil and start filling them out. You'll quickly notice that just organizing your thoughts about your finances and your expenditures can make a huge difference.

	Example 1	Example 2
What You Own		
Value of Home	$ 450,000	$ 200,000
Value of Car	$ 50,000	$ 10,000
401(k)	$ 100,000	$ -
Savings Account	$ -	$ 2,000
Total you <u>OWN</u>	$ 600,000	$ 212,000
What You Owe		
Mortgage on Home	$ 340,000	$ 185,000
Car Loan	$ 40,000	$ 9,000
Credit Cards	$ 20,000	$ 25,000
Total you <u>OWE</u>	$ 400,000	$ 219,000
Net Worth:	$ 200,000	$ (7,000)

Woof Woof... What You're Really Worth

Once you have a handle on how much money you have coming in and the money you've been spending, the next step is calculating your net worth. Normally, companies are judged based on their net worth, or the assets of the company (the things in their possession) minus the debts of the company (everything they owe). If you are evaluating your own finances, you should do the same calculation to see how much you actually have once you subtract everything you owe, all your loans, credit card balances, and any other debts.

Though it might be confusing at first, the definition of net worth is actually pretty simple when you break it down. Net worth is what you own minus what you owe. For example, if you have a $450,000 home, a $50,000 vehicle, and a 401(k) with $100,000 in it, but owe $340,000 on your mortgage, $40,000 on your vehicle, and have $20,000 in consumer debt, then your net worth would be $600,000 of assets minus $400,000 of debts, or a total of $200,000. Your numbers may be much smaller and more complicated or larger and less complicated, but the equation is always the same (Net Worth = What You Own - What You Owe). You always, obviously, want your net worth to be large and positive, but in certain periods of your life, you may not find that to be the case. In some cases, you may have a $200,000 home, a $10,000 vehicle, a savings account with $2000 and a mortgage of $185,000, a car loan for $9000, and consumer debt in the amount of $25,000. When you were first starting out, a scenario like that might have been the case. In this second scenario, the net worth would still be calculated by taking the assets of $212,000 and subtracting the debt of $219,000, for a total net worth of negative $7,000 – meaning that if you sold all of your possessions, you would still owe $7,000. In this situation, someone is praying for a magical goose to wander into the fenced backyard where it can take up comfortable residence and start laying golden eggs, or that a handful of magic beans with a rich, sleepy giant at the top will sprout in the garden – anything to catch a financial break. But if you find yourself in a situation like this, don't despair. With careful budgeting and a desire to improve your situation, you'll be amazed at how much you can achieve.

Sometimes, like in the second scenario, you might wonder why you even need to know your net worth. Although it can sometimes be disheartening to see your current situation, you can't start making adjustments or strategic plans about how to do better if you're not even sure where the problems are. It's like walking up to the mirror in the morning (not a magic, ego-stroking mirror, but a real one) and realizing that maybe it's time to hit the treadmill, but in this case a budgeting treadmill that helps you pay down your loans and lose some debt!

The truth will always set you free and help you make better decisions. During my continuous battle with dieting, my mom told me something that I will never forget: "Honey, you only have two best friends who will always be true to you in this area: the mirror and the scale. They will never, ever lie to you." And you know what, she was right! Unlike my actual friends who kept telling me that I looked great, the mirror and the scale were never going to feel bad for me and lie just to make me feel better. The mirror and the scale weren't going to say, "Don't worry, you don't look like you gained that much weight," or "You are skinnier than you think!" Well, I realized that what my mom said was so similar to what I tell my clients about their net worth. Your Money Diary and bank accounts are never going to lie to you. They will show you exactly what you need to see so that you can make the necessary changes to be more successful!

As you are looking at your expense sheet in combination with your net worth calculations, you can decide where to shift your money so that you can make strides toward financial freedom. Perhaps you'll decide that you want to focus on paying off your mortgage faster, or that you want to build up your 401(k) more quickly. Something about consciously knowing your net worth, in combination with tracking your expenses, will help you begin to make better, wiser financial choices for yourself. And that "something" is really nothing

more than seeing the truth about your financial situation. The thing is, most people already know the right decisions that they need to make for themselves, but it can be difficult to make the right choices if the uncomfortable truth is not staring you right in the face.

Get on the MoneyFast!

Once you have begun tracking your fixed and flexible expenses, and have an accurate picture of your net worth, you can start to improve your buying behavior in order to make smarter money decisions. If you have looked at your net worth and your expenses and have decided that you want to save more each month, you'll likely find room to do so in your flexible expenses category, and you can start by money-fasting today! I know everyone is doing all kinds of fasting diets these days and starving themselves to lose weight. But I promise, the MoneyFast is much easier than saying "no" to a delicious midnight snack that is reaching out to you with those sweet carbohydrate arms, saying, "Just one bite... No one will ever know... It will be our little secret," and this MoneyFast will leave you feeling much more fulfilled. The strategy that I teach my clients is the 30 Day MoneyFast, which will really open your eyes about whether you are buying the things you want because they are important to you, or if you are just buying them impulsively, without really thinking through the decision to spend your hard-earned money.

The 30 Day MoneyFast is pretty straightforward. Instead of buying something right away, start window shopping, make a list of the things that you see, like, and would normally purchase right away – but don't buy them. Just make your list, perhaps on the same piece of paper where you are tracking your expenses. Include dates on the list, and tell yourself that after 30 days you can buy the items on it; but until then, they are off-limits! You are not depriving yourself. You are simply waiting to see if an item is as important to you as building your net worth or paying off some of your debt. Once the 30 days are up, you can go back to the Apple Store and buy that iPad Mini or go back to the mall and buy those Jimmy Choos or that smart new gadget you can't live without, if you are still dreaming about it – but only after the 30-day money-fasting period is over!

I will promise you this: two-thirds of what you write down in your 30 Day MoneyFast list will stop being important to you pretty quickly. Sometimes, we just buy things that we don't really need or even truly want, simply because we are caught up in the moment. By taking the time to evaluate your true desires, by giving yourself some time, you will make sure that you are only spending your money on the things that you really, truly want. Again and again, this strategy has worked brilliantly for my clients who have tried it, and they are always astonished by the results. Each and every one of them who tried this, while in the store, really thought that they wanted some item; 30 days later, their true desires became much clearer and, as a result, they were able to make better and wiser money decisions, rather than just impulsively throwing money in the trash.

Another step that I encourage my clients to take in order to feel empowered in their financial lives is education. As I mentioned earlier, many women, because of cultural messages and habits, simply don't take control of their finances. They feel that it's not their place or that they are not capable of managing their money effectively. I hope, by this point, you realize that's absolutely not true. Educating yourself about the areas of financial planning and management that still feel like personal weaknesses is one way to truly ensure that you have all of the tools you need to take control of your own financial future. Look for interesting workshops in your area, podcasts that you can listen to at the gym or in your car during your commute, instructional courses, books – all of these can help you proactively plan for your own financial happily ever after.

Keeping a good habit, whether it's eating healthy, spending wisely, or playing volleyball to stay in shape, takes determination and continuous, positive reinforcement. That is one thing you cannot forget; creating a budget to keep track of your expenditures is not a one-time thing. It requires your regular attention and effort. Look at Maria Sharapova; she's an amazing tennis player. Don't you think this is because she is always practicing her skills and trying to get better? What would happen if she practiced a bit here and there and stopped? Do you think she could win a competition again?

Investing IN Your Money

When Snow White's stepmother stepped in front of that devoted magical mirror every morning, she didn't say, "Mirror, mirror on the wall, who's the most hateful, horribly ugly, woefully ignorant stepmother with bad fashion sense of them all?" No. She stepped up with swagger and confidence, and said, "Who's the fairest of them all?" – and believed, without a shadow of a doubt, that the answer would, and should, be her. While I don't think the Evil Queen should be our model for healthy, productive relationships or moral judgment, at least in this particular area, I think she got something right. She put out into the world what she expected to get – her confidence and her ridiculously huge sense of self-worth were infectious.

If you're hesitant to get behind the Evil Queen's confidence model, ask yourself if you've heard people joke about their financial future in negative ways. "Oh, I'll just end up eating cat food when I'm 80" or "I'd better get used to this shopping cart, because this will be my home when I retire." Maybe you laughed at the time, because the person saying it seemed like they were joking as well. I wish you wouldn't, and if these were your jokes, I'd like you to stop.

Think about what you are telling yourself, subconsciously, about your future every time you say negative things like that, or even think them. You're not suggesting wealth or privilege, certainly, and it's fine if that's not your ultimate goal. But you're not even suggesting that you will be comfortable or have sufficient money for your needs. You are telling yourself that you will be impoverished, and if we tell ourselves enough times that we will be something, well then we shouldn't be surprised when that's exactly what happens. Of course this isn't what you intend, but our lives are the result of our attitude and words. So, create a self-fulfilling prophecy that works for you rather than one that works against you by wholeheartedly believing that you will have an amazing retirement, and this simple attitude change will drive you to take steps that will get you there!

Imagine if you did this with any of the other relationships in your life – your marriage, your children, your colleagues... If you consistently showed no real interest in what was happening, put no thought into the future, didn't invest in that relationship, or spoke negatively about the future constantly, the relationship would likely not last. Nobody wants to be in a relationship with Sleepy or Dopey or Grumpy for very long. Whether you have thought about it in these terms or not, you do have a relationship with your money. If you keep telling yourself that you don't care about where your money comes from or where your money goes, then you will not have a healthy relationship with your money either. Money will stay and work for you so long as you work to create an environment where it is appreciated (pun intended). It may sound silly, but what does it hurt to try? Working to be more focused on positive, constructive actions and attitudes about your financial future can change your entire outlook on what is possible, and will help you take more positive steps to get there. You might be really surprised. Treat your money with respect, and it will respect you by sticking around longer. You can start by listening to financial inspiration CDs or reading positive books about money. Change your negative and frustrated thoughts about money, and start thinking of Money as a loving life partner, who only wants to make you happy. This way, Money will be your loyal companion for the rest of your life!

When you start the budget planning process, you may feel a bit like the girl in the dungeon in the Rumpelstiltskin story. Desperate for success, you may feel that by tracking your expenses and limiting yourself on the 30 Day MoneyFast, you are signing away your firstborn child for something that may not even be successful. The reality is just the opposite. Unlike that miller's daughter, you'll be entirely in control of your future, and won't depend on an ugly elf-like creature for your survival, a creature who will force you to give away the things that are most precious to you just to be able to pay the bills after retirement. Instead, you'll be the one creating your success and building your wealth, one little step at a time!

Things to Keep in Mind

- Realize that budgeting is an important foundation of your financial future.

- Recognize that budget planning *makes* you money rather than takes it away.

- Know the difference between your fixed and flexible expenses, so that you can better estimate your income needs.

- Track all of your expenses, by writing them down every day, so that you can get an accurate snapshot of how your money is currently working for you.

- Calculate your net worth and ask yourself if it's where you want it to be.

- Take steps toward making wiser financial decisions, like participating in the 30 Day MoneyFast and educational opportunities that will help you be more in control of your cash.

- Think positively about your financial future! Create a successful, positive self-fulfilling prophecy.

Making and working a budget plan is really like spinning straw into gold – with a little bit of effort, you get a big return on not much at all. And the best part? *You* will have done it – no magic required, and the amazing returns will help you be much further along in your plan for a financial happily ever after.

MY NET WORTH

ASSETS	AMOUNT
CASH	
Savings Account	
Checking Account	
Business Account	
Money Market Account	
Foreign Currency	
Other	
INVESTMENTS	
Government Bonds	
Other Bonds	
International Investments	
Stocks (Domestics / Foreign)	
CD's	
REAL ESTATE	
Domestic	
International	
MISC.	
Vehicles	
Precious Metals	
Luxury Collectibles	
Furniture	
Electronics	
Tools / Machinery	
INSURANCE	
Cash Settlements	
TOTAL:	

LIABILITIES	AMOUNT
LOAN	
Home	
Investment Property	
Car	
Education	
Credit Cards	
Tax	
CURRENT BILLS	
TAXES	
MISC.	
TOTAL:	

ASSETS	LIABILITIES	NET WORTH
TOTAL ASSETS - TOTAL LIABILITIES = NET WORTH		

These are the pages from Your Personal Money Diary. If you want to download the usable lite version, go to http://www.CrystalMoradi.com/money-diary-lite

MY APPROXIMATE FIXED & FLEXIBLE EXPENSES

EXPENSES	MONTHLY	YEARLY
HOUSING		
Rent / Mortgage (Principal, Interest, Taxes)		
Home Association Fees		
Parking Garage or Space Rentals		
Electricity		
Gas		
Home Telephone		
Mobile Telephone		
Internet		
Home Improvement		
Utilities (Water / Sewer / Trash)		
Other		
TRANSPORTATION		
Car Payment(s)		
Car Registration(s)		
Gas / Fuel		
Maintenance (Regular Oil Change / Service)		
Repairs		
Public Transportation		
Other		
DAILY LIVING		
Groceries		
Dining / Eating Out		
Clothing / Shoes		
Cleaning Services (Dry Cleaning)		
Housekeeping		
Salon / Barber		
Other		
INSURANCE		
Life Insurance		
Health Insurance		
Dental Insurance		
Car Insurance		
Home Insurance		
MISC.		

MY APPROXIMATE FIXED & FLEXIBLE EXPENSES

EXPENSES	MONTHLY	YEARLY
HEALTH cont.		
Emergency		
Medicine / Drugs		
Other		
EDUCATION		
Tuition Fees		
Books		
School Supplies		
Lunch		
Clothing / Uniforms		
After School Care		
Other Specialty Courses		
Other		
SAVINGS		
Emergency Fund		
Savings Account		
Retirement (401K, IRA)		
College Fund		
Investment(s)		
Other		
CHARITY / GIFTS		
Religious Donations		
Medical Donations		
School Donations		
Charitable Donations		
Other		
DEBITS		
Alimony / Child Support		
Student Loan		
Bank Loan(s)		
Credit Card 1		
Credit Card 2		
Federal Taxes		
State Taxes		
Other		
ENTERTAINMENT		
DVD / CD		
Movies / Theaters		
Rentals		
Concerts / Plays		
Toys / Video Games		
Electronics		
Books		

MY APPROXIMATE FIXED & FLEXIBLE EXPENSES

EXPENSES	MONTHLY	YEARLY
ENTERTAINMENT cont.		
Film / Photos		
Sporting Events		
Outdoor Recreation		
Other		
Other		
BUSINESS		
Office Supplies		
Office Equipment		
Restaurants		
Travel		
Gas / Fuel		
Mileage		
Other		
VACATION		
Travel		
Rental		
Lodging		
Food / Dining Out		
Entertainment		
Fun Activities		
Gifts		
Other		
Other		
HOBBY		
Supplies		
Collectible Objects		
Tools / Equipment		
Other		
Other		
SUBSCRIPTIONS		
Magazines		
Newspapers		
Internet		
TV / Cable / Satellite		
Gym / Health Club		
Other		
MISC.		

CHAPTER 14

THE GOLDILOCKS METHOD

"At the center of your being you have the answer; you know who you are and you know what you want." — Lao Tzu

D o you remember the story of Goldilocks? Goldilocks was the girl who went into the forest, stumbled upon a cabin, and decided to make herself at home, while the inhabitants, the three bears, were away. While she was inside their house, Goldilocks helped herself to their food, and took a nice, relaxing nap in their beds. First she came up to the table where there were three bowls of porridge. Instead of just having one bowl, she tried all three to find one that was just the right temperature. Then, instead of just sitting down and eating, she sat on all the chairs in the house until she found one that was just the right height. And after her meal, she felt sleepy, but instead of just lying down in a bed to take a nap, she tried all three beds until she found one that wasn't too hard, wasn't too soft, but "just right."

Although in the fairy tale, Goldilocks is made out to be a completely inconsiderate girl who just helped herself to others' stuff (she really *was* kind of rude!), there *is* one thing about this girl that is actually very commendable: she didn't like to settle for things if they weren't to her satisfaction. When you decide to set out on your quest to find a financial advisor who will listen to your needs, will answer your questions, and will take your future seriously, you can greatly improve your chances of a successful match by using what I call the "Goldilocks Method." Now, when I talk about the Goldilocks Method, I'm definitely *not* saying you should start breaking into people's homes and eating their food. Although it might initially seem like a great strategy for saving money toward your retirement, you will eventually get in trouble. I also don't suggest trying to steal food from actual bears, as they tend to get cranky when you do that. What I *am* talking about is searching for a financial advisor with the same pickiness that Goldilocks had for food or a bed to sleep in. She didn't just settle for the first thing she saw! No, she knew what she liked, and wouldn't accept anything less than that.

To be successful in your search, it's key to figure out what qualities you are looking for in an advisor and what questions to ask as you interview potential advisors to ensure that you can find the right fit for you and your financial needs. Yes – I said *interview*, because you are hiring this person to help you care for your finances. When my dentist moved and I was looking for another one, I literally went to three different dentists before I hired one. I went to what they thought was a standard dental checkup with my list of questions and, through X-rays and discussions about flossing, I interviewed them to see if they were the right match for me. I was looking to find the dentist with the right personality and a methodology/approach that made sense for me. I am very picky about who I have in my life, professional or personal. So whether it's a doctor, a lawyer, a massage therapist, or even a friend, I always make sure they have the qualities that I am looking for before I commit to a relationship.

You likely feel the same way about the important things in your life. You certainly wouldn't hire a nanny without thoroughly checking references and making sure that they were a good fit for you and your family. You wouldn't hire a contractor without seeing the work they had done and speaking with other customers – so there's absolutely no reason to act any differently with your financial advisor! In all these cases, you are hiring a professional charged with maintaining the safety and security of the things most precious to you: your family, your home, and your future. Your investments and portfolio are more than just dollars and cents; they are the key to achieving your dreams and turning your vision of a happy retirement into reality.

Deciding What You Need in a Financial Advisor

So it's time to strategize and create a plan of action. There are lots of financial advisors out there – you just have to find one who's right for *you*, who fits well with your personality and takes your future as seriously as you do. That's why one of your first steps in this process should be deciding the qualities that you would like your financial advisor to have. Now, the best way to go about this is to write this out on an old-fashioned piece of paper. So dig out that dusty notepad where you used to make your shopping lists before they became digital. You're going to make a list of qualities you hope to find in your new financial advisor. If this process is feeling very familiar, it's probably because you already do this kind of comparison list-making for many important decisions you make in your life. Think back to when you bought your home; before you were wooed by the beautiful marble in the kitchen or the incredible closet space, you probably sat down with your family and decided what you loved about your prior home and what features were important to have in the new one. That way, you could keep those things in mind as you were shopping around. When you write it down, that list becomes a concrete, unemotional compass to keep you on the right path.

If this process isn't feeling familiar, or maybe even feels silly to you, don't worry. No one is looking over your shoulder, and no one else needs to see this piece of paper, so just write without thinking about right or wrong answers – in this situation, there aren't any. What you like and don't like is as personal and unique to you as your fingerprint or taste in shoes; no one can replicate it, even if they tried! You can go back and reword your descriptions later, if you want to. Right now, just commit to writing what comes to mind.

Your Mission Statement

When you begin, at the top of the page, write a few short sentences about what you want your relationship with your financial advisor to accomplish. Think about goals and objectives, but also think bigger! Think about this statement as your mission statement for this new financial planning relationship. A series of questions might help you take these thoughts and turn them into a clear statement of objectives:

- What do you want your financial advisor to do for you?

- How would you like to be treated?

- What would you like to understand better about your finances?

- What financial goals do you have that you'd like your financial advisor to be working toward?

- What would you like your relationship to be like? (Think of specific, descriptive words here.)

Your statement should be about two or three sentences long,

and might look something like this: *I want my new financial advisor to explain investment strategies to me. I'd like to know my risk tolerance as well as my worst-case scenario. I want to be able to be comfortable during retirement and to be able to have an efficient, professional, and friendly relationship with my financial advisor.*

You can see here that, as you write down this statement, what you want in a new relationship starts to become clearer and clearer. The more specific you are, the clearer the vision of what you want will become; you should be as clear about this list as Goldilocks was about the height of the chair she wanted and the ideal temperature of her porridge. This is not being demanding or unrealistic – this is simply being clear about what you want your advisor to do, what you'd like to understand, what goals you have for your future, and the kind of interaction you want to have with your financial professional. It's important to be this specific, so that when you find that person, you will recognize him or her right away. Goldilocks knew immediately when something didn't fit her criteria, and she dismissed it without another thought. You want to be able to do the same thing, quickly and without worry that you're making the wrong decision. Think about how helpful that clarity will be when you are interviewing potential candidates!

List of Qualities

If you had an amazing opportunity to have a world-class fashion designer create a one-of-a-kind outfit just for you, and that designer asked you for your input, would you just sit there and say nothing? Of course not! You would be a fountain of helpful and thorough suggestions, based on your personality and your vision for yourself. You might suggest what silhouettes you thought looked best on you, the details you liked and wanted to have on this piece. You'd probably be as specific as possible, because that would mean the difference between a classic outfit you could keep forever and a piece that might be better suited for a garage sale because it didn't work for you at all. To put this in perspective, that's just a dress! Something you wear a few times a year, at the most! When we're talking about choosing the right financial advisor, we're talking about ensuring the possibility of buying *every* dress you will need during your retirement, taking *every* vacation your heart desires, sleeping easily *every* night, and being certain that you are well taken care of *tomorrow* because you chose so wisely *today*.

Just like with the designer dress input, you must be specific about what you need and want in a financial advisor. Figuring out exactly what you need can be tough to do, but I suggest that you make a list that looks at your past and at your future. It should look something like the three-columned list below, focusing on what you liked and didn't like about your old financial advisor and what you believe you want in your new one. Being super specific matters here too – you're trying to find the financial advisor who will fit your financial goals in the same way that a great dress should fit you.

Jot down the ideas as they come to you and don't worry about putting them in any sort of order or how many qualities you come up with in each column. Just keep going until you feel like it's a complete list, because that's all that matters.

As you're reading this, you might be making the list in your mind already. Go write it down!

THE GOLDILOCKS METHOD

What I <u>didn't</u> like about my old Financial Advisor	What I <u>did</u> like about my old Financial Advisor	What I <u>want</u> in my new Financial Advisor
1. Didn't return my calls	1. Was friendly & upbeat	1. Faster communication
2. Was never on time	2. Brought me chocolates!	2. Prompt meetings
3. Didn't have an assistant to help me	3. Was willing to meet at my house – I didn't have to drive!	3. Would like him/her to have a team/assistant
4. Didn't answer questions clearly	4. I was used to him/her and felt comfortable asking questions	4. Want clearer/better explanations

When you have written down all of the qualities that you can think of, top to bottom, begin to highlight the ones that are really important to you. These are the crucial things that will make a difference in your financial life, so only highlight the must-haves, not the ones that are irrelevant to your main financial goal. Now, cross off the rest. Here's an example of how your list might look:

THE GOLDILOCKS METHOD

What I <u>didn't</u> like about my old Financial Advisor	What I <u>did</u> like about my old Financial Advisor	What I <u>want</u> in my new Financial Advisor
~~1. Didn't return my calls~~	1. Was friendly & upbeat	1. Faster communication
~~2. Was never on time~~	~~2. Brought me chocolates!~~	~~2. Prompt meetings~~
~~3. Didn't have an assistant to help me~~	~~3. Was willing to meet at my house – I didn't have to drive!~~	3. Would like him/her to have a team/assistant
~~4. Didn't answer questions clearly~~	4. I was used to him/her and felt comfortable asking questions	4. Want clearer/better explanations

What you're doing here is working on identifying the essentials. You don't have to forget the non-essential stuff, but think of the non-essentials as extra perks. Even if you loved the little gifts that your financial advisor got you, maybe a box of chocolates for the holidays or the gift certificate to the spa every year on your birthday, you'd probably agree that these things are not essential to your overall financial goals. Instead, when you're making a list of what you need and want in a financial advisor, the focus should be on what will help you accomplish those goals.

Take a look at your new, refined list – these are your personal criteria for your new financial advisor, based on what is most important to you. Your list is as unique as you are. And with this list, you'll be able to start your search for someone who truly is the right fit for your goals. Here are some additional important criteria you may want to consider:

A Top Ten Criteria Checklist

These ten qualities are the things I think every financial advisor must have if he or she is going to help you accomplish your long-term financial goals. Some of these you may already have on your list, perhaps phrased differently, and some may be entirely new to you. Regardless, these are qualities to which you should give careful consideration as you are interviewing potential financial professionals.

1. YOUR ADVISOR SHOULD BE PASSIONATE ABOUT THEIR JOB. For the right financial professional, advising clients about their investments and helping them plan their retirement should be a career. It shouldn't be a side job or a hobby, something that he or she dabbles in with some spare time for extra money. No, this is what they should breathe and eat, every single day. For example, you may think that it's fine to have an accountant who does financial advising on the side. It seems to work, on the surface, since both occupations focus on finances. But trust me, that person is bad at one of those jobs, and it's likely the one that's the side gig. For example, if I asked you if you'd like to go to a cardiologist who is also a gynecologist, would you feel comfortable doing that, or would you hesitate because you'd feel like they're probably average, or below average, in one of those fields? It all comes down to experience, and if your advisor is also your CPA, then they're not spending enough time getting experience in either field. Because of that, one area will definitely suffer, so beware if you gravitate to the jack-of-all-trades types, thinking that you'll get more for your money. Remember the end of that saying: "jack-of-all-trades and master of none." You deserve better.

2. *YOUR ADVISOR NEEDS TO HAVE THE PROPER LICENSES TO CONDUCT TRANSACTIONS AND BE LISTED WITH FINRA.* Here's some technical information that you may not have known about financial professionals. FINRA (or the Financial Industry Regulatory Authority) is the agency that helps the financial industry self-regulate. In addition to conducting audits and other oversight activities, FINRA provides licenses to financial professionals that allow them to conduct certain transactions for their clients. Depending on what investments your advisor wants to work with, that advisor must pass a series of tests and be licensed to help you with those investments. You need to know what licenses your advisor has and his or her standing with FINRA. Don't end up with a financial advisor who seems great on the outside but ends up being just the opposite, like that Dolce bag you thought you got for a steal from a friend, but were shocked to find that it was actually a "Dolce & Cabbana" that she picked up on Canal Street, along with that Rolex that upon closer inspection turned out to be a "Folex." Nobody likes a counterfeit of any kind.

3. YOUR ADVISOR SHOULD HAVE BEEN WITH THEIR CURRENT FIRM FOR AT LEAST THREE YEARS. You want to build a long-term professional relationship with your advisor. If you see that the professional you are considering has frequently hopped firms, this can be a major red flag and a sign of lack of commitment. What you want is the little black dress equivalent in your financial advisor, the person who you can be confident will stick around for years. Someone who is dependable, and always comes through when you need them to. A financial advisor who has roots demonstrates credibility and strength of character. The last thing you want is someone who cannot survive more than a few seasons.

4. YOUR ADVISOR SHOULD HAVE AT LEAST THREE YEARS OF EXPERIENCE IN THE FINANCIAL FIELD. It's great if you find an advisor with whom you really click, but if they're new to the business, chances are that they're not the best fit for you. This is because when it comes to your money, just like when hiring a doctor to take care of your physical health, experience is important. You need someone who has some experience at his or her fingertips, and has seen enough real-life scenarios to be able to use that experience to help you. Even if this new financial advisor has been working under someone's supervision, a senior financial planner or someone who has a solid, time-tested record of successful investments, their supervisor's experience is not their own. Regardless, look for a track record. You don't want a rookie practicing with your hard-earned money.

5. YOUR ADVISOR SHOULD HAVE GOOD COMMUNICATION SKILLS. Anyone who tells you that communication skills are not necessary in the financial world is telling you the worst kind of lie! Finding out about your investments should not be a guessing game with huge consequences. Instead, you want a financial advisor who has the skills of a good teacher: clear explanations, patience, not easily frustrated by questions. Your financial advisor should answer your questions courteously and in a timely fashion, and should make you feel better for having asked them.

6. *THE OFFICE SHOULD ALWAYS RETURN YOUR CALL WITHIN 24 HOURS.* Emergencies and weekends notwithstanding, your financial advisor, or a member of his or her team, should get back to you quickly, every single time. You need to be able to count on their accessibility. Imagine that you are purchasing or refinancing a home. If your financial advisor's office makes you wait days and days for a response to every question or request for information from the mortgage company, you may not only be looking at frustration – you may be looking at an increased interest rate or losing an opportunity for a great deal because your financial advisor was too busy to return your phone calls.

One other note on this: when you do find an advisor who is responsive and returns your calls the same day or within 24 hours, you will likely feel happy and grateful for the attention and service you're getting. But honestly, you shouldn't, because prompt replies to communication from you should be the industry norm. It isn't yet, but seriously, when an advisor is handling *your* money, expecting a callback within 24 hours should feel as obvious as knowing that the sun will rise in the morning.

7. *YOUR ADVISOR SHOULD HAVE AT LEAST ONE ASSISTANT OR TEAM MEMBER AS A SUPPORT STAFF.* One person simply can't do it all, and when your financial professional is a one-man or one-woman show, your needs may not always be met. If your financial advisor is out of town or unreachable during an emergency, if that person has an assistant or a team member who is working to help serve clients, you will always have a point person available. Remember the fairy tale about the shoemaker who worked tirelessly to make all of those shoes but

couldn't quite do it, despite his best efforts? He had a magical elfin entourage that worked all night to finish the work he started. That's what you want – your financial professional should have a back-up system in place so that when he or she is busy and can't quite finish everything, nothing that's important to you slips through the cracks.

8. *The financial advisor should have a clean record.* When you're looking for a financial advisor, it's important to find out their background. Any professional might have a few random complaints, because just like there are bad financial advisors out there, there are also bad consumers. But if you do find out that there is a record of consistent complaints against the advisor you are considering, or issues with consumers and regulators alike, then you should see the red flags flying high. You can look up this information in several ways. One way is through the Central Registration Depository (CRD), which is a computerized database that contains information about individual financial professionals and the firms where they work. You can get the information from the CRD from your state securities regulator or from FINRA's BrokerCheck website. Just like you shouldn't let a plumber into your house without that plumber being bonded and certified, just to make sure your home and valuables are protected, you also don't want to let a financial advisor near your money without taking the time to make sure they don't have major complaints against them.

9. *Your advisor should be able to give you at least a couple of references upon request.* In this industry, advisors cannot have testimonials. It's a rule that was created to protect potential clients from being misled about an advisor's abilities. But you can get references upon request. When you are about to upgrade the appliances in your kitchen, you do the research, read the reviews, and decide which models are best for you. You consider energy

efficiency, think about whether you want stainless steel or standard white, decide whether the whisper-soft feature of the dishwasher is worth the extra money – and then you talk to people who have these items. All of those descriptions can't tell you as much as the day-to-day experiences of someone who actually has them. You should be doing the same sort of investigation when you are choosing your financial advisor. He or she should have a long list of satisfied clients; and if they can't come up with a few that will talk to you, that ought to tell you a lot.

10. IT'S A GOOD IDEA TO WORK WITH AN ADVISOR WHO'S AT AN APPROPRIATE AGE FOR YOUR RETIREMENT NEEDS. You want your financial professional to be available for you at least during the first decade of your retirement, so it's important for you to be aware of their age. You don't have the magical ability to stop the aging process – and if you do, I really doubt you'll have any trouble with retirement funds because you'll be a perpetual money machine, the modern-day goose that laid the golden egg! But since you don't, you need to make sure that the timing of your advisor's retirement won't create unnecessary headaches for you. You don't want someone who is so young that they only realize the mistakes made with your portfolio when you are already retired, or someone who won't even be in business by the time you begin your retirement because they themselves had retired 10 or 15 years before you.

Add these ten qualities and characteristics to the list you already created, and you'll have a dynamic, comprehensive list to use as you are choosing a financial advisor who is a good fit for you. With these elements in mind, you are sure to choose the person who's absolutely right for you.

Asking the Right Questions

Once you've decided what you're looking for in a financial professional, it's time to start the interview process. As I mentioned earlier, this is the person who will help you make major decisions about your finances, so you want to ensure that you are getting everything you need from this financial professional. The interview process can be incredibly incisive – you can find out a lot if you go in with the right questions. Imagine the difference if the first two piggies from the story of "The Three Little Pigs" had chosen a reputable, licensed contractor with whom they had an honest conversation about their building needs. "Well, you see, we occasionally have visits from this Wolf, who likes to try and blow our house down. What can you do for us?" Or perhaps the Emperor who was tricked into believing that he was wearing elaborate clothes, when he was actually walking around naked, should have done some interviewing of his own. Rather than taking the rumor mill at its word about the fashionable nature of those new "clothes" he was ordering, how different would the fairy tale be if he had a conversation with the designers: "Now, what fabric will you be using? How will the design flatter my body type? How will I care for it?" Now, it's possible that mistakes might still have been made, and the two piggies' houses might have still been blown down, and the Emperor might still have strutted naked down the street. But even a wise pig or a fictional, insecure Emperor would be able to see some warning signs of bad professional behavior if the experts they were interviewing couldn't answer their basic questions clearly.

Because you are creating a list of questions that will help you find the right financial advisor for you, you want to take your list of must-have qualities and translate that list into a set of questions to ask. You might start with the sample questions below, as a guide, and add more to them based on your individual needs. Though it may take time and

178

a few initial meetings, these questions will help you assess how well each financial advisor meets the top ten criteria I described above. Remember: take your questions to your first meeting!

Questions to ask

Q: How long have you worked as a financial advisor?

Remember the three-year rule: you want someone who has enough relevant experience, so that they can use that experience to help you – not learn with your money.

Q: How long have you been with your current company, and where did you work before you started with this firm?

You don't want someone who jumps jobs all the time, so get a clear sense of your financial advisor's past job history.

Q: Why did you leave your previous firm?

Don't be satisfied with vague answers. If you get the feeling that they are avoiding the question, you should definitely do your homework. Listen to your intuition!

Q: What made you get into this line of work?

Look for the passion that you hope your financial professional will have. You should hear the enthusiasm in their answer.

Q: Where are you hoping to be in five or 10 years?

You're looking to develop a long-term professional relationship, so if your potential financial advisor is hoping to move across the country next year, you may want to find someone with stronger and more permanent roots in your community.

Q: What are the most important goals for you, as a financial advisor, to achieve for your clients?

As you listen to their answer, think about whether these goals fit with your own. Your advisor should share your philosophy about your investments or, at the very least, respect your goals and risk tolerance enough to follow your direction, and bring ideas to you that match your overall comfort level.

Q: What is the most important goal for you to accomplish within the next decade?

This question can provide a really interesting snapshot into the financial advisor on a professional and personal level. See if the answer resonates with you – if it does, you may have found a person who you can work with effectively.

Q: Tell me a little about yourself on a personal level.

Ask the advisor a little bit about his or her personal life just so you can get to know them better. Understanding personality traits is really important in determining if that person is someone you want to work with. Professional relationships always have a slight personal element, so you need to be able to trust and rely on this individual.

Q: Do you have a team that you work with?

You want to know that your advisor has a support system in place so that your needs can always be met by the professional that you choose.

Sometimes, people feel uncomfortable asking too many questions when they begin working with a financial advisor, or any other professional for that matter. These questions are completely fine to ask, and you're not stepping over any boundaries, or anything like that. Remember, you are interviewing them because they will be handling an incredibly important part of your life. You may even feel like you are kissing a whole lot of frogs to find that one prince, or princess (Note: Please don't actually try to kiss any advisors you are interviewing!), but these questions should help you know which candidate is the perfect one for you.

This is a Marriage, Not a Date

When you think that you've found the right financial professional, realize that this is a long-term professional relationship, not a casual fling. I often see women making a huge mistake when they are in the process of choosing a new professional. They think, "I'll just develop an investment portfolio with this advisor and see how it goes." They plan to wait a little while, reevaluate, and keep changing advisors and portfolios until they find the right person for them.

Look, I totally understand the logic behind that way of thinking, but this is not like trying different hairdressers until you find the right one. Unless you walk in as Rapunzel and walk out with a pixie cut, it won't take too long for your hair to bounce all the way back from trying out a bad hairstylist. But when it comes to your finances, you're dealing with much more substantial consequences for this kind of error in judgment. Your portfolio may not bounce back from all of the mistakes and changes that come during years of trying to find the right advisor through this "wait and see" philosophy. Just think about Goldilocks; what if she tried the first bowl of porridge and said, "Hmm... I'm not sure about this one, it's kind of cold, and there are other bowls of porridge here which might be a better temperature, but I guess I'll just keep eating this one in front of me and maybe it will somehow warm up all on its own, eventually." Nope! She knew what she wanted, and she knew she had options, so if she didn't like something, she continued looking for the right fit.

From the beginning, you need to think about this choice seriously and commit to finding the ideal financial professional for yourself. The goal is to work with one person until, and even through, your retirement. While it may not always turn out that way in the end, if you go into the relationship with that kind of commitment, you will invest in the relationship much differently in the beginning than if you adopt an "I'll try this one out and see" attitude. Doing this will encourage you to do your due diligence when trying to find the right person for you and your financial goals. Think about it this way: when you know that you are looking for a pair of shoes that will last, that will work with many outfits, and will feel fantastic, you're willing to spend a little more time in the search and a little more money on them. You'll probably end up choosing a pair that's made of quality materials, rather than be tempted to buy the pair on the sale rack because no one else is buying it. The initial time investment is worth it because the return is so attractive.

When you create a long-term relationship with your professional, it similarly works to your benefit. The bond grows stronger and stronger, which allows that financial professional to find better solutions to your retirement needs, because they get to know you and your needs. You'll see that same kind of return on your time investment with your doctor. The longer you see the same doctor, the better your doctor will know your health history. Illnesses will be easier to diagnose, and treatments will be quicker. Potential problems will be addressed early on because your doctor will know you as well as possible. Think about that pair of quality shoes that we talked about just a minute ago. After you've worn them enough to ensure that they are broken in, they feel fantastic. We've all had shoes like that – they feel like they were made just for you! No matter how many hours you spend on your feet, you never have to worry about those shoes hurting you, because they are dependable and the perfect fit for you. While I doubt your doctor, lawyer, or financial professional want to be compared to shoes, the similarity is there. The longer you work with your advisor, the better they can cater to your individual needs and become the perfect professional fit for you. But that process takes time.

For example, when I'm working with a client, and I know other advisors who feel the same way, it takes me a good year to get to know her personality and potential problem areas. After the second and third year, I feel like I know her so well that I can begin to see a pattern about what's working and not working in her financial life. I can then help her based on those specific patterns that are unique to her, whether it's budget planning, adding more to her income planning, or adapting her portfolio so that her investments match her true lifestyle better. But I can only do that once I know her well, and this is what helps give my client much more freedom in retirement. With continuous planning comes more income and that leads to a better lifestyle during the retirement years. You just don't get this when you are working with someone in the short term, and constantly switching advisors. It is one thing to set a skeleton plan to fit someone's retirement objectives, but an entirely different thing to keep clients motivated and encouraged to stay on the right track, so that they save more and contribute more toward their retirement nest egg. Remember, it's not just about the investments you have, but about following a budget that is right for your situation, so that you can actually reach your retirement goals, and make that dream a reality! To find that perfect fit, you need to spend time and effort initially and invest in the relationship with your advisor. When you do, you'll reap tremendous financial and personal rewards.

Tomorrow Will Be a Direct Reflection of Today

After you've invested the time and energy to find the right professional fit, your work isn't done. You need to make sure that your professional is not only helping you plan for your future but is also managing your finances right now. What this means is that you can't have your eye squarely set on the future alone. Your current spending habits, income projections – every element of your financial life should be a part of the conversations you're having with your financial professional. Developing a long-term relationship with this in mind helps you both. It helps you, because you have a professional who is watching your habits and giving you advice on how to make your money work for you, and it helps the professional, who can adjust and readjust your portfolio based on your short-term and long-term needs.

You want to make sure that your financial advisor is not just investing without aim. I wholeheartedly believe that when you are planning your retirement needs, you really need to understand your expenses today so that you can better predict your income needs in later years. Believe it or not, many people are not 100% percent clear on what their needs will be later on! So their goal becomes to save up as much as they can and hope that it will be enough to meet their monthly expenses when they retire. Worse yet, sometimes people think that they can live on less money than they are currently making, simply because they are retired. It's unrealistic to assume that your tastes and needs will suddenly change just because you are no longer working. You don't want to be in a situation where you are limited in your opportunities for retirement activities – travel with family, hobbies, even shopping and entertainment – because you didn't carefully project your income needs today.

Having worked with many clients over the years, I can tell you that it takes extensive questioning and discussion to come up with an accurate projection of possible income needs, and, as the years go by, to make sure that the projection is set properly to reflect inflation. It takes more than just keeping up with what the client communicates but with what that client is actually doing. I have to take into account all expenses, even something as simple as the weekly manicure or their frequent trips to Nordstrom. All of that goes into the final calculations, making the investment plan better tailored to the real life situation of each individual. For example, when I'm running numbers, I also like to base those numbers on the most modest projected investment growth performance, even as low as 3% sometimes, to review worst-case scenarios. Many financial professionals will run scenarios that include a high percentage of growth paired with low expenses – of course that looks good on paper, but those scenarios are likely not going to happen in reality. Remember the old saying that you should hope for the best and plan for the worst? Make sure that your financial professional is not going to be more interested in looking good rather than in protecting your future by being honest. This is a very common theme in the financial industry and I hear it all the time. This is why it is important that you choose a financial advisor who doesn't just think the way you do because they want to make you feel good, but can also be very direct and honest about the worst-case scenarios that you may face!

Most good financial advisors who are properly educated in retirement planning will help you plan for your income and expense needs now and during your retirement years, because these are the ones who are passionate about what they do. These financial professionals will either do the budget planning themselves or have someone on their team do this for you.

Remember, investing is not just about buying stocks, mutual funds, bonds, or annuities. It's about making sure that you are allocating your portfolio in a way that will help you cover your projected future income needs. If you do this, you will be prepared for retirement in advance and won't have to hope for a fairy godmother or a Rumpelstiltskin to magically improve your financial situation.

The Importance of Your Choice

You can see why finding the right financial professional can make a big difference between a comfortable, secure retirement or a haphazardly planned, fingers crossed, hope-it-all-works-out-in-the-end retirement. Unfortunately, people often just retire blindly and hope that the money will last for as long as they live. Don't be one of those people! Just remember that the most important thing during the interview process is: "Don't Be Such a Girl," unless you're channeling Goldilocks, then definitely be that girl!

Things to Keep in Mind

- Create a mission statement for what you want in your relationship with your new financial advisor.

- Identify what qualities you liked in your previous advisor, and the qualities you hope to find in your new one.

- Highlight the qualities that are essential to you in meeting your financial goals.

- Consider the top ten qualities that your financial professional should have, and add those to your list.

- Interview financial advisors who match your list of qualities.

- Ask a series of probing questions in your first meeting to get a clear sense of how you will work with this professional.

- Choose an advisor based on who best suits your needs and financial goals.

- Work together to create a future financial plan based on your current spending habits and income.

- Remember that your investment planning benefits from a long-term relationship with the right professional.

THE MAGIC WALL STREET GENIE

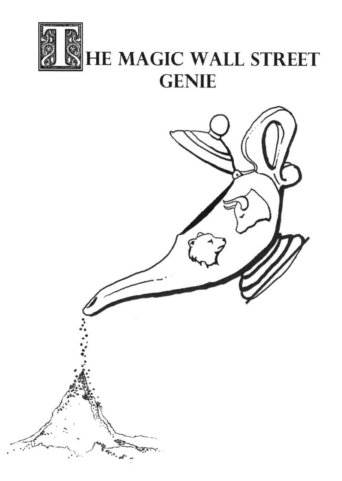

CHAPTER 15

THE GRAND BAZAAR

"Do not seek to follow in the footsteps of the men of old; seek what they sought." — Basho

So now that you understand the basics of budgeting and its importance for your financial planning, let's take a look at the Grand Bazaar, more commonly referred to as the stock market, so that you can have a basic understanding of how it works. This way, the next time you have someone (a friend, a colleague at the water cooler, or the nail salon manicurist) telling you their opinion of what stocks you should be purchasing, you will have a better idea of how to look at the situation. And let's face it, everyone and their grandmother recommends a stock nowadays. I am not kidding you! My last summer vacation I was at the Grand Wailea in Maui, Hawaii, and I was at the stand by the beach getting shaved ice (I *love* shaved ice in Hawaii), and I overheard a surfer who was paying for his order in front of me, talking to the cashier about some stock he really liked. This is how the conversation went:

> THE SURFER: *"Aloha, my friend, aloha! I meant to tell you last week, you should really look into that company I was telling you about, because they're doing an IPO soon. The more I've been checking it out, the more*

I love their ideas. I heard the company produced new tank tops that are going to totally change the surfing industry, and I'm going to get in on this thing."

THE MERCHANT: *"Really, what are they for, the tank tops?"*

THE SURFER: *"Well, they are supposed to help the water slide off of the surfer easier. I was watching Warren Buffett the other day and he was saying that new technology stocks could bring a lot of money, if you look at the company right."*

THE MERCHANT: *"Akamai, what a great idea, thanks for telling me, I'll check it out!"* (AKAMAI, PRONOUNCED AH-kah-mah-ee, means to be very smart, very intelligent, very sharp.)

Really though, this is not a joke; they were discussing something they had no understanding of, and somehow trying to pull Warren Buffett's name into it to make themselves feel like what they were thinking was along the same levels of investment skill. Although, honestly, I'm not sure if the cashier was actually taking the suggestions seriously, or if he was just being nice to his regular customer. I hope that in reality, he was just trying to be nice and never actually invested just because he heard it was a good idea.

In another situation, I had a client who told me that when she was working at a major hospital, she fell for the typical "I know a secret" advice from a co-worker about a medicine that would completely revolutionize the treatment of the common cold. Based on that simple conversation, she invested $30,000 into that company's stock without doing any of her own research. Unfortunately, she ended up losing most of her money, because the company was not very successful. The odd thing was that this was an intelligent woman, who was educated and actually pretty savvy. She became so excited with the idea of making huge returns, that she simply ignored the little voice in her head that was probably pointing out some of the pitfalls in her strategy. What she thought of as "sexy" and being "in the know," and probably plain old greed, got the best of her.

The Grand Bazaar

Oh, the magical land of the stock market, with its wild up and down roller-coaster swings. All this action can certainly make your head spin. There's always something going on, the news almost never stops, and there's no shortage of guys and gals on TV trying to predict what will happen next. But a basic understanding of how the market really works should help you stay level-headed and not get caught up in all the hoopla that makes its way onto the daily news.

When you boil it down to its most bare-bones concept, investing in stocks is a way to easily purchase part ownership in a company. The stock market is like a giant farmer's market, but instead of trading fruits and veggies, this market trades in *ownership*. When you go to this market and buy a stock, what you are doing is buying a tiny slice of ownership of a company – which is represented by the stock itself – and you are sharing in ownership with other people.

The stock market has three very important purposes: 1) It allows companies to go public and raise additional money by selling their previously privately owned shares on the open market (these are the Initial Public Offerings, or "IPOs" you've probably heard so much about). 2) It allows you, and any investors, the opportunity to become a part owner of companies, and, hopefully, share in the earnings and success of these firms. And 3): It provides liquidity, or the ability for investors to quickly sell their stocks. Imagine how difficult it would be to convert your investments into cash if there was no readily available market to buy and sell stocks, and if you had to find a buyer yourself whenever you wanted to sell your shares.

Let's take a look at how this actually works. A very enterprising young woman named Little Red Riding Hood decided to open her own company, Red Wolf Coats Inc., making coats out of wolf fur (after all, she wanted to finally make some good use out of all the wolves in the forest so they would stop scaring little girls). People absolutely love these coats, and Little Red decides that she needs to expand her business. After thinking about it carefully, she decides that the best way to raise money is not to borrow, but to go public. By going public, Little Red will sell some of her ownership (up until now, she owned 100% of her factory) in exchange for money that she can use to expand the business. This process is called an Initial Public Offering, or "IPO." So, after all the attorneys and the brokers hash out all the magical legalities, they set the IPO date and decide to divide the company into 100 equal pieces, or shares. When the IPO date finally arrives, all the forest's critters, elves, gargoyles, toads, and beautiful chupacabras decide to get in on the action and buy some ownership of Red Wolf Coats Inc.

Whenever one of these magical creatures buys one out of the 100 shares of this stock, what they are really doing is buying 1/100th of the company, because, in this example, the ownership was divided into 100 pieces and they just bought one of them. Some critters maybe bought just one share, which equals 1% of ownership in this case (1/100), while others bought 10 shares (which happens to be 10% of ownership in this case, or 10/100) and some maybe even more. Now, that doesn't necessarily mean that the critters were paying a fair price when buying, or getting a fair price when selling the shares; it simply means that they can buy and sell those shares with relative ease because there is a market where everyone who wants to buy is matched with everyone who wants to sell. And of course, this example is very simplified. Publicly traded companies will usually issue millions and sometimes billions of shares. So it's very difficult for the average investor to actually own even 1% of a publicly traded company, but the idea of ownership is very much the same as with the Red Wolf Coats example above; it's just that the percentage of ownership that an average investor can buy in the real world is much smaller. This is also referred to as having equity in the company, however it does not give you any right to make any management decisions; you just get to participate in the upside if the company does well.

The Stock Market Roller Coaster

So if buying a stock means buying a small piece of ownership, why do stock market prices move about so much sometimes? Can the values of companies, and what it costs to buy ownership in them, really change that much in a day? Well, here's the thing: if purchasing a stock means that you're purchasing part ownership in a company, then in an ideal world, it should mean that the price of the stock should be based on how much money the company is expected to make in the future. For example, if you wanted to invest your money in a business and decided to buy a beauty salon, you would most likely try to first figure out how much that salon can make in profits. And then, based on how profitable you think it would be, you would figure out the kind of price you're willing to pay to buy it. So if you thought it could make $10,000 a year in profit, you might be willing to pay $50,000 for the business, or whatever you thought was fair. If it was going to generate $100,000 a year in profit, well then it obviously would be worth a lot more. And in an ideal stock market, it's supposed to work the same way; investors are supposed to look at a company and buy shares (i.e., become part owners) when they believe that it is a good deal based on the potential future earnings of the company. But even though most people and money managers don't have pointy ears or fluffy tails, just like fairy-tale creatures, they sometimes behave in even stranger ways than their make-believe counterparts.

As I've mentioned before, the stock market has a serious mood disorder, and sometimes I honestly think that it's on drugs. You know... erratic behavior, unexplained actions, and everyone who knows the stock market seems to be concerned with its well-being. Hey, from time to time Congress even tries to hold an intervention, but nothing seems to help! Here's the deal: the stock market provides liquidity and makes it super easy to trade stocks, which means that people can buy and sell on a whim! And because of that, especially in the short term, stock prices often move up and down based on what buyers and sellers are feeling and thinking. So, in the short term, the stock market can almost become more of a psychological barometer rather than a logical market that has anything to do with the actual value of the companies being traded. Think about it; would it make sense if you went to the farmer's market, and the price of tomatoes kept going up and down while you were standing in line? Of course not, because a tomato is a tomato and nothing is going to change much about it! But the stock market is a different story because professional and individual investors keep changing

their estimates about how profitable a company is going to be based on every bit of news that comes out about the economy and politics in general. And so, as they keep changing their points of view about the potential profitability, they keep buying and selling stocks at different prices. In that sense, the market is like an immediate barometer of people's fear and greed; stock prices can move up and down simply based on people's feelings, without truly being based on a company's future earning ability; or on an incredibly misinterpreted view of what those earnings might be.

Just imagine in the farmer's market example, if a farmer who was selling grapes kept looking at the line of customers while holding a few grapes out in his hand and having people just guess what they think they should pay, or if he raised or lowered the price according to the length of the line! Can you imagine the chaos that would ensue? People guessing if there were 20 pounds of grapes left or just one pound, if the farmer is able to grow any more, or if there was going to be a grape shortage; or if they thought there would be better grapes and more of them tomorrow, and how would the European debt crisis affect those grapes. This emotional guessing could go on and on! You think this sounds outrageous? Well, guess what? This is what happens in the stock market a lot of the time. Obviously, it's more complicated than guessing the price of grapes, but it's the same idea.

A lot of the time it's not even people that are trying to guess, but computer algorithms that try to make stock market predictions – and sometimes they're very wrong. A great example of that occurred on April 23, 2013, when the market dropped about 1% and no one could understand why, until they realized that some private stock trading computer programs created a mini stock crash after automatically reading a fake tweet from an Associated Press Twitter account, that had been hacked![23] So when the average investor is trying to figure out what is going on within the company they are holding stocks in, and whether it's a good time to buy or sell, a lot of the time it unfortunately becomes almost a guessing game – an emotional game! If you want to play emotional games, go to Vegas. I promise it will be more fun, and at least you'll get free cocktails!

When the market began its meltdown in 2008, it created a chaotic scene for investors. Everyone had an opinion, and everyone had some explanation or prediction of what was going to happen. In hindsight, it's pretty easy to see that the disaster didn't just happen overnight, but was brewing for several years, and some would argue that the meltdown had its real beginnings over a decade earlier![24] But that's in hindsight. And if you pay close attention to various stock market gurus and "experts," you'll notice that there are tons of people who are great at explaining what *happened*, but not all that great at predicting the future – even huge drops, like that of 2008, which seemed to catch everyone completely by surprise. When it comes to building a long-term nest egg, you also don't have the benefit of hindsight, which makes it all the more important to keep reminding yourself that in the short term, the markets can swing wildly all over the place based mostly on investor psychology. If you are a long-term minded person who is 20 or 30 years away from retirement, the fact that the Dow dropped 200 points, and Joe Schmo on television is saying that the country is at the brink of default, these situations, in my opinion, are probably not the best reasons to start selling your holdings. I also don't believe that it's time to buy just because Josephine Schmo is saying that the market will rally. Reacting to *any* major news in this way without doing your own research is likely a bad idea. I believe a better approach is to proactively diversify and allocate your investments in a way that makes sense for your specific situation, your risk tolerance, and your time horizon until retirement, and looks at your overall picture, without trying too hard to jump in and out of the market based on what other people are saying or doing.

A Monogamous Relationship With an Individual Stock – "Do" or "Don't"?

As I mentioned in the previous paragraphs, the stock market is literally like a huge market where large and small investors alike can buy and sell small pieces of companies. When you are buying or selling a stock, you are really trading a small portion of a company. It's very important that you keep this idea in mind, because you can understand a lot about the markets by logically thinking about buying stocks as becoming a part owner in a company, rather than looking at it as some confusing lottery.

I strongly believe that, under normal circumstances, it is very dangerous to allocate more than a small portion of your portfolio into individual stocks. I cannot stress this enough, and I say this because to make money by investing in individual stocks, a person has to be great at analyzing them. Analyzing stocks takes a lot of time, and a lot of experience to do well, and even with all that knowledge and experience it's still easy to make huge mistakes. You would really need to spend many hours every day following the markets and reading company annual reports (You think budgeting is boring? Try analyzing corporate balance sheets on a daily basis!), which still wouldn't even guarantee that you could do better than average. And because of that, for most people, investing into specific individual stocks simply increases their risk for very little additional reward. When you're making a bet on individual stocks, you're losing the benefits of diversification (more on diversification in Chapter 17 and the Appendix), and are hoping that your analysis is good enough not only to offset the higher risks of not being diversified, but that on top of that, you will also earn a much better return (are you really *that* good?). Most people don't think about it this way, but I urge you to keep this in mind before you venture into individual stocks because there's so much to consider.

However, if you just can't help yourself, and absolutely must try your luck, I strongly suggest that you only use a very small portion of your portfolio to do this. This way, if you make the wrong decision on an individual stock, and its value goes down instead of up, you will only lose up to the amount you have invested. A good way to figure out if you should be choosing your own stocks is to look at the worst-case scenario, losing the entire amount invested, and decide if you could live with that risk.

(Many people have confusion about stocks, mutual funds, and bonds. The Appendix section of this book has more information on these topics, and will help you gain a better understanding of how they fit into the context of investments. If you decide that you'd like extra education on this subject, then please refer to pages 263-289.)

Tips and Tricks, Smell Their Deceits!

Over the last several decades there have been lots of books about how to choose stocks and make millions of dollars. There are literally thousands of books out there, and all have some sort of system. If you've happened to stay up late at some point in time, you probably also had the opportunity to see infomercials for stock market systems where grinning testimonial people are gushing about all the money that they made from whichever system is being sold.

I want you to please, please, please keep this particular point in mind any time your advisor, or broker, or in-law, or whoever, tells you that one stock or another is a great bet. There are no sure things in life, and because the stock market is part of life, there are no sure things in the market either. No one has a magical system for making money, no one. There have been millions, if not tens of millions, of investors over the last 100 years who didn't just passively invest in the stock market, but actually thought that they could pick investments in a way that would let them beat the overall stock market returns. Some spent time devising their systems, and some were moderately successful, but not many have been able to consistently outperform the market over the long term. And even for those that did outperform, you have to ask yourself if it was because of their system or just plain old luck; even in a lottery, someone eventually wins the prize, but no one can consistently be #1 no matter how great their "system" is. Even in fairy-tale lands it's not possible. Rumpelstiltskin always had some magical solution that was to solve the some poor princess's problem, whether it was love, money, or power, but there was a price for the magic that was given, let's not forget that. Rumpelstiltskin never actually helped the poor souls, rather they helped him and he came out happy and laughing. And the same goes for the so called "We-got-it-figured-out get-rich-quick" systems.

So whenever someone comes to you with some great tip or system, it is important that you are skeptical and thoroughly investigate before pursuing. These tips and systems usually stem from someone thinking that they are smarter than everyone else, and that they see something in the stock that no one else does. With millions of investors trading in the market on a daily basis, you have to ask yourself: "What are the chances that this particular person that I know just happened to understand this particular stock better than everyone else on Wall Street?"

Likewise, if someone comes to you with a great system for selecting stocks (that is, if you're only willing to make ten easy payments of $39.99), you have to ask yourself, "What are the chances that this system actually works, and why is this company selling their system if it's so amazing? Why won't they just use their system to make money for themselves instead?" Think about it; you know those late-night infomercials that I mentioned earlier, where the people in testimonials say how they doubled their money in a week? Most people see that and think "Whoa! I can make *that* much money – amazing!" But not you, because you are a savvy, confident woman who does not need to jump on every opportunity she sees. So you stop and do the math on this one, and this is what you'll figure out: if you can double your money in a week with this system, and you started with $100, then after 20 weeks you would have over $100 million! And when you see these numbers, you then ask yourself if this is realistic; if someone could actually have developed a system that could create such amazing returns, and if after that, these people would give away their amazing system for just a few easy payments of whatever dollar amount. And I'm sure that by this point, your answer to this "opportunity" is a resounding "No Thank You!" and "Get your hand out of my purse! I'm not giving you my money!"

So whatever system or great investment tip that's being thrown your way, you can weed out most of the poisoned apples by simply thinking logically about the situation and asking yourself a few common-sense questions. Most of the time, you don't need much investment knowledge to avoid making foolish decisions, just a little bit of common sense and the ability to think before you act.

Things to Keep in Mind

- Stocks represent ownership in a company. Buying some means that, in the simplest terms, you become a part owner.

- Even though stock prices are ideally supposed to be related to the earnings ability of a company, in many cases they are not! Especially in the short term.

- Stock tips and investment systems are not a valid investment strategy! Always do your own research!

CHAPTER 16

THE ART OF RISK

"Strategy without tactics is the slowest route to victory. Tactics without strategy is the noise before defeat."
— Sun Tzu

Risk is always a chance that we take. Whether it's good or bad really depends on what it is we are risking. I remember once when I was going to a charity benefit, and I decided that I would risk wearing these brand-new red suede pumps that I had just bought. They looked ah-maz-ing! But the great looks didn't match how they felt on my feet. These pumps were super high, and really uncomfortable, but at the time, because they really looked gorgeous, I felt that it was a risk that I was willing to take. I thought to myself, "What if I can't walk in them for too long? What if they hurt too much? Can I keep a straight face while being so uncomfortable?" Well, I weighed all the options and decided that how I would look in them was well worth the risk! After all, they were Ferragamo Fabulous. So the good news was everyone loved them and I got lots of compliments. The bad news was that I actually broke my little toe. The damage wasn't too bad, and I recovered from the pain within a couple of weeks! And even though this outcome was not the one I planned for, my decision to wear the pumps was nonetheless a calculated risk that made sense at the time. Now what if this had been going to a dancing party instead of a benefit? Well, then maybe wearing those pumps would not have been a risk I would be willing to take! There are numerous factors that need to be considered when we are thinking about taking a risk.

Asking the Right Questions

Most women just don't ask the right questions when making investment decisions, especially when it comes to understanding the risks that are involved. I think that this is mostly because the idea of how risk affects our lives is very much misunderstood and has an undeservedly bad reputation. Most people either look at risk as something that is inherently bad, and something that should be avoided at all costs, or they completely ignore that it exists! The key to becoming a better decision-maker, and to being smarter about the risks you take, is to 1) never ignore risk, 2) realize that risk is not necessarily a bad thing, and 3) train yourself to ask the right questions. Taking risks is what moves our lives forward and helps us achieve our goals and dreams, but risk becomes a dangerous thing when you ignore it and don't devote the time and effort to try to manage it in your favor.

Here's what you need to remember: we are surrounded by risk! Every day, pretty much with every decision you make, there is always a chance that something could go wrong. You could say that our entire life is just one humongous risk! You decide to wear bright red lipstick to a job interview; you're taking a risk. You change your highlights into lowlights; you're taking a risk. You ask your boyfriend if that dress makes you look fat, well, you're also taking a risk – a risk that you will soon be single if he dares say anything other than "Of course not, honey! You look amazing! As always… my beautiful princess." And just like there are two sides to every story, there are both good aspects and bad aspects about risk.

For example, imagine that you are planning this year's holiday dinner and you decide to try a brand-new approach; you are going "turkey chic," and by that I mean you are abandoning the turkey altogether this year, because you're going to cook stuffed quail! That's right, that's the new hot thing on the Food Network, and you want to shine in front of your entire family as an amazing cook! You're giddy with anticipation about everyone's reaction, all the compliments you're going to get, and all the questions about this yummy dish that you will so expertly prepare. You probably even have pictures from the magazines cut out with many different side options showing you the best ways to visually present the dish, and you're hoping that this holiday dinner will be a smash! Oh, how all your friends and family will be jealous! They will bow to your feet at the sight of your dinner table, and will all chant, "We're not worthy! We're not worthy!" And the party poopers who dare complain, "Umm... Where is the turkey and the stuffing? I don't like trying new, exciting things, because I'm boring," well, they'll just have to sit there hungry and bitter, while everyone else is partaking in this amazing feast.

But here's the thing, although you don't really know until the actual dinner party if this new feast will make you look good, you also understand that if you're not willing to take the risk of trying a new, modern extravaganza, then you'll never know for sure. So as you are sitting at your kitchen table glancing through the food magazines and the quail recipe books, you are wondering to yourself if taking this risk is a good or a bad thing. Well, unfortunately you really wouldn't be able to answer that question because it all depends on what happens at the end. You might have a breathtaking holiday dinner party and get many genuine compliments, or you might look like a wolf that stole the golden *turkey* and everyone will point their fingers and accuse you of ruining the holiday. Okay, maybe that's not really going to happen, but at least that's how you'll feel if you don't get the reaction that you want – like you ruined things for everyone.

Of course, taking a risk with your new holiday dinner is so much easier than figuring out the riskiness of an investment and if it's a good fit for your portfolio, right? Wrong, you'd be surprised how much your everyday decisions have already prepared you for making smart investment choices, because the underlying thought process is the same for almost all the decisions you make! Let's look at your decision-making process by continuing with that holiday dinner example in more detail…

From the moment you got the idea of attempting this holiday feast, to the moment you are trying your new recipes in the kitchen the morning of the holiday, you've already asked yourself all the important decision-making questions, but you likely did this intuitively without fully realizing it! You subconsciously analyzed all the aspects of the situation, looked at the pros and cons, and considered all the costs before making your decision.

Now, the key to making better investment decisions is to take your usual daily decision-making process, break it down into its individual parts, and then apply it to evaluating your portfolio. Throughout your life you've already had lots of practice making everyday decisions, so you usually don't need to think about your decision-making process too much – you're already a pro. But you probably haven't practiced analyzing potential investments all that much, so you'll definitely want to approach them with a much more structured thought process. Let's take a look at some of the most common points to consider when you're thinking about any kinds of investments and the risks that come with them.

Upside, Downside (Risk/Reward)

As you pondered if you should try to replace the traditional turkey with the new exotic stuffed quail dish, one of the first things you probably did is think about how much of an impression it would make on everyone. This is really nothing more than just considering the potential upside of trying quail instead of turkey. Quail is a bird just like a turkey, it has wings, but even though it's smaller than a turkey, it's somehow even bigger in your mind because of the potential upside. You saw the different recipes in a magazine or on TV, imagined how perfectly it would taste, and probably even thought about how great it would make you feel to get all those compliments from all your loved ones. But you didn't just stop there and hop in your car to go to the grocery store, right? Instead, you must have considered the risk that something could go wrong, which is the potential downside of your decision. What if you burn it and never get the recipe perfected in time for the holiday fiesta? What if it really doesn't fit with your family's image of what a holiday dinner should be? What if you mess the whole thing up and ruin the holiday forever and no one will come over to your house ever again? Well, maybe not that extreme, but you get the point, right!?

When presented with an investment decision, you should think about it in the same way. Consider the potential upside and potential downside.

First, you need to have at least some understanding of how much an investment can *realistically* generate in growth, your up-side. Why invest any money if you have zero idea about how much you *could* earn on it, right? One way to do this is to look at how much growth this type of investment provided in the past, on average. Think of it this way: there really isn't any logical reason to believe that an investment can somehow magically give you a return that's significantly higher than what it consistently did in the past. While past performance is never, ever a guarantee of how much you will make in the future, it can be a good way to approximate the *maximum* that you could hope to earn, on average. For example, if an investment provided 5% average growth per year for the last 50 years, it is unlikely that it would suddenly provide 40% per year for the next 50 years, unless there was some huge change in the market and the economy. Not to say that this isn't possible – just probably unlikely.

So one of the first things you need to do when you're considering any kind of investment is to look at the potential gains and the potential losses that you could experience – your reward and your risk. These are questions that you should ask your financial advisor, and try to focus on getting concrete answers. If you do this enough times, what you will notice is that, usually, investments with higher potential returns will have higher potential losses. And investments with lower risk of loss will provide you with a lower return, on average.

Probability of Making Money

So once you've taken a look at the potential rewards and risks associated with an investment, the next step is to figure out what the actual probability is that the investment will turn out in your favor. Going back to the quail example: this obviously doesn't happen very often, but what if the recipe you wanted was so complicated to achieve, and required such an incredible amount of skill that only a highly trained chef, with decades of experience, could actually pull it off? Maybe it required a special kind of cooking technique, or special exotic spice or sauce that had to be applied in just the right way. In that case, you might wonder if you could really pull it off, and you would ask yourself, "What are the chances that I actually can make this amazing new dish?" (Well, if my fiancé was the chef, those chances would basically be zero – he can't even get toast right. But I *will* say that he's great at making dinner reservations.)

Think about the lottery. You only need $1 to buy a ticket, and you could win hundreds of millions of dollars! How great is that!? But the reason why you haven't cashed out your 401(k) to buy thousands of tickets is because you clearly understand that the probability of winning the jackpot is very low. Sure, your downside isn't all that high – just a buck, and your upside is amazing (Shopping spree! A Cartier watch, anyone?), but the chances that you will ever win big are close to zero.

When you're considering a possible investment, and you've

thought about the possible reward and the possible risk, the next step is to figure out the probability that you will actually make money, or at least will not lose anything. For example, if your neighbor's daughter offered you a chance to invest in her start-up social networking company that's operating out of her garage, you could potentially make lots of money, but what's the probability that you actually will? In the same way, if you're considering investing in a couple of stocks that your advisor suggested, what are the chances that these companies will give you high returns?

These questions are always very difficult to answer. Figuring out the probabilities of these things occurring has been kind of like the holy grail of finance – people try really hard to figure it out, but no one has been able to find the exact, 100% correct approach, and I believe no one ever will. There are just too many uncertainties to account for. But you don't really need to know the exact formulas for doing this; you can often get by just on a little common sense. If your advisor is suggesting that you buy stock in a print newspaper company, and tells you that print newspapers are going to overtake the internet, well your common sense would tell you that the probability of that happening is questionable, because newspaper subscriptions have been experiencing declines. It *could* happen, but how *probable* is it?

Again, this question is meant to be almost rhetorical in many ways because it will be difficult to answer completely. But if you keep asking yourself this question every time you're thinking about an investment, and try at a minimum to make a list of the reasons why an investment may go bad, it will put you in the right frame of mind and will train you to constantly ask questions when it comes to your investments. It will get you to think more critically about the opportunities you come across, and will begin to change your way of thinking about these things.

Balance Between Risk and Reward

In addition to looking at the risks and the potential rewards, it's also important to see if the two are well matched. Is there too much risk for very little potential reward? Now don't get me wrong, the entire topic of measuring the balance between potential returns and potential losses can take up volumes upon volumes of books. It's a subject with many different moving parts and many theories, some of which are still very much debatable. But you don't need a PhD in Economics to understand the basic idea, and just asking yourself whether the balance between the risk of loss versus the potential reward actually makes sense can help you see if something about an investment just doesn't seem right.

Think about it this way: you've probably heard that old saying that "There is no such thing as a free lunch," which means that something can't be created out of nothing. In other words, if you are sitting down to have lunch, *someone* is paying for it. Either you are, or your friends are, or that handsome prince who asked you on a date is paying, or if you had a coupon for a free lunch, then the restaurant is absorbing that cost. But the idea is that whenever there is a benefit (the lunch) there is also a cost (the payment), no matter who it is that actually pays.

A good way to look at the risk of losing money is to see the risk itself as a sort of payment for the *possibility* of making money. Even though you are not actually opening your wallet and paying anyone, just the simple fact that you are agreeing to the possibility of losing money is a sort of payment. Whenever you are making any type of investment, the potential return on that investment is the benefit that you are getting (your lunch), and taking the risk of losing some money is basically how you pay for that lunch.

213

Why is this so important? Because if taking on risk is a way to pay for a possibility of earning a return, then the bigger the return you would like to earn, the more risk you would usually need to take – if you want more, you have to pay more. For example, if you put your money in your savings account, you might get 0.10% in annual interest (one tenth of one percent), which is basically... nothing. But the reason for such a small return is because the risk of loss is almost non-existent! On the other hand, if you decided to invest in a pharmaceutical company that had an untested drug that could potentially cure the common cold 100% of the time, you could end up being a very rich woman if that drug eventually proved to be all that it promised. But the risk of failure would also be very high. The company could fail miserably since their drug hasn't been tested yet. You could lose your entire investment if their new drug never ends up working. With any investment opportunity, this will always be true: the bigger the potential return, the bigger the risk. And the smaller the risk, the lower the potential return.

In other words, you will almost never encounter a situation where you can make a lot of money with very little risk of losing, and most of the time when the situation appears to be too much in your favor, it is probably because you're not seeing all the negative aspects of the investment.

Other People's Abilities

Whenever you make an investment, I want you to be completely clear that it is other people's abilities that will play a big part determining whether your investment is successful or not. Again, going back to the holiday dinner example, before you decide to finally go through with the new holiday cooking plan, you probably thought about your past dishes and whether, based on your previous experience, you could cook a brand-new dish and not make it into a complete mess. And you decided that, yes, you do think that you can pull it off. But since quail isn't a common item you can just buy at your local supermarket, you realize that you'll probably have to order it online. Since the dinner is just a few days away, you ask yourself, "Will the shipping service deliver them on time? Will they be fresh, and won't spoil on the way here? What if they're delivered a day late, and I can't cook the meal at all – no turkey, no quail, nothing!" You might even look for a specialty food store, and find one that's quite a drive away. "Is it worth the drive? Will they have good quality meat there?" And you go through the questions to figure out if *someone else* in the process could end up letting you down and messing up the entire holiday dinner plan.

That's the same thing that should be on your mind when you are considering an investment. If your advisor suggested a mutual fund for you, you might want to look into how successful the fund managers have been before. One way to do that is to look at the mutual fund's returns over a long period of time and compare them to the overall performance for that specific investment type. For example, if you are going to buy a mutual fund that invests only in stocks, then it's a good idea to compare how well that fund did over the last few years to how the overall stock market did. After all, if a mutual fund is supposed to give you more value by selecting better-performing stocks, then it should give you a better return than the stock market would. Now, good historical returns don't ever guarantee good future results, and you should never, ever invest in something just because it did well in the past. But on the flip side, is it worth it to buy a mutual fund that all the time performs worse than other similar funds?

These are questions that you want to ask your financial advisor, and try to get concrete answers. Whether you're investing in mutual funds, or individual stocks, or your friend's new bakery, you have to ask yourself whether the person running the show (mutual fund manager, CEO of the company whose stock you want to buy, or your friend) has enough experience to make the investment a success.

Considering Costs

So as you're thinking about whether to change the typical holiday dishes, you probably also thought about how much your new recipes will cost to get it all done as perfectly as you see Cat Cora or Bobby Flay whip it up on *Iron Chef America* in just an hour.

Quail is more expensive than turkey, and if you have a big family, it might end up costing you quite a bit more. Especially since you could get away with just one huge turkey for everyone, but since quail is smaller, you might have to make one for every single person attending! The more people attending, the more money you have to spend. And what about all the side dishes? Will you have enough time to make mashed potatoes, or gravy, or will you have to spend more money and buy them ready-made because there's no time to do it all yourself, because you're stuck in the kitchen making 15 quails? What about other side dishes; will you have to make them yourself or will have to buy those as well? And after figuring what it would cost, you might realize that it's probably quite a bit more expensive than just a simple turkey dinner.

Well, you guessed it, whenever you're making an investment you also have to figure out what it will cost you, just like you figure out the costs when planning your holiday dinner.

There are fees associated with many types of investments, and they can add up to a nice chunk of money over time. Mutual funds, for example, have various types of fees that can be charged when you make an initial purchase, or sometimes when you sell your holdings, as well as annual management fees. You have to understand ahead of time what you're going to pay (refer to the Appendix for more details on mutual fund fees, pages 268-270). Or, you might have to pay trading commissions, and you'll want to know beforehand how much that will be. Whatever the investment you are considering, you want to make sure to check the fund prospectus or ask your advisor all these questions. It will give you a much better understanding of the investment, so you can make a truly educated decision, rather than just hoping that your advisor will make the best decision for you.

Lock-Up Periods

We all know that trying new things, especially at traditional holidays, can sometimes turn into a longer than expected ordeal. Depending on what you are preparing, and all the things that need to be done ahead of time to make the dinner, what starts out as "just a couple of hours" can eat up your entire day. And just like you'd ask yourself, "Do I really have the time to cook for that long in the kitchen? Is it worth the time to try this new dish?," when thinking about an investment, you have to find out how long your money becomes "locked-up."

You won't see this with too many regular investments. With stocks, you can buy and sell pretty much any time you want. But with other investments, like REITs and similar funds, you may have to commit to keeping your money in an investment for a certain period of time. With some mutual funds, you are charged a fee if you sell your holdings before a certain number of years have passed. If you don't want to pay the fees, then you are locked into that investment.

Mutual funds do this to encourage people to keep their money in the accounts longer, and to trade the fund less, so as to save money on administrative expenses. But as an investor, you need to understand these time periods because if you know you will need to withdraw your money after three years, but the fund eliminates the selling fee after five years, then you might want to consider a different fund because you already know that you will not be able to hold your investment for the minimum amount of time required to avoid those fees.

Understanding what the minimum holding periods are, if your investment has one, before you commit your money, is very important because if you have an emergency, or just decide that you hate the investment, you may be forced to pay penalties to take your money out early, or you might not be able to take it out early at all! Just imagine how long it takes to prepare 15 individual quails. What would happen if you had to leave in the middle of the process? It would be a horrible, terrible mess of a dinner. Your portfolio will look just like that horrible disaster of a dinner if some of your investments require a lock-up period, and you need to take your money out earlier.

Risk Tolerance

Cinderella's mean stepsisters tried really hard to make their huge feet look like they could actually fit into the glass slipper. But no matter how hard they tried, reality just would not let it happen. The bottom line, the glass slipper was not the right option for them. And just like people have different shoe sizes and can't shrink their feet on command, in the same way, different people have different comfort levels when it comes to taking risk, and can't force themselves to change it on command. That's why knowing your own comfort level is essential, and will go a very long way toward making you a savvy decision-maker. After all, it's not just about how much your portfolio earns over the years, but also about your own quality of life and your ability to sleep well at night.

There are people who are completely fine with seeing ups and downs in their portfolio, and don't fret much about the risks they're taking. They have no problem plunking a large chunk of their portfolio into a few mutual funds (or even a few individual stocks), and then not really worrying about what the investment is doing for the next few years, until they need to take the money out.

Then there are people who hate seeing any drops in value, no matter how small. It doesn't matter to them that their retirement is 30 years away. What matters to them is being able to look at their latest account statement and not cringe at the sight of any losses. You'll be surprised, but there are folks with millions of dollars in the bank who feel extremely uncomfortable when they see their investments decrease even $5,000 or $10,000 in value. They have millions, but a loss of just a few thousand dollars (less than half a percent of their portfolio!) makes them cringe! Because even though it's such a small proportion of their overall wealth and they are financially secure, they simply hate to experience any kinds of losses and that's just how they feel about it – and who's to say they should feel otherwise?

The reason for people having different risk tolerances is because we all have very different personalities. We all see the world a little bit differently, we come from different backgrounds, and we all have preconceived notions of what may or may not happen in the future. All of these things mesh together to create our comfort level when it comes to risk, and there's not much we can do about it – after all, we can't tell ourselves how to *feel*, right? Knowing your risk tolerance and having a genuine understanding of what you are comfortable with is very important because it will help you make better decisions, and will make you a much more confident decision-maker. I can't stress enough that it's about knowing your risk tolerance, *not* your advisor's risk tolerance! Many people just assume that as long as their advisor is comfortable with the risk level of a particular investment, it somehow means that it is a safe investment for them. Nothing is further from the truth, and this way of thinking has gotten many people into big trouble.

Some people are perfectly comfortable trying new investments, just like some people are perfectly comfortable with unusual dishes like oxtail or uni (sea urchin), while others would never even consider eating such food because they would feel too uncomfortable. You don't even need a logical reason to feel uncomfortable; you just know that you would never eat certain foods because they're too far outside your comfort zone – and it's the same way with your investments. If you don't feel comfortable with a specific investment, then there is no reason to jump into it. If you don't understand the investment, you might want to take the time to learn more about it; but no matter what your reasons are, you should only stick to the types of investment that have risk low enough to allow you to sleep well at night. That is my test method of measuring risk comfort; if the stock market is crashing and you hear it on the news, can you sleep that night comfortably or are you up tossing and turning? If the answer is yes, you can sleep, then you are where you should be, and if not, then you better reconsider your portfolio allocations while you still have your sanity!

If you make your decisions not only by weighing the pros and cons of investment opportunities, but also by carefully considering if you are comfortable with the level of risk that you are about to take, then you will also allow yourself to remain calm and to feel in control of your retirement, rather than fretting every day about what the future holds. The reason why this is important is because being calm and reasonable will prevent you from making rash decisions that often occur when a person is invested in a way that's beyond their comfort level, and starts making decisions based on emotions instead of a clear understanding of the situation.

Don't assume your advisor knows what your risk tolerance is or that they have studied your situation so closely that they know exactly what is best for you! Cinderella's stepmother thought she knew what was best for her, too, and had Cinderella listened to her, she would have missed the biggest ball of them all, and she and the prince would have never lived happily after. But all fairy tales aside, you really need to take this point seriously. No one knows you better than you, or cares about you more than you care about yourself!

Is this Investment Right for Me?

After you've done all your homework on an investment, you have to ask yourself the most important question of all: "Is this investment the right choice for my particular situation?"

You see, asking questions about the various attributes of an investment, and understanding your risk tolerance, helps you get a general understanding for how the investment works and how it fits within your portfolio. But the most important step is to combine all this information together and ask whether that particular investment makes sense for where you are in your life right now. It's important to remember that you are not asking whether the investment itself is good or not (that part you do when you're considering the risks, rewards, and the probability of making money), but in this final step you are asking if the investment makes sense for you in particular, based on your goals in life and your ability to tolerate risk.

Think of it this way: every year around the holidays, tens of thousands of women will think of trying some new, and even unusual, recipe to make for their holiday dinner. Some will maybe even consider the same one that you had in mind, especially if you watch the same cooking shows, but not everyone will actually try to get it done, even if they all thought they could pull off that recipe and would like to try it. This is because everyone's situation is different, and even if something is a great idea in and of itself, it doesn't mean that it's a great idea for everyone in the same way. You may choose to try this new recipe because you feel it's worth a try in your specific situation, and you have the time and the extra money to go for it. Someone else might not have the time or the money to do it, or they'll spend the money on new soap/bath bubbles (or some other home thing) instead, because that's just what they would prefer to do with their money. Why? Because it's all a matter of what's right specifically for *you*.

This way of thinking is something that you already do every day, with every decision you ever make – and it's a matter of just applying the same approach to your investment process. Try it: the next time you're at a store and decide to buy something, stop for a moment and trace your thoughts backward. You'll realize that pretty much with any personal decision you make, you think about the upside and the downside, and then you ask yourself if it is the best decision for *you*. So you might see that delicious cupcake, consider the upside of eating something yummy versus the downside of not being able to fit into your clothes, and then you'll ask yourself if buying and eating that cupcake is the best thing for your specific situation. If you work out three hours a day, seven days a week, well then it's probably not a big deal; but if you're always busy and have little time to get any exercise, well then you'll probably think long and hard about whether eating that cupcake is worth the trouble. Most of the time these thoughts happen in the background as your mind subconsciously thinks about all the pros and cons and then all of a sudden you've decided what you would like to do.

Remember, you get lots of practice doing this with your everyday decisions. From the time you're a little girl to the time you grow up into a strong and confident woman, you're practicing this decision-making over and over again. Remember when you first started wearing makeup? You probably didn't do so well in the beginning. You either had way too much foundation and your face looked a different color than your neck, or the combination of eye shadow, lipstick, and blush made you look, well, a bit clownish (hey, in the beginning it happened to most of us, just check your yearbook pictures!). The reason why you ended up with those ridiculous looks was because you didn't have enough practice with making the decisions about how to apply your makeup. You considered the pros and cons of the different makeup styles, you considered your own abilities, and you decided to take a risk because you thought it was worth it, and sometimes it turned out much worse than you expected. With time, as you practiced more and more, you found the look that made sense for you, and learned what looks good on you. In the same way, with practice, you will be able to make better investment decisions. You will be able to understand what works better for your specific personality, and most importantly, you'll learn how to think critically about every opportunity that comes your way. It may be difficult at first, but worthwhile things are rarely easy.

Here is a fun quiz to help you understand good risk versus bad risk!

Personal Risk Quiz

1. Wearing red lipstick for the first time to a family gathering?

2. Trying a brand-new sun lotion on your Hawaiian vacation?

3. Eating Indian food for the first time on your first date?

4. Wearing a short, sexy dress at the company holiday party?

5. Going on a blind date that your co-worker set up?

Personal Risk Quiz Answers

1. Good risk. Even if you don't look as good as you thought, you are only exposed to your family, who are more forgiving and won't blackmail you with pictures!

2. Bad risk. You never want to try anything new that you can have an allergic reaction to on your vacation, because your vacation could get totally ruined.

3. Bad risk. Can you imagine how that date will go if the Indian food doesn't agree with your stomach!? Your date might just leave by the time you come back from your third trip to the ladies room.

4. Bad risk. Can you imagine the reputation you will have the next day back at the office?

5. Good risk. Hey, sometimes your co-workers may know you even better than you know yourself. After all, you do spend half of your life at work – so it's worth the try!

Investment Risk Quiz

1. Trying a new investment that you heard about at the water cooler?

2. Investing all your money into one technology stock IPO when you are 61?

3. Investing your entire nest egg into the stock of the company you work for when you're 55?

4. Investing a small portion of your portfolio in a technology stock when you're 40?

5. Investing a small part of your portfolio into a stock you think is undervalued?

Investment Risk Quiz Answers

1. Probably a bad risk. The hot tip could possibly pay off, but the chances that your co-workers know the secret to making bundles of money is pretty slim. Stick to restaurant tips at the water cooler only!

2. Probably a bad risk. If you are close to retirement, you absolutely do not have the time to recoup your losses should this hot new stock fizzle out. And if you have your entire portfolio, or a significant portion of it, in a highly risky investment, right when you're about to retire, you're taking a huge risk that your retirement will be ruined.

3. Probably a bad risk. Sure, the company where you work could

end up being the next big thing and your shares could make you a millionaire, but if that doesn't happen, then there are two problems with having all your money in company stock. First, putting all your retirement money into just one stock is a bad idea – it's like betting all your money on one number at the roulette table; it may pay off, but most likely the house will always win. Also, what will happen if the company you work for hits hard times? You'll lose your job, *and* your entire life savings will be in jeopardy because if they're laying you off, then they're probably having profitability issues, which will affect the stock price. So you're putting your livelihood (your paycheck) *and* your retirement into the future of just one company.

4. Probably a good risk. As long as you're not putting all of your eggs in one basket, your portfolio has the time to recuperate should an investment go south. Of course, again, this is only if you invest a small portion of your portfolio into something so risky, have done your research, and clearly understand that you could lose the entire amount invested. Betting your entire retirement savings on one thing is never a good idea.

5. Probably a good risk. You can always take a bit of your portfolio and take advantage of a stock that may be undervalued, as long as it is not going to harm your retirement plans if it completely loses its worth. However, identifying undervalued stocks takes lots of practice, so just because you think it's undervalued, doesn't mean that it actually is.

When it comes to risk, the most important thing to remember is how much you are willing to pay. Picture opening your purse, and literally handing money out if things don't go your way!

CHAPTER 17

THE GOLDEN RULE

"The cautious seldom err." — Confucius

When it comes to their retirement portfolios, most people already understand that investments can be risky and that they can lose money. With all the hype about the stock market on the news, it's easy to forget that the stock market is not the only risk out there.

I remember one of my clients telling me about her past experience, a story about her plans to purchase a retirement home 20 years ago, because she wanted to live in Big Bear when she retired. Her plan was to buy the house and rent it out until she was ready to move in, but as it happens a lot of the time, life got in the way. She got busy with work and family, and kept putting off the purchase, until she just stopped thinking about it. It was still one of her retirement goals, but every time she thought about it, she would just put off taking action until next month or next year. By the time she was telling me about it, the kind of home that she wanted was worth about four times the original price, and she could not afford it.

She had missed out on the opportunity to have the kind of retirement she wanted, because her salary and ability to afford the home certainly did not quadruple in that amount of time, and it would put too much of a strain on her budget. On top of that, she unfortunately kept most of her 401(k) allocated in stock funds when the 2008 meltdown happened, and she lost a big chunk of her nest egg (over 40%!). The worst part… she was about six years away from retirement.

Let's take a look at some of the other common risks that may not be directly related to your investment performance, but which can eat away at your portfolio nonetheless. Remember, it may seem daunting at first, especially if you haven't paid much attention to the details of your portfolio before, but you will get the hang of identifying these risks and asking the right questions as you get more practice. There are quite a few common risks out there, and I will touch on some of the more prominent ones here. As you read about them, make a mental list for yourself of any other risks you can think of, or that you unintentionally may have exposed your portfolio to.

Inflation

Most people know about inflation and understand the basic idea that our money becomes devalued over time. As prices rise over time, our money loses purchasing power, and we can't buy as much with it. What has always surprised me is that although most people understand that inflation is a bad thing, they don't look at it as an actual risk. Let's take a quick step back; if risk is the possibility of you losing money in an investment, and inflation is one of the ways that you lose money over time, because money loses purchasing power, then when you make an investment, inflation will definitely affect your actual return at the end of the day – any losses that you may experience will be made even worse by inflation and any gains that you may make will be diminished by inflation.

When you make an investment, you are taking the chance that

228

it may not even give you a strong enough return to keep up with inflation. For example, if you decided to keep all your money in a savings account, you might not lose actual dollars, but would lose money anyway, because inflation would eat into your purchasing power. We haven't experienced strong inflation in the U.S. in several decades, and we've become somewhat spoiled because of that. However, there will eventually come a time when the rates of inflation will start to rise again and you will need to find ways to battle this particular risk by finding investments that can help your purchasing power stay intact. It's important to keep inflation in mind, because it will always be there and it can hurt you significantly even if you're not making any actual risky investments.

Fraud and Pyramid Schemes: If It Sounds Too Good to Be True, It Definitely Is

Okay, maybe once in a great while you will have an opportunity to make an investment that will provide you with amazing returns without much risk. Such opportunities do happen once in a blue moon, but they usually happen in very unique situations where you are able to buy something at a huge discount because it is more important for the seller to get rid of the item rather than to get a fair price (think of a moving garage sale, where someone will pretty much take any offer for their big screen TV because they're leaving in the evening and can't fit the TV in their truck, so their only choice is to either sell for the best price they can get right now, or just leave it on the side of the street and get no money at all). Such situations are rare in life, and never really happen in the financial markets, because no one will give you some valuable item, or an investment, at a significant discount just because you have pretty eyes. So when you hear of amazing investment opportunities, you need to be aware that most of the time either one of two things is happening: 1) you are not seeing or understanding all the risks, or 2) someone is trying to cheat you out of your money.

Let me give you a recent example where a client of mine came across an opportunity, which really ended up being a pyramid scheme. This particular woman came across a penny auction website that sold everyday items at deeply discounted prices, but on top of that, touted itself as a website that was a completely new and amazing business model. It also did one funny little thing: if people wanted to, they could become members of this website by "investing" some money, and if they promoted the website a certain number of times per day, they could get as much as 1.5% return on their money *daily*. Now, I want you to really think about this: if you became a member of this website, and gave them $10,000 and posted free ads on message boards, you would earn 1.5% daily on that $10,000 of yours. A great investment, right? Well, that's what my client thought when she told me about it. The moment I looked at it, it was pretty obvious that it was a scam, and I arrived at that conclusion by simply looking at the situation from the Risk/Reward Balance perspective that I described in the previous chapter.

I tried to explain to her that this opportunity was not real. "Why would anyone pay you 1.5% daily interest on your money to spend 20 minutes a day promoting their website? Really think about what they're offering you... 1.5% daily on a $10,000 'investment' is $150 *per day*." So I reasoned with her and pointed out to her that if she invested $10,000 with this firm, they would essentially pay her $150 *daily* for 20 minutes of work. "Why would they do that, when they could just hire someone for minimum wage and pay them $8 for an hour's worth of work and save the other $142?" But that didn't convince her. "If they needed money to expand, why would they just not borrow money from the bank, and maybe pay 10% interest for the *entire year*, rather than pay you 1.5% *daily* to use your money?" This reasoning didn't convince her either. So finally, I ran some numbers for her in an Excel spreadsheet, which showed that if she invested $10,000, based on what that company promised, after two years she would have about $3 million, and I asked her, "Does this seem realistic to you? Do you believe that someone will seriously pay you about $3 million two years from now? That if you just give them $10,000 and post message board advertisements for 20 minutes a day for the next two years, that you will actually receive a check in the mail for $3 million? That instead of hiring someone at a salary of even $100,000 per year to post messages all day long, this company would rather give you $3 million to post advertisements a few minutes a day?"

Still my client oscillated for a while, because she had already put in a few hundred dollars before running this idea by me, and she just didn't want to believe that she had made such a silly blunder. But I could see that the reality of the situation was slowly starting to make sense to her. She just had a difficult time letting go of this idea because in her mind, this was a solution to all her problems. Her mind was at ease, thinking she'd stumbled on a goldmine of an opportunity and that she'd finally have the kind of life she wanted – that everyone else was too foolish to understand what an opportunity this really was. But eventually she realized that indeed no one was going to give her $3 million for doing very little work with no risk. She understood the basic tenet of investments and the basic idea behind sound decision-making, and it finally became clear to her that no one was stupid enough to offer huge returns for no risk, and that this had to have been a scam.

Sure enough, less than a year later, the Securities and Exchange Commission shut down the website that offered this "opportunity," labeled it as a Ponzi scheme, and froze that company's assets. Thankfully, my client did not "invest" any more money and listened to reason. But you will undoubtedly come across such "opportunities" at one point or another, because people will never stop trying to cheat other people out of money. Every time you do come across these magical investments that promise amazing returns, just ask yourself if the potential reward matches the risk that you are being shown. If the scale is skewed too much into the reward aspect (like getting $3 million on a $10,000 investment), and you are being presented with a no-lose scenario, then chances are that you're being scammed. If you can't quite tell right away, another trick to use is to role-play, and

ask yourself: "If I was in this person's shoes, would I offer this invest-ment at such favorable terms? Would I give away all these potential returns to people for basically no risk to them at all? If yes, then *why* would I do that?" And if you think about the situation logically, from all angles, and don't allow yourself to be blinded by the promise of amazing returns, then it's pretty easy to spot when people are trying to cheat you.

The Ostrich Risk (Keeping Your Head in the Sand)

Nearly every time you go to the grocery store, the mall, or even a car wash, you get a detailed receipt showing you exactly what items you have purchased. This itemized list is the proof of exactly where and how you have spent your money. And the reason why you want to always check your receipt is so that you know you're not being overcharged. Just imagine if you left the store one day and the ca-shier just told you, "Don't worry about the final amount, ma'am, just check your credit card statement and you'll know exactly what you were charged." Now obviously you'd never go to that store again. After all, if you are paying money to someone, then you have every right to know what the amount is, and what specific items you are paying for, but people do this all the time with their investments be-cause figuring out what their portfolio is costing them can seem like a daunting chore.

For example, if you are invested in mutual funds, then you re-ally need to figure out how much you are paying in fees. All mutu-al funds have fees associated with them, and they can vary widely. There are annual management fees, for example, that can range from about half a percent per year to as much as 1.5% per year or even more. Or there may be 12-b-1 fees, which are a way for mutual fund managers to offset their marketing costs. And let's not forget the loads, which are fees that can be charged when you buy or sell a mutual fund. Why does all of this matter? Because you need to know when someone is taking money out of your account, because it's *your* money, and you need to be sure that these fees make sense for your situation and are worth the additional services or earning potential, instead of just assuming that you're not paying too much. (For more details on mutual fund fees, please refer to pages 268-270 in the Appendix.)

Think about it this way: if there was a fund in your portfolio that consistently gave you a worse return than the overall stock market (went up less than the market during a market upswing, and dropped more than the market during a downturn), and on top of that you paid 2% every year in management fees, would it make sense for you to keep your money invested in that fund? Because if that were the case, then you would be paying someone to give you below-average results. It's like paying full price for a purse only to realize that it's a designer knock-off! And the only way to catch these types of situations is to carefully review your account statements, and get a good understanding for how your investments performed and how much you paid in fees. Even though it's not always easy, because these fees aren't always clearly broken out on most account statements, just a little bit of time, effort, and research can help you get the answers that you need. It's easier than you might initially think – you just have to keep asking questions until you get an answer and not let any initial frustration or confusion stop you. You can get this information from your advisor, or you can call the mutual fund company directly. You can also find this information online by looking up the funds on the finance pages of websites like Yahoo or Google, for example.

You'll be surprised how many people pay lots of money on a regular basis through their investment accounts, without even realizing how much they are being charged or what they're paying for! Many people take this approach when it comes to their retirement accounts. They just take their statement out of the envelope every three months, take a quick look at it, and that's it! They don't try to figure out how much they've paid in fees for the period. And they don't try to figure out what their actual returns were for a period of time. Instead they just take a quick look at the numbers and take an "Umm, I think this looks all right, I'm sure nothing is wrong" attitude.

Let me give you an example from many years ago. I first became exposed to the world of finance when I was still in high school, in my economics class, where our teacher teamed us up with a partner and we used Monopoly money to pretend to purchase stocks. We had to research all the investments and various companies and pretended to buy our favorite stocks. After the research, we followed the stocks that we chose every day, and after about a month we had to report our losses and earnings. We could buy and sell just like you would in the market; we just had to do it on the tracking board and the only money exchanging hands was our Monopoly money.

Even if I didn't fully appreciate it at the time, this was a valuable experience when I think about how it affected my way of thinking and my outlook on the real world. Suddenly, the movie *Wall Street* wasn't so glamorous as I saw most of my classmates lose their paper money, and realized that it could have very well been real money. This was a very educational experience for me, and I'm glad that it happened while I was still a teenager, because it opened my eyes early about investments and taught me the importance of good research and pushing for meaningful answers, even when they were hard to obtain. What was also great is that my teacher didn't favor the boys versus the girls in this class just because it was economics. He actually encouraged the girls to be just as involved and not to sit this exercise out!

In any case, as part of this assignment, our teacher asked us to research brokerage companies and brokerage fees so that we could get a much more real experience of not just the fun aspect of researching stocks, but to gain an understanding of how to open accounts, and how it all works. At first, I thought it was one of the most boring things in the world. I even asked my dad to help me figure it all out, but he told me that it was important for me to learn this on my own. The internet was in its infancy back then, and most companies didn't even have websites. So without much help, my team and I had to do our research the old-fashioned way – Yellow Pages! But as tedious as this little project was, it was extremely eye-opening, and here's why: almost every broker I called could not give me a straight answer as to what commissions they charged! Mind you, this was before cheap online trades were available, and you could only trade by calling your order in. I would ask, "So, what kind of commissions would I pay to buy some stock?" and the answer I would get was something like, "Well… it really depends, I mean, there's usually a base amount, and then there's extra fees depending on the volume being traded." I'm sure that hearing a teenage girl on the other end of the phone didn't help the situation much, but I would press forward, "Okay, what is usually the base, and how do you calculate the volume-based charge?" And the answer I would get was, "Well… you know… we'd have to see what your account balance is first, and then we'd have to figure out the tier where you'd fit in." By the way this was still the time when most financial advisors were being referred to as brokers.

Long story short, no matter how much I would press with my questions, I was never able to get a clear answer, and I could see that the brokers I spoke to were trying to be as ambiguous as possible. Even though I didn't fully realize it at the time, this was a huge learning experience for me because instead of just accepting the highly ambiguous information, our teacher made us call these brokerage companies again and again, until we were able to clarify the answers. And at that time, I was really annoyed with this assignment, and even more annoyed with our teacher, because I didn't understand how it would help me, a teenage girl at the time, to deal with this pointless school project. After all, he already knew the information, so why wouldn't he just tell us about it? It wasn't until a few years later that I realized that what he was trying to do was to help us learn how to be self-sufficient and to solve frustrating real-world situations (thanks, Mr. H!).

Don't Be a Guinea Pig!

As I mentioned earlier, looks can be deceiving. Just as Snow White was deceived by a beautiful red apple, in real life, danger to your financial future can come in many forms.

Unfortunately, many people think that the larger, well-known financial firms will have the best financial advisors, that the name and reputation of the firm automatically makes the advisor knowledgeable, and that this will ultimately protect them and get them the highest returns on their investments. But advisors are just people, and people tend to make mistakes, especially if they are inexperienced at what they are doing. If you happen to be blindly trusting someone because they have the name of a big financial firm on their business card, you're making the same mistake that Snow White did when she bit into that apple; you're not taking the steps to check if that apple might not be what it seems.

Keep in mind at all times that just because a financial advisor happens to be from a large, reputable firm, it does not mean that he or she is actually experienced in advising clients. It also doesn't mean that their management is carefully watching over their every decision to make sure that they don't make any mistakes on your behalf. What you may not realize is that many firms specifically hire advisors with *no experience*, so that they can train them from the ground up.

So you may be expecting an experienced financial advisor just because you are meeting with someone from a reputable firm, but you might actually be getting a recent college graduate who hasn't done much in terms of managing people's money and therefore hasn't seen enough situations that would prepare him or her for effectively advising their clients. And that previous experience is essential, because without experience, an advisor won't be able to caution you about pitfalls that you may be encountering, and won't be able to help guide you in your thought process as you work on your retirement plan and try to align your portfolio with what your retirement plans are. Even someone who graduated from an Ivy League university needs experience. Most people don't realize that having received an education from a four-year university is very different from having the tools and experience needed to excel within the financial field. So don't let your financial advisor learn on your dollar!

It's really the same thing as going to an inexperienced tax preparer at a major accounting company. Sure, they may be very intelligent, and they may be trying hard, but unless they have done a certain number of tax returns, there is no way that they can be as effective as someone who has done 1,000 tax returns. No matter how big the firm where they are working is, that big, reputable name cannot translate into actual experience for that individual person, no matter how hard they try. Of course, everyone was a novice at some point (yes, yours truly was a novice at one point as well, but I was lucky because I was extensively mentored by a senior advisor for several years, before I handled my own clients); but if you have a choice between an experienced advisor and a novice at a big firm, then you should always go for experience because that's what helps you better cover your bases when it comes to putting your retirement plan to work.

One more point about experience: it doesn't just come in the number of years. I once heard a great quote that went something like this: "When hiring someone who says that they have 20 years of experience, make sure that you're not hiring someone who actually just had one year of experience 20 times in a row." Think about the implications of what that means... Think of a doctor who doesn't take the time to learn new procedures or doesn't take the time to practice with new medical instruments. Not only that, but a doctor who doesn't go to medical conferences to share ideas with other medical professionals, doesn't take a genuine interest in innovation in medicine, and doesn't try to learn anything new. That would be crazy, right? You'd never go to a doctor like that because no matter how many years of experience they have, they don't actually understand the latest developments in medicine that could save your life! Well, this same scenario happens over and over again with financial advisors who refuse to educate themselves about these new financial products and methods for reducing risks to their clients! They're basically stuck in the cave age of finance, and so are their clients. An experienced financial advisor is someone who continually seeks self-improvement and goes the extra mile to stay on top of the latest research, so that his or her clients are not stuck in the cave age.

It has always been my opinion that the best advisors are the ones that help you acquire wealth, while simultaneously helping you sustain the wealth you have acquired. You simply cannot attain the wealth you desire through cookie-cutter or outdated investment plans that are right off the shelf, which you will likely receive from a rookie. Your investment plan should be specifically tailored according to your financial needs and your personal financial risk tolerance. And as I always say: retirement planning is not just about the investments that you make; it is about your overall financial picture, spending habits, goals, and lifestyle. You cannot do one without planning for the rest.

Incorrect Diversification

You've probably heard this word already many times before. Diversification, or "not putting all your eggs in one basket," is the idea that you want to spread your portfolio over many different types of investments. By spreading your portfolio over a large number of investments, you are helping reduce the effect that any one bad investment will have on your nest egg. For example, if you invested in 100 different stocks, and one of those companies went bankrupt, it would be annoying, but at least most of your money would still be there because you were spread over so many different stocks. But if you invested only in two companies and one of them went bankrupt, your portfolio would take a real hit and your retirement dreams might be ruined at that point.

One of the biggest reasons why diversification is supposed to help is because different investments will perform differently in the same economic situation. Let's compare this to your closet, shall we? A good stylist will tell you to have a variety of clothes in your closet so that every occasion is covered, and you are always well prepared. Does this mean that you should go and buy 20 different styles of jeans? Of course not! Even if they are all in different colors, styles, or patterns, no matter how great and fantastic those amazing pairs of True Religions are, you can't just wear jeans to every event. What would happen if you had to go to a formal event, or to a business gathering? You wouldn't have anything appropriate to wear! The same danger can occur if you are all in one type of investment; an occasion will come up and you may have nothing left in your savings.

After our economy became a mess in 2008, stocks of discount clothing stores actually performed pretty well because their sales rose, because more people began to shop there as they lost their jobs and had less income. Companies that sold luxury items had a harder time because less people were spending money on their products. The idea is that if your portfolio is well diversified, then big drops in the stock market shouldn't affect you as much because some of your investments will go up while other ones are going down, and the gains and the losses will offset each other a little bit.

In order for diversification to really help you, it's important to allocate your portfolio over a large variety of investment types. You can own 1,000 stocks, but if the overall stock market crashes, then you'll experience some serious losses. You can own thousands of bonds, but if the bond market experiences a major jolt, then your portfolio will suffer as well.

Things to Keep in Mind

As you work toward building a secure retirement, you will need to continuously protect your retirement nest egg from various risks. Some of these risks will come directly from the stock market, or from other investments you make. Other risks will be more indirect, like working with an inexperienced advisor, not being able to keep up with inflation, or not understanding all of the fees that you are being charged. To protect yourself from all these risks, you have to practice asking the right questions, to pay attention to your portfolio, and when you don't understand something (like the math on your account statement doesn't make 100% sense), to ask questions until you do understand. This will not happen overnight. Your ability to protect yourself is something that will happen over time if you stay involved in your finances, and question everything that you don't understand. But you know what? It's worth it. After all, your portfolio won't protect itself – only you can take the steps to keep it safe. Most importantly, when it comes to your retirement portfolio, if you're going to take a risk, make sure that you open your purse just enough to risk losing a few coins, but not so wide that you lose your entire wallet.

- Inflation can really eat into your overall nest egg. In the U.S., we haven't experienced high inflation in quite a while, but a time will come when inflation will again become high, and could hit the double digits. Imagine if you are retired, and are not earning money anymore; what will happen to the real value of your nest egg after five or 10 years of double-digit inflation?

- Make sure that you are working with an experienced advisor, who has seen enough real-life situations to be able to actually help you.

- Don't keep your head in the sand, and assume that everything is okay. Check on your nest egg regularly and ask lots of questions. Your relationship with your money is very much like your romantic relationships; what would happen if you paid no attention to your spouse or partner? Eventually, they would leave, right? Money is the same way. If you don't pay attention to it, it could very well leave for good.

- Make sure you are properly diversified for your age and

risk tolerance. This is very important and this is something you must bring up to your advisor on a regular basis. It's very risky to be invested into just stocks, or just bonds, or any single investment. Even if you keep your money under your mattress, you're still facing a risk, right? Inflation! So make sure that you pay special attention to working with your advisor to diversify your portfolio for your specific situation. You can learn more about diversification in the Appendix at the end of this book.

YOUR INNER FAIRY GODMOTHER

CHAPTER 18

HAPPILY EVER AFTER!

"We are what we repeatedly do; excellence, then, is not an act but a habit." — Aristotle

We are creatures of our own habits and I choose to believe in fairy tales and the idea of a happy, prosperous ending, and a Happily Ever After! Just because things in life don't work out exactly how you expected, that doesn't mean that you can't change things for the better when you come to the realization that you're not satisfied with where you are in your life. Whether it be your physical health, your relationships with others, or your finances – you have a lot more power to change things than you give yourself credit for.

As Albert Einstein so eloquently said, the definition of insanity is "doing the same thing over and over again and expecting a different result." This applies to everything in life. I have a close friend who hasn't yet found the "right" guy in her life. Whenever she does date a guy, she always has the same exact problems, which she shares with me. When I look at all her actions and relationships, it's no wonder that she can't find the right guy! She dates the same type of men, she does the same exact things that make her unhappy, and yet she doesn't see where the problem lies! Seriously, it's like watching re-runs of the same show over and over again; you already know what's going to happen next, but the main character in the show, in this case my friend, is oblivious to what's happening – no matter how many times you watch that episode, it doesn't change! I even confronted her one day about this because it became so ridiculous, and she was not happy with me! She even stopped talking to me for a while, because she felt offended, but all I did was tell her the truth. Well, we all know that the truth hurts sometimes. But being really honest with yourself from time to time is the only way to make a change and move forward.

Even in our financial life, and all of our professional relationships for that matter, we sometimes do the same exact thing, over and over again, and then can't figure out why we keep falling into the same trap! I have seen many clients who repeated these same mistakes time after time, and expected that eventually things would work themselves out! Remember Mona, who was stuck with the wrong financial advisor, and kept trying to talk things out with someone who was manipulating her? And every time she tried to leave, she'd "talk things out" with him and expect that, somehow, everything would be different this time. I bet you anything that even when I gave her advice to just focus on herself and dig deep to find out what her expectations were for herself, before getting involved with yet another unsuited advisor, she probably didn't, and is probably still repeating her mistakes. The reason I say that, is because I noticed that she had a hard time breaking this unhealthy and unproductive trend. Her destiny won't change until she decides to break away from those habits. And the only way to break away from bad habits is to stop dwelling on all your previous mistakes, or all the things that could go wrong, and to focus on the positive. To focus on the success that you know you will have.

Focus Your Mind on Success

Personally, I am all about the power of intention; deliberate, educated action to make changes and improve your life. Every single person can change their financial destiny, should they desire it enough! Because it's not just about what you do in the physical world, not just about what investments you choose, and not just about your career and how much you earn. Instead, the biggest part of your success and your future depends on what you do in the mental world first. If you think positively, and if you train your mind to refuse to think negatively or to draw you into feelings of fear or insecurity, then there's genuinely very little limit to how much you can change your life for the better. Your attitude creates your thoughts, your thoughts create your actions, and your actions create your future!

In this book, I showed you the importance of budgeting, explained investment basics, and gave you a roadmap for how to ask for what you want, and the questions to ask yourself when you are making a decision. Most importantly, I did my best to teach you how to think differently, because the right mindset, and learning how to ask the right questions, is the only way to achieve the kind of future that you want. But, you know what? All of it means absolutely nothing if you don't take that first step and decide to make your life better – genuinely better. Now, you don't have to do it all in one day, right? The best changes in life occur from small, deliberate steps that help you change your habits, and change not only the way you act, but the way you think. The only thing required for changes to occur is your determination to not settle for the status quo, determination to stick with your goals through thick and thin, through easy times and more importantly, through the difficult, and sometimes heartbreaking, times.

In many ways, making changes in your financial life is very much like dieting. I started many diets: the South Beach diet, the Atkins low-carb diet, the juicing diet, and so on. But none of them worked!

Why? Is it because they were all bad? No, the truth is that I wasn't successful at them because I never fully committed to any of them! I would think about how great it would be to lose 20 pounds, or how great I would look, and I would start a diet, but I realized that I was only doing these things to tell myself that I was doing something good for myself, but I never actually resolved in my mind to stick to the plans. Once I made that real commitment to change my lifestyle, when I decided that my plans were more important than just freely indulging in whatever food – things changed. I was no longer just getting hyped up at one diet or another, just to feel like I was making a change. And you know what? Other successes followed. I was no longer just dieting, but eating healthier, exercising more, and had more energy than ever before. One little success led to many more!

Just like with any positive change you want to make in your life, this mental determination to make a change and achieve your goals applies to making real improvements to your financial planning. If you just get hyped up and say, "If I only just budget right," or "If I only invest smarter," or "If I only get the right advisor," you won't get very far, because it's not about just one thing or another, but about changing the way you think and feel about your financial future. It's about changing your lifestyle and outlook, and doing it with 100% dedication.

Your Financial Intuition Zone

Many of us experience things in life as they come. A lot of the time it's because of the way we were raised. We learned from the way our parents talked about money, or the way that our friends and others around us expressed their opinions about money. To that, add in the way that society has portrayed men and women, as well as all the negative and disastrous stories that are projected into our daily lives from watching TV or hearing news on the radio, and many women end up feeling weak, insecure, and constantly worried that something will go wrong. We are surrounded by so much negativity that we allow it to creep into our lives, and yes, this can even affect your finances because it affects your outlook on life. If you're feeling sad or depressed, or if you're constantly worried about the economy because some clown on TV keeps talking about how things are just terrible, then this will affect how you feel about your finances, and the decisions you make. Which is why you have to truly watch out for all the negative stuff that makes its way into your life, and not allow it to take over how you feel and think. I refer to this as protecting your Financial Intuition Zone, that spot in your mind that helps you make the right choices, calmly, without letting all the outside hoopla and negativity throw you off balance.

It's really like a broken glass window concept. If a house has a broken window that is never fixed, then chances are that there will be more break-ins. In the same way, if your mental "windows" are broken, and you don't fix or fortify them with self-confidence, then negativity will always make its way inside. And when it comes to your financial intuition, you have to protect it and fortify it with all the inner strength you've got. Because, just like a burglar, negativity and insecurities will sneak in when you least expect them, rummage through your stuff, and leave you feeling lost and weak. So to make a real change in your life, it is truly about what you do in the inner world that will project what you will accomplish in the real world! If you've had a bad relationship with money, or a bad relationship with financial advisors, and because of that you think that things will never change, then you can rest assured that's exactly what will happen! The state of your finances will continue to be one gigantic mystery, a shapeless mass, which you will never resolve! But if you tell yourself that, "Hey, maybe I never had a great relationship with money, but there's no reason that I can't," then guess what, your attitude will dictate your reality! Like a shapeless piece of clay, you'll be able to mold your financial situation, step by step, until it becomes a beautiful work of art that you will truly enjoy seeing.

Being in Control

Years ago, I read a book by Napoleon Hill, and the following quote really connected with me. I'd like to share it with you:

> "You are the master of your destiny. You can influence, direct and control your own environment. You can make your life what you want it to be."
> — Napoleon Hill, *Think and Grow Rich*

You are truly in control of the choices that you make. If you make that decision to commit and tell yourself that starting today "I will change everything that has to do with my finances that I don't like," and you decide that "Today is the day that I will take everything I know, including what I've learned in this book, and will make that inner change," then you will start yourself on the path to success! When it comes to your financial well-being, you are the master of your destiny, and only you can change your life and make it what you want it to be. First, you have to truly desire it, and only then you can actually conquer it. Because how can you conquer something if you haven't made it the object of your desire? This means going after what you want, kicking pessimism to the curb, and not letting previous setbacks get in the way of the new you. This is about today, and what you will do going forward! Forget yesterday!

If you've had a hard time with your finances in the past, or have worked with a financial advisor who you didn't like, then just make a decision that you will now have a better relationship with whoever you choose to manage your money. That you will find a person who you have the right professional chemistry with and that it's going to be the right fit for *you*, because you will accept nothing less than that!

More importantly, if you've never been able to save enough or you lost quite a bit in the market crash of 2008, or whatever the year was that put you back financially (there were quite a few of them), learn from it, accept that it happened and that you can't go back in time to fix it, and then move *forward*. So many people dwell on the misery of their losses, their painful memories, things that happened in the past, but that accomplishes nothing. Unless you are on a *Star Trek* episode, and you can find a time machine to travel back to fix all those mistakes, then sure, dwell all you want! But since we are in the real world, you don't have Captain Picard or Captain Kirk to help you find that precious time machine, so why not focus on the present and find your future instead? What's done is done, and you need to let go of it and think about the future, and how you will start making the right choices for yourself *today*, and get yourself on the right track!

Love Your Future

You have to encourage yourself to really love your future, and that means loving your finances, and loving to learn more and more about what you can do to have a better financial life. Okay, maybe you don't have to love your finances, but at least have a cordial relationship with them. You know… invite your money for tea regularly, ask it about how things have been going, if it has any news for you. Your money is just like a good friend; it wants to be in your life, but you've got to make a regular effort to be there for it, and to make sure that it's all right. By having that positive energy, having a positive attitude toward your money, and being proactive, that is how you will accomplish whatever you want when it comes to your finances and well-being!

If you look through history, over and over again you'll find people who were able to accomplish what they wanted, what they desired, against really difficult odds. But even though they all had different situations and different goals, what makes them all alike is that they all believed wholeheartedly that they were going to accomplish their dreams. They saw what their future held, and they *loved* their future enough to work for it. This is exactly the same determination and faith in your future that you've got to find within yourself in order to achieve the kind of life and retirement you want. When it comes to your finances, regardless of where you are now, regardless of how old you are, *today* is the day that you will begin to shine. It will start off as a faint light, which can quickly grow into a roaring fire of determination if you feed it the fuel that it needs: confidence, desire to succeed, and a refusal to just do what everyone else does. Today is the day that you will start to conquer all of your fears, and will begin to master everything that you have learned about yourself, your money, and your future. If you want it badly enough, and stop dwelling on the past, nothing can stop you.

Esther's Story

Let me tell you one last story that really embodies what a positive attitude and a desire to succeed can achieve for you. I remember one of my clients, Esther, who I met about seven years ago. Esther was 61 and she was in a very bad situation. When I first met her, I saw that she did not have very much in her 401(k) and not that much in overall assets for retirement. She had made mistakes, a lot of mistakes, but she wanted to make a change. I told her that what's done is done, and if she decided to change it all, then she could still achieve a lot for her retirement. And surprisingly, on her own, she had already prepared herself! She knew it didn't matter what had happened in the past, she had already accepted it, and told me that she was meeting with me to change her life. That she didn't want to think about the past, but finally wanted to plan for the future.

Even though she didn't have very much in assets, she was confident that she could build it up again. She wasn't sure how she would do it, but she knew that she would. The crash of 2000 (the tech bubble) had left her with only about $80,000 at that time, and she was still working and contributing to her 401(k). She started looking at her savings, and mind you again, this is someone who at the time was 61 – most people in her shoes would be sitting in sorrow, thinking it was too late for them to do anything about it! But oh no, not Esther! She had made a conscious decision to be positive in her way of thinking, and made a commitment to herself that she would do whatever necessary, and sacrifice her lifestyle in the short term, but that she would take the right steps and get to her ultimate financial goals! Well, guess what? She is now 68, and has over half a million in retirement assets! Not just because of her contributions or market returns, but because her positive attitude brought her more than she could imagine! It's really amazing how things can start to align themselves in your favor if you just take the first steps forward!

So here is what happened: she was contributing about $15,000 a year to her 401(k) (she had almost doubled it from the previous contribution amount), and on top of that, she was adding substantial amounts to her savings, because she became fanatical about budgeting, and she was also able to build up an emergency fund by adding almost $6,000 to it every year. And she was the one driving the whole process forward, because she realized it was her life, and her destiny. But here's the real kicker: as she was doing all this, she made a great discovery! As she was going through all of her old paperwork and statements, she found actual paper certificates of shares that her mother, who had passed away a few years earlier, purchased several decades earlier! Unfortunately, when her mom passed away, Esther was so distraught about it that she never really looked through all of her financial documents. Her mom had Alzheimer's, and for the last eight years of her life, and even well before the onset of her illness, she never talked much about her finances. She had casually mentioned some shares she had from her old phone company where she worked, so Esther never took it seriously. Because it was never mentioned significantly enough, Esther never paid much attention to it.

This was a big break for Esther, and a bittersweet turn of events that didn't just help her find money, but helped her find closure. In a way, it was almost like a final gift that her beloved mom was able to give her, and it couldn't have come at a better time. If she had not sat down to look at her financial papers, didn't decide to get organized, then she would have never found those certificates! The only reason she made the discovery was because she had made a commitment to herself to be organized, and to make her life genuinely better! This didn't happen overnight. It was about two years after she met with me and started this commitment, but she took regular steps forward, and eventually went through all the boxes of documents, and that's how she stumbled across them! I remember telling her at the time that the only thing cooler than that would've been if she had found the certificates in her couch cushions or under the mattress! Remember, when I met her, she was 61 and woefully unprepared for retirement, and then two years later, at the age of 63 she finds these stock certificates that were now worth, drum roll please… just under $280,000!!! At that time, it basically tripled her net worth!

But her late mother's shares didn't just magically appear, and

I know these things are not just a coincidence! I do believe in the power of intention. If Esther had not gotten herself on the right track, I have no doubt that she would have never remembered about the existence of those shares, because the certificates would have remained stuffed away in the old dusty boxes in her garage. The same boxes that throughout all the years before she just didn't want to see because it was too painful to go through all that stuff. Imagine what would have happened if there was a fire or something, and all those boxes burned – a mini-fortune would have been lost forever! But because she looked at her future with a new eye, and then applied positive action, it all worked out!

Now, I'm not saying that this is something that happens often. But what I *am* saying is that positive, deliberate actions to improve your future will definitely help you uncover opportunities that you didn't know existed. Through careful budgeting, you might find that you can save a whole lot more money than you thought. By reviewing your 401(k), or other account statements, you might find that your investments have seriously underperformed over the years. Whatever you do, you will find additional money simply because you'll be able to take advantage of opportunities that you couldn't before, because you will now know everything about your financial situation, and will be able to make well thought-out, educated decisions.

This is YOUR Fairy Tale

I did say at the beginning that I do believe in fairy-tale endings. I may not believe the magic, and all the fluffy fuzziness, but to me, fairy tales are just inspirations of what *could* be. They are the final result of hard work and preparation, and of being on the right mental track! That is how our destiny and our real-life fairy tales are written! Many times we look at successful people, self-made million-

257

aires, and we think, "Wow! I wish I could have that level of success! I wish I had enough money to retire, so that I could do what these successful people have done! I wish I could have their life, their business, their career…" Well, it's time to stop wishing, and time to start doing. You have your future in your hands, and you're the only one who decides what happens next. How will you write your fairy tale? How will you reinvent yourself? How secure and independent will your retirement be? If you believe, truly believe, that your life can, and *will* be better, if you love yourself and your future, and if you take action, then there's no reason, no matter where you are in your life, that you can't make the right plans and help your dreams become a reality! I know you can! You know you can! So, make the commitment to yourself and go ahead and live happily ever after; it's all within your reach!

So I would like to leave you with three rules to remember every time you think of your money!!!

1. <u>DO NOT LET ANYONE TAKE MONEY OUT OF YOUR PURSE</u> – you worked hard for it, so only hand it over when you know what you're paying for!

2. <u>DON'T BE SUCH A GIRL</u> – when it comes to your professional relationships and more importantly *your* money!

3. <u>LOVE YOUR MONEY</u> – because it can do a lot for you and your family; don't just have a casual friendship with it, have a long-lasting relationship with it so that it will want to stay with you!

I know books usually end with the cliché "The End" or "Your New Beginning…" Instead, I want to leave you with two words that are from one of my new favorite songs and they can mean whatever you want them to mean to you!

Let's Go*

HE END?

APPENDIX

Mutual Funds – the Basics

Mutual funds are a nifty little tool that can make your life easier if you know how to use them correctly, or that can become a headache if you happen to invest in those that have high fees and consistently underperform the general market. They may or may not be right for your situation, and you definitely want to speak with a financial advisor before making any major decisions, but in either case, it's important to have a general understanding of mutual funds and how they work.

A mutual fund is basically a huge pool of money. Many investors buy into it by investing their money in the fund, and then the mutual fund manager will invest all this money according to the fund's overall strategy. The pool of money managed by a typical mutual fund can be hundreds of millions or even billions of dollars, with thousands of investors, and the pool of money is managed as one big portfolio. Because of this, all the investors are pretty much invested in the same way, and share in the profits and losses proportionately. For example, you might have $1,000 invested with the fund, while another investor could have $10,000, while someone else might have $500,000 invested. And as the fund makes or loses money, you all share in it together. So if the fund makes a 5% return, you'll make $50 on your $1,000 investment, while someone with $10,000 invested will make $500 on their money, which is still 5%, same as you (of course, this is a static example that doesn't take into account any charges or fees you may incur due to fund management or redemption).

The easiest thing you can compare mutual funds to is a buffet! Instead of ordering one entrée, you just get a little bit of everything! Now each buffet at each restaurant is different; you may have a brunch buffet or a seafood buffet or a dessert buffet, depending on what style of food you like. When it comes to mutual funds, the style is based on what type of risk you are willing to accept, and the kinds of assets you would like to invest in.

An Easy Way to Invest in Many Investments at Once

The great thing about mutual funds is that, in a lot of ways, they have the potential to make your life much easier. The fund itself can hold hundreds of different stocks, bonds, or other investments in its portfolio. When you buy a mutual fund, what you're doing is buying a tiny piece of that mutual fund's portfolio and therefore tiny little pieces of stocks. So if you invested $100 into a mutual fund, you might have 10 cents worth of stock in Coach Inc., 10 cents in Chico's Stores, another 5 cents in Revlon, and so on. And by doing this, you saved yourself lots of time because you didn't have to research each and every company on your own, and you are easily able to spread your money over a whole lot more investments than you could if you tried to buy all of them one by one.

Understanding Mutual Fund Lingo

You can get a very rough idea about what a mutual fund does based on its name. Definitely don't just stop your research there, but here are some basic terms that often come up in mutual fund names:

266

Growth Funds: These types of funds will usually buy stocks of companies that are currently expanding, and companies that tend to reinvest a big chunk of their profits into growing their business. These companies are not as likely to pay dividends, and when you buy this type of mutual fund, you are focusing more on the potential growth of the investment, rather than the current income.

When you're younger, and have more time until retirement, under normal circumstances, growth funds would usually make up a larger portion of your portfolio because you are focused on building up your nest egg. They are riskier and their prices can fluctuate, so you'd want to have a long-term time frame when holding them, because you are accepting more risk for a potentially higher return. As you get older, and closer to retirement, you could still have a part of your portfolio in this kind of fund, but you would typically decrease their proportion in your overall portfolio because you can't afford to take on as much risk. If you're one year away from retirement, for example, and have 100% of your portfolio in growth funds, then if stock prices drop, you could experience a big hit to your money with no time for your portfolio to recover.

After you retire, these kinds of funds typically wouldn't be in your portfolio anymore, because at that point your focus is on your money generating income for you, rather than trying to make your portfolio grow. But that, of course, would depend on your overall situation and your wealth. If you were no longer working, and the stock market went through a jolt, having a large part of your money in growth funds could be a disaster. Think of a growth fund as a big balloon that is getting filled with water; it can grow bigger and bigger, but there is always a big possibility of it bursting. So it's important to remember that growth does not mean *guaranteed* growth!

Value Funds: These kinds of funds also focus on capital appreciation, but instead of buying companies that are growing quickly, the portfolio managers of these funds will focus on buying stocks of companies that they think are currently undervalued in the market. What the managers are doing is analyzing the price of the stock, and comparing it to where they think the price *should* be, based on the company's profitability, etc. They purchase those stocks when they think there is a temporary mismatch between the price in the market and what they think the stock is really worth. Now, the important thing to remember here is that a big part of the fund's performance depends on how good the managers are at identifying undervalued stocks. So just because the fund says "value," it doesn't necessarily mean that the fund managers are going to be good at finding profitable opportunities.

It's common for value funds to have dividend-paying stocks in their portfolio, so when you buy a fund like this, you're betting on capital growth as well as hoping for part of your portfolio growth to come from dividends paid by the companies in the mutual fund portfolio.

Think of a value fund like buying a painting from a no-name artist on the streets of Paris. Others have heard of him, but he is not famous. You think his paintings are good, and are being sold cheaper than they should be. Further, you think he may become big one day and then those paintings will be worth so much more! You are hoping for this outcome, but risking that you may be wrong.

Income Funds: These types of funds are usually focused on, you guessed it, current income. Because of this, they will primarily invest in either stocks that pay large dividends, or in bonds. The major point of these funds is to give you a steady stream of regular income. These are meant to be a lower risk than growth or value funds, and can be in your portfolio at any stage in life, but you'd be more likely to own them as you get closer to retirement, because they are meant to be less risky, and to provide you a more steady return on your investment. However, because the return is expected to be steadier, and less risky, you'll also likely have a lot less capital appreciation.

Remember, mutual fund returns are only as good as their managers' abilities, and bad managers as well as dramatic events in the financial markets can hit your portfolio in big and unexpected ways. Just because you have an income mutual fund that's had a steady price and has been paying you steady dividends for years, it doesn't mean that one day it won't experience a big drop in value or an interruption in dividend payments. Keep in mind that diversification is very important.

Think of investing in income funds like going to Costco. There are always those fun stations giving away free samples. In this sense you can think of the samples as dividends, and your investment as the money you spend on your shopping trip. Now, every time you go to Costco, you expect your free food samples – it's part of the shopping experience! But one day, you may very well walk in, and the samples won't be there, because they're not guaranteed. In the same way, owning an income fund doesn't guarantee dividends, and they may not always be there.

Mutual Fund Fees

As I already mentioned, a mutual fund is like a huge pool of money from lots of different investors. Since the pool itself has to be managed by someone, mutual funds can charge different types of fees which they use to pay the management of the fund.

- *Loads* (I'm not talking about doing laundry, so don't worry.)

   Mutual funds will usually have transaction fees when you are either buying or selling fund shares. If you're buying a stock, you'd usually pay a commission to your broker to make the transaction. Mutual funds use a different method by charging *loads*. These loads are calculated as a percentage of the total dollar value of the transaction, and include front-end loads and back-end loads, which are fees to buy or sell the mutual fund. Some funds will charge front-end loads, for example, which are a percentage of the dollar amount you are investing, as a way to cover the cost of the transaction. Others will charge back-end loads, which are fees that you would pay when selling the mutual fund.

   The thing to keep in mind about these loads is that they hit you directly in the pocket without any relationship to the fund's performance. Just because a fund is charging a high load doesn't mean that it will actually do better than another fund. In fact, if you really think about it, loads directly decrease your returns. For example, if you invested $1,000 into a fund with a 3.00% front-end load, you would immediately give up $30 for the transaction ($1,000 x 3.00% = $30), so now your account would have $970 in it, and it would have to grow by $30 just for you to break even!

In the same way, funds may charge a back-end load, where instead of charging a percentage when you buy the fund, they will charge you when you sell it. The good thing about it is that you put your entire investment to work (nothing gets deducted when you buy the fund), but the bad thing is that you're still paying a fee at some point. Still, other funds don't charge a load at all. There are lots of funds out there with different fee structures, and this is something you definitely want to consider carefully. You can find information about specific funds in their prospectuses, or ask your advisor to help you obtain this information.

- *Management Fees:* These fees are regular fees, calculated as an annual percentage of your account value, that are used to pay the fund managers for their services in managing the portfolio. So if you have $1,000 in a mutual fund, and it charges a 2.00% annual management fee, then you can expect to pay about $20 per year.

- *12-b-1 Fees:* These fees are also charged as a percentage on an annual basis, and are meant to help cover the costs of the mutual fund for advertising and distribution to new potential investors. These fees usually range from 0.25% to around 1.00%, and not all funds have them, but they can hit your account, and can add up over many years.

As you can see, mutual funds can have a lot of fees associated with them. Some try to limit these fees, while others end up charging quite a bit. That's why you should always carefully understand the fees that a mutual fund charges *before* you invest. Think about it this way: if a fund charges a lot of fees, it automatically means that any growth in investments you get will be that much smaller, because you're already losing money in fees. This means that you could potentially accept a smaller return in another fund, that has less fees, and still earn just as much because you're saving money by paying less in costs.

Just remember, there's no such thing as a free lunch. Whether you're paying upfront, or at the end, or in the middle, you are *always* paying. This is not necessarily a good or a bad thing, because what matters is how much your portfolio grows when all is said and done. It's like going on a cruise; some cruises are all-inclusive but that doesn't mean it was not all calculated ahead of time in the cost of the ticket! Do keep in mind that you have to consider all of this before making a decision to buy any mutual fund!

Things to Keep in Mind

Overall, there is a lot to know about mutual funds, and the information in this chapter just scratches the surface. But there are two major things you want to keep in mind as you ponder the mutual funds in your portfolio: 1) what kind of investments do they make, and 2) what kinds of fees do they charge. These two questions will go a long way in helping you make better decisions.

Don't forget that mutual funds can be just as risky as stocks. Depending on their strategy, and the kinds of investments they make, you could end up losing a lot of money, just as you could with an individual stock. It's important to remember this as you decide how to allocate your portfolio, because you don't want to invest your money thinking that it's safe just because it's in a mutual fund! Work with your advisor to see if, and what kind of, mutual funds are right for your specific situation and your risk tolerance. As I like to say, "Always make sure you know exactly what amount of money is getting taken out of your purse," as in: 1) the fees that you'll pay, and 2) the potential losses you're exposing yourself to.

MUTUAL FUNDS AND DIVERSIFICATION

As I've worked with many clients over the years, I've noticed a consistent problem: most people don't understand how diversification really works, and so they end up placing their retirement portfolios in risky situations, all the while thinking that they're doing the right thing.

I've noticed the biggest misconception about diversification is when it's viewed in the context of mutual funds. Many people think that just by buying mutual funds they are well-diversified, but few people realize how proper diversification is supposed to work. This lack of understanding, and lack of explanation on behalf of the financial industry, has gotten some people in a lot of financial trouble. During the crash of 2008, many people thought that they were safe simply because they were invested in mutual funds instead of individual stocks, but their mutual funds weren't diversified. As you work with your financial advisor to build your nest egg and allocate your money, it's important to keep the following in mind, especially as you get closer to retirement.

Let's look at diversification in more detail.

Mutual Funds – A Way to Spread Your Bets

Investing in mutual funds is a good way to spread your bets

across lots of different investments, such as stocks, to help minimize the risk of any one stock destroying your portfolio. But there's a difference between spreading your bets and diversification. For example, when you buy an individual stock, you're making a bet that a specific company is going to be profitable and your stock will go up in value. What happens if that company isn't successful and goes bankrupt? You'll lose your entire investment! That's where mutual funds come into play, because they're a great way to lower the risk that any single investment will completely destroy your portfolio. This can be compared to making bets on the roulette table in Vegas.

Think about it this way: what would happen if you walked into a casino with $1,000, walked up to the roulette table, and bet the entire amount on just one number, all at once? Of course, you could be right and win a heck of a lot of money, and spend the rest of the day partying and drinking mimosas. But I'm sure that you would agree that making this bet would be a pretty risky thing to do because you could also instantly lose everything in one fell swoop, right? So instead, you might bet a couple bucks on a few numbers here and there, and maybe put $5 or $10 on red. Or you might go to the slot machines and play a couple of penny games, or you might play a few hands of blackjack. What happens in that second scenario is that you're spreading your money across many different bets so that you don't risk everything you have on just one single event.

In the same way, if you were going to bet your entire retirement savings on one stock, you *could* be 100% right, and end up rich and retire in a mansion, or you could end up losing absolutely everything. Notice that the real point is that you're trying to lower your risk by avoiding the possibility of losing everything if you were to place all of your trust in just one investment. Instead if you make lots of small bets, it's unlikely that every single one of them will be a loss.

When you invest in mutual funds, what you're really doing is trying to decrease your risk by spreading your bets so that your entire portfolio isn't just dependent on one stock. Some stocks within the mutual fund will go up in value. Other stocks will go down. But the idea is that even if some of the companies in the mutual fund portfolio go bankrupt, it won't completely destroy your nest egg. Of course, that's the *idea*, but just buying a mutual fund doesn't guarantee that you actually made the right decision.

Diversification is **NOT** the Same Thing as Spreading Your Bets

As I just mentioned, mutual funds are a great way to spread your bets across lots of investments, so that your portfolio isn't dependent on any single stock or bond. But here's where most people make a huge mistake; they assume that spreading their bets or not putting all their eggs in one basket automatically means that they are diversified – it does not!

Here's how diversification is supposed to work: as I mentioned in Chapter 15, when you buy a stock, you're buying a piece of ownership in a company. There are thousands of companies out there, and they operate in different industries. Some companies are in real estate, others are in retail, others are in manufacturing, some are technology firms, and so on. Now, this is very important: different industries are affected differently by the overall economy. For example, when the economy drove off a cliff in 2008, stocks of banks were hit hard, because many of them issued or bought mortgages that would end up pretty much worthless. So investors were rushing to sell their bank stocks because they expected these banks to experience huge losses. In the same way, companies that were involved in home construction were also hit hard because if the economy was in a recession, then less people would buy houses, and construction companies wouldn't be making profits. So, investors started selling the stocks of these companies as well, and the stock prices fell. During the same time, stocks of companies that were in the business of selling cheaper everyday products actually did better! Discount clothing stores and discount retailers saw their stock prices increase during the economic mess. That's because as the economy was faltering, and people were being laid off left and right, folks weren't willing to spend as much on clothing or other items. So companies selling cheaper products actually saw their profits rise, because more people were buying their products, and investors started buying up their shares.

The idea behind diversification is about spreading your portfolio across lots of different investments that react differently to what's going on in the economy, and help balance each other out. So if, let's say, one stock goes down by 20%, another one, in a different industry, might go down only 10%, while a third one in yet another industry might go *up* by 5% – *all at the same time*. That's why just buying mutual funds without taking the time to understand what their strategy is can be dangerous and can give you a false sense of security. For example, there are many mutual funds that will invest in technology stocks only. Others might invest in retail stocks only. Some might just invest in real estate stocks. Some only in small growth companies that haven't proven themselves. So if the mutual funds where you allocated your savings invest in the same types of stocks of companies within the same industries, then all you're doing is spreading your bets, but definitely not diversifying your portfolio!

When you're selecting mutual funds for your portfolio, you have to check the kinds of investments that the mutual fund makes. You can pull up their prospectuses online, and then read about their general investment strategy as well as take a look at the most recent allocation of their portfolio. That's the only way to really understand what the mutual fund is doing, and the only way to see if it actually fits your comfort level, and if it will help you diversify your portfolio.

Full Benefit of Diversification

In the previous section, I only talked about the idea of diversification from the standpoint of stocks, and the idea that shares of companies in different industries don't always react in the same way to economic events and will sometimes move in opposite directions. But diversification doesn't end there. You see, even if you buy several mutual funds and diversify across lots of companies and lots of industries, you're still facing a diversification problem, because your portfolio is 100% in stocks! The issue with this is that stocks are all in the same asset type – equities. As I mentioned in Chapter 15, when you buy shares in a company, you're buying a small piece of the ownership, or in other words, a small piece of the equity. At a certain point, no matter how many stocks you own through your mutual funds, you reach a limit as to how much more you can reduce your risk, and the only way to diversify your portfolio further is to invest in other asset types that are different from equity – for example, fixed-income (bonds) or money market accounts.

The basic idea of doing this is that just as different industries react differently to the economy, different asset types will react differently to economic developments as well. So a good mix of stocks, bonds, money market funds, and other asset types can give you even better diversification. You can go a step further and diversify even more, by adding funds that invest in foreign stocks and bonds as well, so that your portfolio isn't strictly based on the U.S. economy, but is also diversified geographically across the economies of other countries.

Diversification and Age

Here's one final important note about diversification: because proper diversification is meant to decrease the overall risk to your portfolio, it's important to pay more and more attention to this as you get older. I've seen women who in their early 60s had the majority of their money in mutual funds that invested in small-cap growth stocks, because no one told them otherwise! They had no business being in such risky allocations, but they thought that just because they were invested in mutual funds that they were safe, all the while having their entire retirement savings exposed to humongous risk. In the same way I've seen people invested 100% in bond mutual funds, and they also thought they were safe – sure thing, right? And they were very happy because they were getting a good dividend payout. But the bond funds they owned only had lower-rated U.S. corporate bonds! They didn't realize what a dangerous situation they were in! What if interest rates went up and caused their mutual funds to fall in value!? What if there was another credit crunch like we had in 2008? That's why as you get closer to retirement, it becomes more and more important to carefully plan out your allocations to make sure you're not exposing yourself to unnecessary risks, by being stuck in just one asset class.

Things to Keep in Mind

Diversification is not as simple as just buying up a bunch of mutual funds. You need to figure out exactly how much time you have left until retirement, if you'll continue to work part-time afterwards, and what your comfort level is when it comes to losing money. Doing all of those things, and working closely with an advisor who will take the time to explain all the pros and cons to you, is what will help you figure out the proportion of the various types of funds that you should have in your portfolio.

- Diversification is not the same as spreading your bets.

- Different companies in different industries will react to economic developments differently.

- It's important to consider how you are allocating your money across various asset types as well. Different asset types will react differently to the same economic events.

- The closer you get to retirement, the more important it is for you to be diversified intelligently, in a way that helps lower the overall risk to your money.

THE BASICS OF BONDS

It's important to know a little bit about how bonds work because they could end up in your portfolio, especially if you happen to invest in mutual funds that invest in bonds as part of their investment strategy.

A bond is an IOU, and is a way for companies, the government, and government entities to borrow money. The most basic way that it works is you give the bond issuer your money, and they give you their promise that they will make regular payments to you, the bond-holder. This may sound kind of like a car loan or a mortgage, but it's not really the same thing. With a car loan, for example, each and every single payment will be the same, and after you make your last payment, you don't owe anything else. But with bonds, payment terms can vary quite a bit, and can have different ways of paying you back. Usually, a bond will have regular payments of interest, and one final payment of the principal. So, for example, if you buy a five-year, $1,000 bond that pays 7% interest, then you can expect to receive $70 per year for five years (the 7% interest), and when the five years are up, your $1,000 will be repaid in one lump sum payment. So the company, or the government, from which you bought this bond gets to use your $1,000 for five years, and you get to earn the 7% interest rate, and at the end of it all, you get your money back.

In simplest terms, companies and governments need money to use in their different projects and one way to do that is to issue these

IOUs so they can accomplish their goals and you earn something on your loan to them. What is important is that you realize that a loan is a loan. Things could go bad, and you might not get your money back.

Bond Types

Overall, there are many different types of bonds out there that are designed for different purposes and can have very different overall terms.

- _PAYMENT TERMS_

    One aspect in which bonds differ is in how they make payments to the bondholders. Some bonds will only pay you regular interest until they mature, and will repay the principal as one payment at the very end. Other bonds will actually work like a car loan, where every single payment will be the same, and every payment will consist of interest _and_ some principal. So there's no lump sum payment at the end because you're getting your principal back regularly, piece by piece. There are also so-called _zero-coupon_ bonds, which have no monthly payments at all, and will instead accrue interest over the life of the bond. You would receive just one lump sum payment at the end of the loan, which would contain the principal as well as all interest together, in one big payment. Overall, bonds can vary a lot in their payment terms, so make sure you clearly understand what those terms are before you invest your money into a bond.

- _BOND DURATION_

    Bonds can also vary based on their durations (from a year to several decades). If you've considered buying a bond before, you may have noticed that longer term bonds will usually have a higher interest rate. There's a reason for that. Later in this chapter, I will talk about how interest rates affect bond prices. But if you consider buying a bond, keep in mind that usually, if all other things are equal, a longer term bond will be riskier than a short-term bond. This is because as your money is tied up in a long-term bond, a lot more things can happen in that longer period of time, including rising interest rates and political instability. Because of this, if you look at two bonds that are 100% the same in all respects except their duration, the longer term bond would likely be more risky since you're tying your money up for a longer period of time.

Think of a bond's duration as a serious relationship. Unlike stocks, where it's more like dating (you can break up any time), with bonds, time can become an issue if you want to get your full value. With stocks, it depends on the price of the stock that day if you want to dump it or not. But with bonds, the price depends on interest rates, which can take a lot longer to change. It is much easier to end a date than an actual relationship, right?

- *BOND RATINGS*

One thing that bonds usually have, that stocks don't, is credit ratings. Just as credit reporting agencies will issue a FICO score for people, there are also agencies that will rate companies and governments (federal, state, city, etc.) on their ability to repay a loan. These ratings are usually done with letters and can range from ratings such as AAA all the way down to a C, or even lower. This is basically a way to show investors what the likelihood is that the issuer of the bond will actually have enough cash flow to be able to repay it. It's important to note that a rating of AAA doesn't actually guarantee that you'll get your money back. The mortgage crisis that sent our economy into a tailspin was partly due to credit rating agencies issuing high quality ratings to mortgage-backed securities that ended up being nothing more than junk. So do take these kinds of ratings with a grain of salt.

- ### _Bond Coupon_

A bond's *coupon* is the interest rate that the bond is paying. However, this interest rate is calculated on the original price, or *face value*, of the bond. So if the original face value of the bond is $1,000 and it has a coupon of 5%, then it pays $50 in interest per year. However, it's again important to remember that this rate only relates to the face value, and the *dollar amount* of the annual interest is set at the time the bond is issued. If you end up buying a bond in the open market, after it was issued, you may not actually get the same *interest rate* on your money as the coupon. This is because you may not be buying it for the original $1,000 face value. So if you buy it in the open market for $1,100, for example, you'll still just get the $50 that's spelled out in the terms of the bond, but for you it will be less than the 5% interest rate because you paid more than the original price. Or you might be able to buy it for $900, and if the coupon is 5%, then you'll still get the $50 per year ($1,000 face value x 5%), which in your case would be a return of more than 5% per year, because you only paid $900 for it. Keep this in mind, and by the way, if this is completely, 100% new to you, then you definitely want to stay away from bonds until you learn them in more depth. Bonds only *seem* safe, but they are an entire animal all of their own, and they could, in some situations, give you disastrous losses, like any investment can.

Bonds vs. Stocks

Bonds also have their own set of advantages and disadvantages. Here's something to remember: because bonds are loans, they don't participate in a company's upside when the company does well. Bondholders are entitled only to the predetermined amount of cash payments that come with the bond, and that is all, even if the company does amazingly well. On the flip side, bondholders are often first in line if a company goes bankrupt. For example, if Little Red Riding Hood's company (from Chapter 15) issues bonds and then goes bankrupt at a later point in time because wolf coats are just not selling any more, all lenders, including bondholders, have priority over stockholders when it comes to sharing in whatever money is left. So the bondholders may not participate in the upside of the company doing well, but they're also taking on less risk than regular investors because they have priority claim to any assets the company may have in case of bankruptcy.

And when you think about it, it makes sense from a risk-reward perspective. Bondholders do not get to participate in a company's upside when it does well, the way that stockholders do. If a company does poorly, then its stock might drop in value, and investors won't receive any dividends that year, but the bondholders have to be paid no matter what. In that same exact way, when a company does well in a year, and the stock doubles, the bondholders will still receive the same payment that they were scheduled to receive, according to the original terms of the bond, and nothing more.

Now remember, this doesn't mean that bond holders are 100%

protected when the company goes bankrupt. Let's say you are a bondholder in Little Red Riding Hood's company and poor Little Red's wolf fur business went bad, and she has only a few furs on hand and her little cottage and a few sewing machines. Well, first her staff has to get paid, then she has to pay village taxes, then all the creditors like the famers, the banks, possible vendors that gave her credit, all have to be paid, and then once all that is done, then you, the bondholder, might get paid. So you can see that by the time it comes to you, maybe there is not as much as you thought left to pay you fully or anyone else for that matter!

Bond Prices and Interest Rates

But here is one thing that I want you to really keep in mind, because most people don't truly understand how bonds work, and if you have any bonds in your portfolio, understanding the relationship between bond prices and interest rates is very important, especially if you may at some point need to sell your bonds early, before they mature.

Let's say you're back in magical make-believe land, and Little Red's company, Red Wolf Coats Inc., wanted to borrow $1,000 for a year, by issuing a bond, and pay you 10% interest on it, which just happened to be the average interest rate for these kinds of bonds based on Red Wolf Coats' credit rating. At the end of one year, you would receive $1,000 plus an extra $100 in interest ($1,000 x 10% = $100). And let's say that you looked at all the risks, thought about it, and decided to buy this bond for $1,000 with the expectation of receiving all your money back, plus an extra $100 at the end of the year, or $1,100 altogether.

Now, let's pretend that the very next day interest rates went through the roof, and now Red Wolf Coats was selling some more bonds with everything being exactly the same, but instead of offering 10% interest, like on the one you bought, they were now offering 20% per year in interest. That would mean that any new bond purchasers would now get $200 per year ($1,000 x 20%), while you would still only get $100 ($1,000 x 10%). So there you are, sitting with your bond, for which you paid $1,000 and will receive $1,100 at the end of the year, but if you bought the bond just a day later, you would be receiving $1,200 at the end of the year. Besides making you feel like you made a mistake buying the bond when you did, how does this affect your money?

Well, if you're going to hold the bond until its maturity (until the final payment), it doesn't directly affect how much money you'll get, since you'll still receive the exact same amount of money you originally thought you would. That's very important to keep in mind, because if interest rates change while you are holding a bond, if you are expecting to hold the bond until it fully matures, then the situation doesn't really affect you from the perspective of the number of dollars you will receive. The amount of money you will receive is still exactly the same as you thought it would be when you made the purchase. Yes, you'll get the same amount of dollars, but depending on what happens with inflation during that time, those dollars may not be able to purchase nearly as much as you thought. And if interest rates are rising, then inflation is likely to increase as well. But what if a week later you have an emergency and you now need to sell your precious bond? Well, remember, all the bonds that are out there that are now paying 20% per year, or $200 for every $1,000 in principal. So if you try to sell your bond, which pays only $100 a year, no one will want to buy it for the full $1,000 price. Instead, you would have to ask your broker to sell this bond for less money than you paid, in order to make it more attractive, so that the person who does buy it from you can still make 20% a year.

Think about what's happening here: the person who takes it off your hands will buy it for less than what you paid for it, but will still get the $100 in interest at the end of the year. So you have to drop the price of your bond so that the amount of money that the buyer would get at the end of the year would still give them 20% in interest. In this case, even though you paid $1,000 for this bond just a few days before, you would now need to accept only $917 for it, if you wanted to sell it. This is how it works: if you sold your bond to someone for $917, and at the end of the year they collected what you were originally going to collect, which is the $1,000 face value + the $100 interest, or $1,100 altogether, then they will have earned 20% on their money ($1,100 they will receive, minus the $917 that they paid to you, is $183 dollars they will receive on top of their investment, which is a return of 20%, or $183 / $917 = 20%).

This relationship between bond prices and interest rates is crucial to remember if you hold bonds in your portfolio. Bond prices and interest rates are like two friends on a seesaw – when interest rates go up, bond prices go down, and when interest rates go down, bond prices go up. Also remember that if you hold bonds until their maturity, changes in interest rates won't usually affect the original amount of cash flow that you were going to receive. However, if you need to sell your bonds early, a rise in interest rates can significantly reduce the amount of money that you will be paid for your bonds. Therefore, although bonds are considered to be safer than stocks, if you are forced to sell when interest rates have risen, you may still end up losing money simply because you needed to sell at the wrong time.

Therefore, if you do choose to buy bonds for your portfolio, you want to make sure that you're not forced to sell them for one reason or another, when you are close to retirement. For example, if in your mid-60s you decided to buy 30-year bonds with all of your money, it's likely going to be a problem because if interest rates rise unexpectedly, and you need to sell some of your holdings to cover medical costs or long-term care costs, then you'll probably end up needing to sell your bonds at a discount.

Things to Keep in Mind

Bonds are not the simple, straightforward investments that many people think they are. Bonds can be very dynamic, and as our financial system gets more and more complex and intertwined, bonds can react in very significant ways. You could, in fact, lose lots of money in bonds, especially if you have to sell them before their maturity. Even if you own bond mutual funds, you can lose money just as easily, the same way you can with stock mutual funds. Of course, generally speaking, under normal circumstances, bonds are not as risky as stocks. But what I'd like you to clearly understand is that even though bonds have certain guarantees, it doesn't mean that they can't hurt your portfolio. *Any* investment can potentially hurt your nest egg, and it's important to understand this, and not just operate on the common misconception that bonds are safe. In fact, whenever a client asks me if a bond, or any other investment, is safe, my first answer is always "It depends." Your personal circumstances, your cash flow needs, jolts in the economy, lots of things, can have an impact on the riskiness of an investment as it relates specifically to you.

I will leave you with one thought: "Be sure who you bond with, because once bonded you will never know if they will ever be out of your life!"

OTHER INVESTMENT TYPES

Over the last half century, the financial industry has created many kinds of investments that are meant to have unique features so that they can be used for specific investment strategies. As a result, today you have many choices about how to allocate your money, beyond the simple decision of what stocks or bonds to buy. Some of them are very complex and can be confusing, while others are simpler and are much easier to understand. The key is to realize that there are a lot of products out there to invest your money in, and they have different features that may or may not be right for your specific situation. If you understand the features, and can work with your advisor to understand how these can affect your retirement goals (beyond just the returns, but liquidity and risk, etc.), then you will be able to make better decisions for yourself as you try to navigate the waters toward a well-funded retirement.

Certificate of Deposit (CD)

CDs are round disks that contain music and can be placed into your Walkman to play exactly the kind of music you want – if you're still living in the '90s! Okay, okay, "CD" stands for "Certificate of Deposit" which can be purchased through many banks. Think of certificates of deposit the same way you would think about a savings account, but with a slightly higher interest rate and limitations on your ability to withdraw your money. What happens with a certificate of deposit is that you give the bank some money for a certain amount of time (3 months, 6 months, 1 year, or more), and the bank pays you a pre-agreed upon amount of interest in exchange for your promise not to take the money out. Because you are agreeing to give the bank your money for a certain amount of time, the bank can pay you a higher interest rate than you would get in a savings account because the bank can better plan its own cash flow (although sometimes longer term CDs may actually offer a lower rate than a savings account will, because future interest rates are expected to fall. It doesn't happen too often, but don't be surprised if you see this from time to time).

Of course, if your plans change, and you need access to the money sooner, you can still withdraw the funds in most cases and pay a relatively small penalty, which usually equals a few months of interest that you would have earned. This penalty is a way for the bank to encourage you to stick to the original agreement to keep your money with them for a certain amount of time.

CDs are a great place to park money that you won't need immediately, but would still like to have access to in case of emergencies. In fact, having your emergency fund in a CD makes a lot of sense because you don't really plan on using the money unless something unexpected happens, and you get to earn a slightly higher return because of the higher interest rate. This way you are keeping your emergency fund secure, without risking the principal, while still being able to earn at least some sort of return, even if very little.

However, one thing you want to triple-check when putting your money into a certificate of deposit, is that the CD is FDIC insured. FDIC stands for "Federal Deposit Insurance Corporation," which is an organization designed to help protect the general public's deposits when banks go bankrupt. This way, if something happens to the bank, and it has to close its doors, you have a much better chance of recovering your money.

Lastly, here is one final important note: when banks quote their CD rates, they will usually quote what a CD will earn on an *annual* basis, and if the CD you are being offered has a duration of less than a year, you have to divide the interest rate by 12 months, and then multiply it by the number of months of the CD duration to figure out how much you will actually receive in interest. So if they're advertising a 2% CD for 6 months, that means that you will earn only 1% in interest, because the CD duration is only half of one year. So the 2% annualized rate of return that is being advertised would give you 2% after 12 months, but will bring you only 1% actual return over a 6-month period. Banks quote CDs this way so that it's easier to compare CDs of different maturities.

Not too long ago one of my clients called me with very exciting news because she saw an advertisement for a 3-month, 1.5% interest CD, and so she thought she could earn 6% per year because she thought that she would get 1.5% every three months, and could reinvest the money again! I felt absolutely terrible when I had to explain to her that she wouldn't earn the full 1.5% in just three months and that the rate quoted was an *annualized* rate. So instead, she would earn 0.375% for the three months. This is because 1.5% was the *annualized* rate that she would earn if the CD was of a 12-month duration. But because she was only committing her money for three months, she would only earn a quarter of that amount (three months out of the year is a quarter of the year. One quarter of a 1.5% annual return is 0.375%). After I explained this, she felt a little silly, but she did exactly the right thing by asking questions and trying to figure out the situation before investing her money. So even though she may have felt somewhat embarrassed asking the question and then learning that she misunderstood the offer, now that she knows how to interpret these offers correctly, she won't make the same mistake again. That's precisely why it's so important that you feel comfortable asking your advisor all these questions, even when you may feel silly for not knowing the immediate answer or misunderstanding something, because the only way to learn is to ask questions and not be afraid to sound silly. Everyone is a novice at one point or another, and there's absolutely no shame in that.

Exchange Traded Funds

An Exchange Traded Fund ("ETF") is an investment product that is similar to mutual funds in some ways and to stocks in other ways.

Just like investing in a mutual fund, when you're buying an ETF, you are investing your money into a portfolio that contains a variety of other investments. For example, if you bought a mutual fund that invested in a certain type of stocks, every dollar you invest would be spread across many different individual stocks. If you bought a mutual fund that invested in certain kinds of bonds, every dollar would buy small pieces in many different bonds. With an ETF, it's a very similar concept in that you're buying a small portion of a larger portfolio that could have lots of different investments in it.

But there is one big difference between mutual funds and ETFs. A mutual fund will usually be actively managed by a portfolio manager, who will make regular decisions about how the portfolio should be allocated. Of course the portfolio manager has to stick to certain guidelines, but he or she can make active decisions about buying one investment and selling another, how much to buy, and other similar considerations. ETFs are different because they are not meant to be actively managed, and their portfolios instead mirror an index. For example, an ETF might follow the S&P 500 index, or the price of gold, or the price of silver, or a bond index, and so on and so on. Instead of making decisions about how to invest the money in the fund, the manager's job is to try to get the fund to copy the performance of the index as closely as possible, regardless of whether the index is going up or down.

One of the reasons why ETFs were designed this way was to make it easier to diversify your portfolio over different asset classes. Remember the discussion about diversification in one of the previous chapters? ETFs were meant to make asset-based diversification easier to achieve. Because an investor can buy ETFs that follow all sorts of indexes, she can diversify her portfolio across stocks, bonds, precious metals, international investments, and many other kinds of assets, and can usually do so at a significantly lower cost than a typical mutual fund with comparable assets. The reason for this is because a majority of ETFs are not actively managed, since the funds follow an index and there isn't any real research or stock picking involved on the side of the fund manager. This keeps the management fees lower. In some instances these fees might only be 0.10% per year. When you compare it to a mutual fund, where management fees can be 2% or more per year, that can be a huge savings. At the same time, though, because there is no active management of these funds, if an asset class, like stocks, begins to drop in price very quickly, there is no one there to try to soften the situation. So if you own an ETF that follows the S&P 500 index, for example, and the markets begin to crash, your ETF will experience pretty much the same price movements as the index that it follows. Now, as you've probably seen, having money in a mutual fund with active managers doesn't mean that they can actually protect you in case of a downturn in the markets, but it's definitely an important point to keep in mind when considering ETFs.

Another difference between ETFs and mutual funds is in the way you buy them. Whereas you would buy a mutual fund by investing a specific dollar amount and (usually) paying loads (sales fees), an ETF is bought and sold like a stock. You would buy a certain number of shares of an ETF and pay the same commission to your brokerage as you would for stocks. And also, you could sell them just as quickly, without any sales fees (like Back-End loads in some mutual funds) other than the brokerage commissions.

Lastly, it's important to note that recently a new kind of ETF has been appearing that is actively managed, like mutual funds, and charges higher annual management fees. It remains to be seen how these kinds of ETFs will fit into portfolios, as they become more commonly used over time.

REITs

Real Estate Investment Trusts ("REITs") are financial instruments that allow you to invest in real estate without actually going out to purchase and manage properties yourself. REITs purchase and operate commercial real estate for profit. There are many types of REITs out there. Some invest in apartment buildings, others in office buildings, others in industrial properties, and they can specialize even further by focusing on operating specific types of buildings (like medical office buildings, hotels, and other more targeted real estate properties).

When you purchase a REIT, just like with a mutual fund or an ETF, you are purchasing a small portion of the overall portfolio and get to share in the potential profits that correspond to the number of shares you own. Except that in this case, you are buying a small piece in a portfolio of properties. One thing that you will notice about these trusts is that they pay out a large chunk of their income in dividends, 90%, because they have to do so by law. So when someone purchases a REIT, a big component of the total return on investment would come from the regular dividend payments that are a direct result of the income produced by the properties that the trust owns. To a degree, some of the profits will also come from the properties appreciating in value.

Having said that, it is important to understand the kind of REIT you are buying and what its drawbacks are before you decide to invest your money. There are three main types of REITs: equity (those that purchase and operate actual properties), mortgage (those that generate income by buying and owning mortgages), and hybrids (those that operate actual properties, as well as invest in mortgages). As I mentioned before, the broad categories of REITs can also specialize significantly in subcategories of property types, and if you're going to invest in one, it's a good idea to research not just the REIT itself, but to have an understanding of how the property types it owns are likely to perform in the future. If the underlying property type is not expected to perform well, then it will directly reflect on the share price of the REIT as well as its ability to make dividend payments. Just like when buying a stock, if a company whose stock you own does not do well and cannot generate income, the stock price will likely suffer. In the same way, owning REITs that have properties that are not generating income and have high vacancy rates because of a bad economy, or overbuilding, is likely to also make the REIT share price suffer.

Another thing to keep in mind about REITs is that there are two ways of purchasing them. Some can be purchased just like a stock, within your brokerage account. Other REITs are not traded on the markets and investments have to be made directly with the REIT itself – these are referred to as *non-traded REITs*. If you ever do choose to purchase a REIT that isn't publicly traded, keep in mind that this becomes a very illiquid investment, meaning that you may not be able to sell it as quickly if you need to. A publicly traded REIT can be sold just a like a stock, directly from your brokerage account, while a non-traded REIT cannot always be sold easily. So if there is a high probability that you will need to withdraw your money, a non-traded REIT may not be the best strategy because of the lack of liquidity.

Overall, REITs can be a useful tool if you choose to diversify a part of your portfolio into real estate, but they can also be highly risky. Keep in mind the recent real estate bubble and the effects it could have on your portfolio. That's why it's very important to do thorough research when considering investing your money in a REIT, and to work with your advisor to make sure that the investment actually matches your portfolio goals. REITs can be very attractive and can sometimes offer very lucrative dividend yields. But the higher the possible return, the higher the risk you are likely taking. So if you see a REIT that's offering a very attractive dividend payment, don't make your decision to buy it just on that fact alone. That dividend payment could drop significantly, and the price of the shares could fall as well.

Things to Keep in Mind

As an investor, you have many options available for investing your money. There are lots of financial instruments out there, and more of them are being created all the time to give investors more choices. I will be releasing books soon on some of the other investment topics, like annuities, to provide a more detailed discussion on these investment types and to take a more detailed look at how some of them work. However, the two questions that you always have to ask yourself are: 1) what are the particular features of this investment and how do these features fit into my overall situation, and 2) what are the risks and costs associated with these features? It's really like looking at the risk and reward aspects that I discussed in Chapter 16. Just like with stocks or bonds, every investment has a potential upside and a potential downside. When you're considering various investment types to include in your portfolio, such as ETFs, annuities, REITs, or whatever other investment you come across, you always have to ask yourself how the features of that investment will affect you and what are the risks and costs associated with it. If you do that, then your decision-making process will become more structured, no matter what investment idea your advisor presents to you.

Annuities 101

The subject of annuities is too complex to cover in one chapter and I soon will be releasing a book on this topic where I will cover annuities in greater detail. However, in this chapter I will focus on the basic features and concepts to help you get a better feel for how annuities work.

You've probably already heard about annuities, but there is quite a bit of confusion surrounding this topic because there are many different types of annuities that can work very differently and can have a variety of features. On the one hand these features can make annuities somewhat difficult to understand the first time around, but it's these same features that can make them a versatile tool that can address a number of concerns the way that stock and bond investments can't. That's why when it comes to annuities, there are a lot of suitability issues to address, and if you ever consider an annuity, it's important to understand all of the features before you commit to anything.

The Basics

Annuities are meant to be a financial product that an investor would buy with a long-term view in mind, and one of the main reasons why investors usually put their money into an annuity is to generate income at a later point in time. In the simplest of terms, some annuities can be compared to a defined-benefit pension plan. If you have a defined-benefit pension at your job, you put in a certain amount of money every paycheck and you get a promise from your company that based on the number of years you work and how much you earn in wages, you will receive a certain amount of money every month after you retire. An annuity could be set up very much like a defined-benefit pension, except that it's a stand-alone product where you can invest your money with the goal of eventually receiving regular monthly payments once you retire.

Now, there are many types of annuities that do not necessarily have to be turned on as an income stream, and can instead grow and be taken out as a lump sum amount or could just remain liquid after maturity without having to actually turn on the income stream. Some retirees may not be looking for stream of income but may just want to protect their nest egg against market volatility, so they choose certain annuities, such as equity-index annuities, to protect their principal and still enjoy growth potentials based on index options available.

To better understand how annuities work, let's first look at some of the relevant concepts. Unlike stocks or bonds, annuities are a contract between the annuity owner and an insurance company. Every annuity will have an annuity owner, an annuitant, and in most cases a beneficiary of the contract.

In its simplest form, when someone buys an annuity (creates an annuity contract), the insurance company receives money, either as a lump sum, or a series of payments, and in return, they promise growth potential depending on what type of annuity you get. The *owner* of the annuity is usually the person who purchases the annuity contract with the insurance company, and the *annuitant* is the person who will receive the benefits of that annuity, whether it's a lump sum amount or a stream of regular payments, depending on what is chosen. Usually, the owner will purchase the annuity for themselves, to either help supplement their income during the retirement or to simply to have principal preservation with growth potential, and in that case, the owner will also be the annuitant. However, this doesn't always have to be the case, because an annuity owner could also be someone else like a spouse or even an entity such as a trust. The key here is to understand that an annuity will have an owner and an annuitant, but that they don't always have to be the same person.

An annuity will usually also have a *beneficiary,* the person who is entitled to receive any death benefits of an annuity, if there are any. This is very similar to listing a beneficiary on your IRA or 401(k) account, where you would designate a person who would receive any remaining money in your account in case of your death. With an annuity it's very much the same thing. The beneficiary doesn't receive any money from an annuity while the annuitant is alive and is only meant to receive any remaining benefits of the contract should there be any money left once the annuitant dies.

How an Annuity Works

Once an annuity contract is purchased, it will go through two phases: the accumulation phase, and the annuitization phase, if that is chosen. The accumulation phase comes first after the contract purchase. During this phase, the money that was invested into the annuity grows. This phase is very important because it will directly affect how much income your annuity will pay out in the future if you choose an income payout option. The growth during this phase can vary significantly based on the type of annuity you purchase and all the features that you requested it to have. During the accumulation phase most annuities will have a penalty-free withdrawal option, and as long as you are over 59½ you can use that option should you need to. For example, you may put $100,000 in an annuity and may be still able to withdraw $10,000 a year (10%) after the first year anniversary, even during the accumulation period.

Once the accumulation phase is over, you can decide to annuitize it, and the annuitant will begin receiving regular payments (annuitization phase). If this option is chosen, the size of the payments will depend on a lot of factors, but two of the major ones will be your total accumulation value and your age when you start receiving the payments. Again remember that it depends on the type of annuity and the reason you decided to purchase the annuity. You might decide not to annuitize it and instead take a lump sum and walk away.

Types of Annuities

There are four main types of annuities: Single Premium Immediate Annuity ("SPIA"), Fixed Annuity ("FA"), Equity Indexed Annuity ("EIA") also referred to as a Fixed Indexed Annuity, and Variable Annuity ("VA").

Let's start with the most basic one, which is a fixed annuity. A fixed annuity is very similar to a CD at a bank. What that means is that a fixed annuity will earn a predetermined interest rate for the term of the annuity, just like a CD would earn a predetermined rate at a bank. Let's say you purchase a five-year annuity giving you a specific interest rate for that time duration, for example 2%. Well, that's the interest rate that you will receive regardless of what's happening in the economy or the stock market. Just like with a CD, a fixed annuity limits what you can do with your money for a certain period of time, because it's a contract between you and the insurance company where you agree to keep your money in the contract for a specific duration in exchange for a specific interest rate. That doesn't mean that you can't take your money out at all. Remember, unlike a CD, there is a penalty-free annual withdrawal amount available on most annuities. But if you decide to break the annuity completely and take all your money out early, then you will have to pay a surrender charge, the amount of which will depend on your specific annuity policy. Again, this is similar to a CD at a bank, where you set aside your money for a certain period of time, and have to pay a fee if you'd like to take it our earlier.

Single premium immediate annuities are contracts where you give the insurance company a certain amount of money and they immediately start paying you regular income payments. So there really isn't an accumulation phase in this kind of annuity, because what you're doing is agreeing with an insurance company that it will immediately start making regular payments to you for a predetermined amount of time. There are several payment options to choose from, and the amount of the regular payments will depend on how long you'd like to receive those payments (the longer you'd like to receive the payments, the lower those payments would usually be).

For example, you could choose a payment option called life pay, which means that you will receive larger regular payments, but only as long as you are alive, and there won't be any money paid to your beneficiaries after you die. This is an option that people with no children or other dependents sometimes choose because they would rather receive more in income instead of worrying about what happens after they pass away. You can also choose a life pay with a certain years option, such as 10-year certain, or 15-year certain, and so on. In these types of payment options you will receive regular payments, but if you were to die before the certain amount of time passed (10 or 15 years, for example), then your beneficiary would continue receiving the payments until that period of time was complete. So if you choose a 15-year certain payment option, and pass away after 10 years, your beneficiary would continue to receive payments for five years after that. On the other hand, if you choose that same 15-year certain option, but live for 25 years, then your beneficiary would receive nothing, because the contract will have already met its minimum requirement to make payments for 15 years. It's important to note that in this second example, you would continue receiving payments no matter how long you live, even after the certain period elapses (whether it's 10, 15 or however many years).

Equity and fixed index annuities are types of annuities that depend on what's happening in the stock market, but don't directly expose your principal to the risks of the markets. This type of annuity safeguards your original principal in exchange for a lower rate of return than the money could earn if it was invested directly in the markets. This provides protection of the principal, but, as you remember from Chapter 16, because you're taking less risk, you will also receive a lower return and in some cases may earn nothing at all for a year, or longer, if the markets are falling. But it also means that you are not losing anything either like you would be if you were invested directly in the market while it was crashing.

These types of annuities usually work by being tied to an index. In the previous chapter I talked about Exchange Traded Funds (ETFs), which basically mirror an index. Fixed index annuities are also tied to indexes, and the growth of your accumulation value will depend on how those indexes perform. Usually, an insurance company that sells you this type of annuity will add gains to your accumulation value annually. So if an index performs well, your annuity will earn a return which will be added to the accumulation value. But unlike a straight stock market investment, this gain will be locked in, so that if the market experiences a loss the following year, you would not earn anything but wouldn't lose anything either.

For example, let's take the crash of 2008. Someone who was invested in a fixed index annuity would accumulate gains all the way up to the crash. When the crash occurred, they maintained whatever the accumulation value was in their fixed index annuity as of the last anniversary date of establishing their annuity contract. So even though the market was deteriorating, someone with this type of annuity wouldn't experience any losses, but because the market performed poorly they didn't experience any returns either.

It's important to remember that in a fixed index annuity, the growth depends on the index options that are selected. A more aggressive allocation can provide a higher return if the markets do well, but can give you 0% if the markets are doing poorly. And as you already know, just because you're not losing money, it doesn't mean that you're in the clear, because your purchasing power continues to decrease due to inflation. That is why it is so important to carefully select the annuity, the index allocations, and the insurance company from which you purchase the contract. Two people can be holding the same type of annuity from different companies throughout the same exact time period, and with similar indexing options, but one could earn 3% while the other could earn 8%. This is because different companies will have different methodologies for calculating returns and different allocation techniques.

The reason someone would choose a fixed index annuity versus a fixed annuity would usually be because they want a higher potential return while giving up the rights to a fixed regular rate of return. On the other hand, someone might choose a fixed annuity because it's more important to them to earn a regular rate of return, even if it's lower, rather than take the chance that they won't earn anything at all if the markets do poorly.

Lastly, there are variable annuities which are a lot like owning mutual funds within an annuity contract. It's similar to purchasing mutual funds in a retirement account, but instead you are purchasing them within your annuity contract. So you are exposing your principal to the upside and downside of the markets, and your annual return depends on how the markets perform. But it's still different than investing directly into the markets because you can choose to attach certain riders (contract options) to help protect the income benefits and the death benefit of the contract. Also, because variable annuities are tax-deferred products (you don't pay tax on the gains until you start withdrawing the money), a variable annuity could be a way for some people to save money for retirement outside of their IRA or 401(k). But of course, make sure to check with your tax preparer to see how this would affect you before making any decisions.

Although variable annuities can play a specific role in a retirement portfolio, they still expose your principal to investment risk and are actually similar to being invested directly in the stock market. Now, granted they have certain riders that you can add to guarantee some features, but exposing your principal to market volatility makes variable annuities more risky. Because of that, even though most annuities are complex and have a variety of features that need to be carefully considered before making the decision to invest your money, special care should be given to selecting a variable annuity. If you choose one, make sure that it fits within your portfolio objectives, and that you don't have unrealistic expectations about its safety and the possible returns it can generate.

Riders

Riders are various options that can be added on to annuity contracts to fine tune the features of the annuity to better fit an investor's specific situation. There are many different kinds, and they are too numerous to be covered extensively in one chapter, but here is an example of one of the more common ones, the income rider:

Remember, an annuity has an accumulation value where your principal grows based on the features of the annuity. Well, eventually you could choose to take your accumulation value as a lump sum out of the annuity and move it somewhere else, or you could choose to annuitize it and receive regular payments instead. But as with any investment, there is a chance that your returns won't be as high as you expected, and because of that, the accumulation value will not grow as large as you had hoped. For example, if you had a fixed index annuity, and the index that it was tied to continued experiencing constant declines, your principal would be safe, but it would not grow either and if you are in a variable annuity you could actually have less money than you invested .The income rider can help address this problem by giving you an opportunity to choose a different rate of return if that was to happen, but it comes with some strings attached.

For example: let's pretend you are 55 and you purchase a fixed index annuity and add an income rider that happens to guarantee a rate of 6% per year. Let's say you started by investing $100K, and now after 10 years your accumulation value happened to grown to $150K, based on the returns of the indexes (not from the income rider). You could choose to take that $150K out as a lump sum amount and put that money somewhere else. But since you had an income rider that guaranteed a 6% return, you also have another choice. At 6% annual return, your guaranteed income value (similar to accumulation value) would have grown to about $179K, which is more than the $150K that your accumulation value reached in mutual funds in this example. At that point you could choose to annuitize that $179K guaranteed income value for a regular stream of payments instead of taking the $150K accumulation value as a lump sum. However, you cannot choose to take that $179K as a lump sum amount.

As the example above suggests, the income rider is a good way to guarantee that your principal can grow at a predetermined rate to give you a higher amount to annuitize into regular income payments during retirement, should you choose to do so. But as with everything, options do cost money, and an income rider will cost a certain fee per year, just like any other riders you might decide to add.

Overall, there are many different riders to choose from that can alter the features of an annuity and will address different the needs you may have. There are, for example, death benefit riders that work by protecting and adding growth to your principal. This is why it's very important to understand what your needs are and select riders that will address your specific concerns.

The Role of Insurance Companies

A big part of selecting an annuity is selecting the right insurance company to work with, because the stability of the insurance company plays a role in the safety of the annuity. That's why it's important to research the insurance company to ensure that it is reputable, stable, and not an operation that will go out of business in a few years. Annuities are getting popular and many smaller companies are beginning to offer them but they do not have the same backing a bigger company has nor the experience to keep their promises to their consumer.

What's important to remember about annuities is that they are guaranteed by the insurance company that issues them, but unlike a CD at a bank, they are not FDIC insured. This makes it vital to select reputable insurance firms that are going to be around for the long term. I personally prefer that a company issuing the annuity contracts has been around for at least five or more decades. To me, this means that a company with a longer reputation has had the opportunity to navigate the financial markets through various ups and downs in the economy, and has the benefit of having experience in dealing with difficult economic environments. It's very important that they have an A rating when it comes to their financial strength, and that they have a good reputation of payouts and keeping their commitments to their clients.

Things to Keep in Mind

Annuities are a complex investment vehicle that has a lot of different options. They can have many pitfalls if they are not chosen carefully, precisely because the options that they have are designed to address many different needs and to fit specific situations and address specific concerns. This is kind of like going to the store and buying a good dress – you have to find one that fits you. It may look good on the mannequin, and it might look good on some people, but it won't necessarily look good on you if it doesn't fit your unique shape and personality. In the same way, an annuity has to be chosen carefully, with the right features to make sure that it actually addresses your needs and helps you achieve your specific goals.

- Understand the strength and rating of the insurance company.

- Understand what type of annuity you are purchasing.

- Understand the terms/length of the annuity.

- Understand withdrawal options during and after the accumulation period.

- Understand how much you will be paying in fees, if they apply.

- Understand riders that are available, and which riders will address your specific concerns and goals.

ENDNOTES

1   Jessica Arons. "Lifetime Losses: The Career Wage Gap," Center for American Progress Action Fund, 2008

2   Current statistics show that women earn approximately between 75% and 86% of what men earn. These statistics vary based on age, occupation, education level, and how average earnings are measured. Even wider variance exists when ethnicity is taken into account.

3   Lilly Ledbetter filed a complaint with the EEOC after having worked as a supervisor for the Goodyear Tire & Rubber Company for about 20 years, and after learning that during all that time she was consistently paid less than her male counterparts. She was awarded approximately $3.3 million dollars in damages. However, the U.S. Supreme Court eventually overturned the ruling on the grounds that the case was filed more than 180 days after the original decision was made by Goodyear Tire & Rubber Company to pay Ms. Ledbetter less, and therefore, her case was filed too late. The Lilly Ledbetter Fair Pay Act of 2009 resets the 180 day period every time a discriminatory pay practice occurs – not just from the original date of the discriminatory practice.

4   Under coverture laws, women had very few legal rights and were either considered dependents of their fathers or their husbands. When a woman became married, she and her husband became one entity, which was fully controlled by the husband. The wife had no legal rights to sue, own property, or make other financial decisions. A woman was simply not considered to be a legal entity under the law. Some of the aspects of coverture laws have been slowly dismantled during the 20th century, but their effects still persist.

5   Texas State Historical Association. "Women and the Law." http://www.tshaonline.org/handbook/online/articles/jsw02 (accessed May 9, 2013)

6   National Women's Business Council. "Businesses Owned by Women." http://www.nwbc.gov/sites/default/files/NWBC%20Women-Owned%20Business-es_FINAL.pdf (accessed August 20, 2013)

7   Catalyst.org. "Women in Law in the U.S." http://www.catalyst.org/knowledge/women-law-us (accessed May 9, 2013)

8   Catalyst.org. "Women in Medicine." http://www.catalyst.org/knowledge/women-medicine (accessed May 10, 2013)

9   Having worked with many women over the years, one of the most common concerns I hear is that their advisor does not listen to them or take their concerns seriously. This is one of the more frustrating hurdles that routinely prevents women from getting the answers they want, and a hurdle that is only reduced if a woman assertively demands that her questions and opinions be taken seriously. I have heard many stories over the years that border on absurd, but that is the sad reality – an absurd reality.

10   United States Government Accountability Office. *Gender Pay Differences: Progress Made, but Women Remain Overrepresented among Low-Wage Workers.* GAO-12-10. October 2011.

11 As described in "Graduating to a Pay Gap. The Earnings of Women and Men One Year after College Graduation," a 2012 report by AAUW, one factor behind the pay gap is that women are less likely to negotiate their salaries than men are, because they feel that employers will not perceive it favorably.

12 Rapunzel is a fictional character in the fairy tales of the Brothers Grimm. She is held captive in a tower by a witch, and has very long hair that the witch uses to climb up to the tower. One day, a prince finds her and she lets down her hair so that he can climb up to the tower. Yet throughout her ordeal Rapunzel never thought to use her hair to escape from the tower and run away.

13 In the 1987 film *Wall Street,* Michael Douglas portrays a greedy and ruthless broker by the name of Gordon Gekko, who is eventually caught in an insider trading scheme.

14 CNNMoney. "Prosecutors: Madoff fraud started in 1970s." http://money.cnn.com/2012/10/01/investing/madoff-fraud/index.html (accessed May 10, 2013)

15 In his early 19th century poem, Marmion, Sir Walter Scott tells a tale of lies, deception, and greed that ends poorly for the instigators of the plot.

16 Bruce Bartlett. "Who Saw the Housing Bubble Coming?" Forbes.com http://www.forbes.com/2008/12/31/housing-bubble-crash-oped-cx_bb_0102bartlett.html (accessed May 13, 2013)

17 Gretchen Morgenson & Louise Story. "Banks Bundled Bad Debt, Bet Against It and Won." The New York Times. http://www.nytimes.com/2009/12/24/business/24trading.html?pagewanted=all&_r=0 (accessed February 18, 2013)

18 In the 1987 film *Wall Street,* Bud Fox, played by Charlie Sheen, was the reluctant hero who brought down his greedy boss Gordon Gekko (Michael Douglas). Unfortunately he, himself, had to get a taste of Wall Street before realizing what a painful and ruthless game it can be.

19 In the tale of "Jack and the Beanstalk," Jack is a boy living with his mother, who asks him to take their cow to the market for sale. The cow was their only asset, and it had stopped giving milk, so they had no choice but to sell it. On his way to the market, Jack meets a man who asks him to trade the cow for some magic beans. Jack goes ahead and decides that it is indeed prudent to trade their only asset, the cow, for magic beans. In the end, Jack finds treasure, but he could have very well traded his mother's only asset for a handful of regular beans.

20 BusinessInsider.com. "FAIL: 84% of Actively Managed Mutual Funds Did Worse Than Their Benchmarks in 2011." http://www.businessinsider.com/84-mutual-funds-underperform-2012-3 (accessed May 13, 2013)

21 Michael Zennie & Eddie Wrenn. "Google overtakes Microsoft in market value for first time (but it needs to work hard to catch up with Apple)." Daily Mail, October 2, 2012. http://www.dailymail.co.uk/sciencetech/article-2211565/Google-overtakes-Microsoft-market-value-time.html (accessed May 18, 2013)

22 In the story, "The Emperor's New Clothes," a ruler is fooled into believing that clothes made for him are invisible to anyone who is stupid or incompetent. When the "clothes" are delivered, neither he nor anyone else can see them (because they don't exist), but everyone pretends that they do see the new clothes, so as not to seem stupid or incompetent. The Emperor, not wanting to seem unfit for his office, ends up "wearing" these clothes in a parade, but really just walks around naked.

23 CNBC.com. "This Is the Worst Thing About Fake-Tweet Stock Dive." http://www.cnbc.com/id/100669021 (accessed May 5, 2013)

24 Bureau of Labor Statistics. *The U.S. Housing Bubble and Bust: Impacts on Employment.* December 2010

Made in the USA
San Bernardino, CA
15 October 2013